D1404833

# Print Preview: A Guide to Academic Writing Success

## Canadian Edition

**Elizabeth McMahan**
Illinois State University

**Robert Funk**
Eastern Illinois University

**Brian T.W. Way**
University of Western Ontario

PEARSON
Longman

Toronto

**Library and Archives Canada Cataloguing in Publication**

McMahan, Elizabeth
    Print preview : a guide to academic writing success / Elizabeth McMahan, Robert Funk, Brian Way.—Canadian ed.

Includes index.
Previously published under title: Here's how to write well.
ISBN 0-321-26963-2

    1. English language—Rhetoric—Handbooks, manuals, etc. 2. English language—Grammar—Handbooks, manuals, etc. 3. Report writing—Handbooks, manuals, etc. 4. Academic writing—Handbooks, manuals, etc. I. Funk, Robert II. Way, Brian III. McMahan, Elizabeth. Here's how to write well. IV. Title.

PE1408.M343 2005          808'.042          C2004-905631-X

ISBN 0-321-26963-2

Vice President, Editorial Director: Michael J. Young
Acquisitions Editor: Patty Riediger
Sponsoring Editor: Carolin Sweig
Signing Representative: Carine Pierzchalski
Marketing Manager: Toivo Pajo
Associate Editor: Jon Maxfield
Production Editor: Martin Tooke
Copy Editor: Karen Alliston
Proofreader: Kathleen Richards
Production Manager: Wendy Moran
Page Layout: Gerry Dunn
Art Director: Julia Hall
Cover Design: David Cheung
Interior Design: Monica Kompter
Cover Image: Photonica

2 3 4 DPC 08 07 06

Printed and bound in Canada.

PEARSON
Longman

for Brian Charlton
— writer and teacher of writers —

"But the Bear knows and he is looking for Angel
to let her in on the secret"
—*Angel and the Bear*

# Table of Contents

# Preface

Writing well is something you will always need to do. Whether for college or university or for work, for business or for pleasure, for practical matters or for personal expression, your writing will always be very important to you. And you will be judged on how effectively you write. *Print Preview: A Guide to Academic Writing Success* is designed to help you become a confident and proficient writer of prose, serving both as a general guide to improving your skills and as a source of ideas, methods, and practical exercises. Writing is often seen as a journey—and this is a good place to start. *Print Preview* is written in clear, straightforward language and takes a logical, sequential approach. The book is organized into three parts.

PART I: PUTTING A PAPER TOGETHER offers an overview of the writing process—from gathering, sorting, and organizing ideas and information to drafting, revising, and editing the final product. Strategies, outlines, and practical suggestions are provided in this section for a variety of writing challenges: approaches to different kinds of writing assignments; suggestions for composing and developing varied sentences and effective paragraphs; ideas for revising and editing final drafts; and hints for improving critical thinking and logic. And to help complete the range of things you might need to think about in putting a paper together, the inside front and back covers of this book feature typical college and university assessment rubrics as well as common revision symbols.

From conducting your research to documenting your sources, PART II: WRITING A RESEARCH PAPER provides a concise but thorough guide for completing a research paper. Along with sample student papers, this section includes detailed instructions for finding and writing from sources, particularly electronic sources, and for using both the MLA and APA systems of documentation.

PART III: MAKING YOUR WRITING CLEAR AND CORRECT explains the rules of grammar, punctuation, and usage. Recognizing, understanding, and correcting common errors will help you carry out that most problematic but vital stage of the writing process: revising and editing. The information included here will make you better aware of the language you use, and thus more effective in the writing you produce. The final chapter in this section provides a listing of many of the words and phrases that writers typically find confusing, accompanied by some advice about standard usage.

The APPENDIXES include a Glossary that defines many of those terms most frequently used in talking about writers, writing, and research. As well, an Answer Key offers best answers to most of the exercises included in the book, bolstering its use as an instructional text and as a self-help guide to writing.

*Print Preview* is a book that encourages active participation. Throughout, boldfaced **TIP!s** emphasize important concepts and reinforce learning. A number of collaborative activities enable students to work and learn together. Overall, the text is filled with Canadian examples and references that make its reading both relevant and vibrant.

This slender book, presented in clear, concise language, offers a straightforward and logical approach to help you on your journey to becoming a proficient writer. Taking that journey is now up to you—*Print Preview* is in your hands.

## Acknowledgments

My sincere thanks to all who have helped in the collaborative effort required to make a book such as this reach its current stage of production. To Elizabeth McMahan and Robert Funk for their original vision; to the following reviewers who provided thoughtful comments and suggestions: Deb Bridge, Mount Royal College; Kent Walker, Humber Institute of Technology and Advanced Learning; Kathleen Shannon, Georgian College; David Brundage, Athabasca University; Lisa Narbeshuber, Acadia University; Adam Muller, University of Manitoba; Jean Clifford, Capilano College; Erika Watters, Mount Royal College; and Susan Reid-MacNevin, St. Thomas University; to the assistants and editors at Pearson Canada for their benevolent guidance, including, in particular, Jon Maxfield, Carolin Sweig, Carine Pierzchalski, Marianne Minaker, Martin Tooke, Kathleen Richards, and Karen Alliston; to so many of my students for the experiences they have afforded me, in particular, this time around, Amanda Phillips, Mikiko Fukuda, and Kara Barfett for the essays they offered; and, as always, to Miriam for her wisdom and support.

—Brian T. W. Way

# Putting a Paper Together

## CHAPTER 1

Do not let anybody fool you: writing well requires both effort and time. Effective writing rarely happens easily or instantly, and sometimes your writing will take you to places you had not planned on going. As Margaret Laurence once said, "Writing is a journey, not a destination." But what an exciting and rewarding journey it can be.

## The Need for Good Writing Skills

The rewards are more than psychological. Writing well is one of the most useful skills you can develop—essential even—and extremely valuable to prospective employers. You will improve your chances of earning better grades in all your subjects and, ultimately, of landing and keeping a good job if you can write clearly, correctly, and convincingly. Face it. You need to be able to write. This book can help you learn.

### Allow Plenty of Time

Because of all the thinking that goes into good writing, the process always takes longer than you think it possibly could. So plan ahead. Get started early and you will have a chance to get your paper done in time to let it cool a day—well, at least a few hours—before revising and proofreading. Otherwise, you will be pulling an all-nighter for sure, and your work will probably show it.

> **T I P !**
> **Remember Mark Twain's**
> **Rule: writing always**
> **takes twice as long as**
> **you think it's going to.**

## Writing Seldom Goes Step by Step

Be advised that although we are going to describe writing as a step-by-step process, it is really a lot messier than that. And everybody's process is a little different. Experienced writers, for instance, often revise as they go. But other writers—especially those who have to struggle just to get their ideas down on paper—save the revising for later. Some people plunge straight into a first draft with no planning whatsoever and then keep doing drafts until they come up with something suitable. Others devise a plan of some sort before they begin. In short, different writers use different writing processes. Whatever works for you is what you should do.

So, bear in mind that we are simplifying the writing process as we explain it. We are going to straighten it out, tidy it up, and take it in steps to make it easy to understand.

## Think Before You Write

Before beginning a first draft, you need to consider three things:

- *Your purpose:* Why am I writing?
- *Your readers:* For whom am I writing?
- *Your main point:* What am I writing about?

All of these questions are important, and your answer to one will often affect your response to the others.

### Ponder Your Purpose

Ask yourself, "Why am I exerting all this energy and straining my brain to write this paper?" An honest reply might be that someone told you to, but that is not a useful answer.

Think beyond that immediate response to find a better reason. What do you hope to accomplish? Are you writing to provide information? Do you hope to persuade your readers to take some course of action or to change their minds on some issue? (You may, of course, be writing in a journal as an aid to learning or just to keep track of your life, but you do not need our help there.)

Your purpose affects your whole approach to writing: how you begin, whether you state or imply your main idea, how you organize the material, what details you choose, how you end, and what words you select. If your purpose, say, is

to explain how to follow a process, you will want to state your thesis clearly up front, arrange your ideas step by step, include easily visualized details, warn about any possible pitfalls at the end, and write the whole thing in easy-to-understand language.

If, on the other hand, your purpose is to entertain with an account of your disastrous visit to Nunavut in midwinter, you will leave your thesis unstated, arrange the details to build up to the worst fiasco, conclude with a vow never to travel again, and use humorous slang and metaphorical language.

### Consider Your Audience

You cannot hope to accomplish your purpose without also thinking about who is going to read this piece of writing. Your audience may be a single person—your

professor or instructor, a coworker, your employer, your member of Parliament, perhaps. Or you may at some time want to reach a more diverse audience—your city council, the urban planning commission, the readers of your local newspaper, or maybe the readership of *Maclean's* magazine, the *Globe and Mail*, or an interest group on the internet. If, for instance, you are writing to explain the hazards of mixing household cleaning products, it makes a huge difference whether you are doing it for a university economics instructor or a grade five health class. Or say you are writing to persuade your readers that physician-assisted suicide should be legalized. Consider how different your tactics would need to be depending on whether you were addressing a gathering of the local Tweedsmuir History Society or a panel of the Canadian Law and Society Association.

## Come Up with a Working Thesis

Keep both your purpose and your audience in mind as you think about finding a *thesis*—that is, *your main idea, the point you intend to make.* Simply put, a thesis is a topic expressed in the form of an argument. We think it helps to have it clearly thought out—and down on paper—early in the planning process. You will be able to use it as you gather information and construct your paper.

### Gain Unity with Your Thesis

All your major ideas will relate to this thesis, and your supporting details will relate to those main ideas. As a result, your whole paper will be effectively unified. Of course, as you proceed with the planning and the actual drafting, you can narrow the thesis, expand it, or even change the focus as new ideas occur to you. On occasion, your final thesis may be quite different from the one with which you started. If you do depart from your original thesis in the process, do not forget to go back, check each paragraph, and, if necessary, make changes, additions, and deletions to be sure you have not drifted away from your main idea as the paper evolved.

### Start with a Topic

First you will choose (or be assigned) a topic or subject to write about. In some university or college courses, you may be allowed to choose your own, or you may be provided with a variety of topics from which to choose. In other situations, you will quite possibly be told specifically what to write about. But whether assigned or chosen, a topic is not a thesis—until you turn it into one.

### Narrow the Topic

Let us assume that in your earth sciences class you have been assigned a three- to four-page paper on the topic of home gardening. Since you are not interested in growing flowers, you narrow the topic to home vegetable gardening. That is still a subject more suited to a book than a short essay. How about organic vegetable gardening? Better, but four pages are not much—only six or seven paragraphs, plus a brief introduction and conclusion. You need to narrow the topic still more. What about the problem of insects eating the tender plants? Should the gardener try to control them with insecticides or find other methods? How about focusing on methods of fighting bugs organically? Now, that sounds promising.

### Try *Freewriting* to Inspire Ideas

If the process of narrowing down does not come naturally, you can try this technique for your paper: just type your topic on your computer screen (or write it on a piece of paper) and then start jotting down all the ideas that come to mind as you think about this topic. Pay little attention to spelling, punctuation, or organization—this is the reason why the technique is called *free*writing. After you have written for ten minutes or so, read over your notes, looking for one idea that sounds suitable as a possible thesis. If all the ideas seem too broad, choose the most promising one and do another round of freewriting. Keep writing and choosing until you discover a thesis idea that pleases you.

You might also ask questions about your topic, such as *why, how, what,* or even *what if*; for example, Why did certain events occur? How was the final decision reached? What was the critical turning point in the tragedy? What if the warning had been received earlier?

Depending on your topic, you may wish to use one or more of the following approaches:

- Trace the chronological development of aspects of your topic.
- List the pros and cons, or strengths and weaknesses, or causes and effects associated with your topic.
- Compare various aspects of your topic. (Are there two, three, or more concepts or ideas involved, and if so, what are their similarities and differences?)

## EXERCISE 1.1: WRITING

Select one of the following broad topics and freewrite until you find a suitable thesis idea for a paper of about 700 words. Then write the idea in a single sentence.

| | |
|---|---|
| Parenting | Soap operas |
| Science | Movies |
| Teen pregnancy | Politics |
| Violence | Fashion |
| Sports | TV shows |

## Make a Point in Your Thesis

Once you have narrowed your idea, you need to find an approach that will allow you to make a point about the topic. Ask yourself: What *about* fighting insects organically? Clearly, the point here is to get rid of the voracious bugs without using hazardous chemicals. So, your working thesis might read something like this:

> Fighting bugs organically allows home gardeners to avoid the dangers of pesticides.

You make your point by writing a complete sentence—with both a subject and a predicate. The subject of the thesis statement is your topic. The predicate includes the verb and states the point you are going to make about the topic. Notice the difference between topics and thesis statements in the following examples:

**Not a Thesis:**    Romance

**Not a Thesis:**    Romance and losing it after marriage

| | |
|---|---|
| **Thesis:** | Several simple strategies can help keep romance alive for married couples with young children. |
| **Not a Thesis:** | Drug abuse |
| **Not a Thesis:** | Drug abuse and abusing prescriptions |
| **Thesis:** | Serious drug abuse can occur even with legal prescriptions. |
| **Not a Thesis:** | Air pollution |
| **Not a Thesis:** | Air pollution and the internal combustion engine |
| **Thesis:** | The popularity of gas-guzzling sports utility vehicles contributes significantly to air pollution. |
| **Not a Thesis:** | High school football |
| **Not a Thesis:** | High school football and raising academic requirements |
| **Thesis:** | High schools should require all football players to maintain a 65 percent average to be on the team. |

> **T I P !**
>
> **Before beginning a first draft, write out your thesis in a single clear sentence with a subject and a predicate.**

## Say Something Solid

Your thesis needs to express an argument worth making. You want your essay to be interesting, informative, persuasive, and insightful. You do not want it to be obvious, predictable, shallow, or boring. If you cannot tell whether your idea is worth writing about, ask somebody—better yet, ask several people. Be especially wary of a thesis that has the ring of a greeting card message: "Happiness is a warm puppy." Think twice about ideas you have heard all your life that may or may not be true: "Playing sports builds character." And try not to bore your readers by telling them something they already know: "Illegal drugs cause a huge problem in our society."

## Positioning Your Thesis

In most writing—especially for university or college classes—you will do well to state your thesis in the opening paragraph. Your readers can more easily follow the ideas if they know where the paper is going. In narrative and descriptive writing, of course, it may be a more effective tactic to leave any formal expression of the thesis unstated: as the old maxim about creative writing suggests, it is better to show, not tell. You should have in mind—and perhaps on paper—what you hope to accomplish as well as how the story or description will develop. But announcing your purpose in advance will take the edge off for your readers.

## Changing Your Thesis in Mid-Writing

Keep in mind that the main idea of your paper can change during the writing process. As British author E. M. Forster once observed, "How do I know what I think until I see what I say?" If you come up with a better idea or a different approach as you write, be prepared to shift gears and go with the new insight. Word processors allow changes—even major changes—to occur easily with a few keystrokes. So do not become locked into the main idea with which you began. Let your thesis evolve when it makes sense to do so.

## Starting Without a Thesis

Some writers, in fact, plunge right into writing in order to discover what they have to say. They just begin putting down ideas about the topic until they have completed a first draft, a discovery draft. Then they begin revising and keep on revising—adding ideas, taking out ideas, rearranging ideas—until they have a finished product. This method strikes us as less efficient than planning ahead, but if you suffer from writer's block, you might want to give it a try.

### ▓ EXERCISE 1.2: DISCUSSION

With a small group of classmates, discuss the following sentences one by one. Some are workable thesis sentences for an essay of two to three typed pages, double-spaced with 2.5-centimetre (one-inch) margins. Some need to be made more specific, however. Identify the successful ones, and decide what is wrong with the others.

Then, writing individually, turn each unsatisfactory sentence into a reasonably good thesis. When finished, compare results as a group.

1. Many Canadians spend so much time in front of the TV that they never really experience their own lives.
2. Personal freedom and independence carry with them responsibilities and consequences.
3. Making a lemon pie is easy.
4. I think university and college students and instructors would be happier with education if people did not enrol in university or college before the age of twenty-five.
5. My dog and my boyfriend are much alike.
6. Thousands of Canadians go through the vicious cycle of eating until they are overweight and then dieting until they reduce, only to gain the pounds back again.
7. I learned not to worry when I was sixteen.
8. The perfect omelette is fluffy, light, delicately browned, and even attainable if the cook follows five practical guidelines.
9. The purpose of this paper is to compare and contrast the Catholic schools and the public schools.
10. The prevailing views on capital punishment are quite controversial.

## Developing Details: Invention Techniques

Once you have established your thesis, your purpose, and your audience, you need to get your mind in gear and come up with plenty of ideas to use in developing your essay. Here are some strategies that will get you started.

## Brainstorming a List

Because you want to come up with as many details as possible, start thinking about your topic, and jot down every idea that comes to mind. Do not be selective at this point. You can eliminate useless or irrelevant material during the arranging stage that follows. You will probably end up with a jumbled list, something like the one generating ideas for gardening without pesticides shown in Figure 1.1.

<u>Fighting Bugs Without Pesticides</u>

– birds eat insects

– some insects eat other insects! (good ones eat bad ones, hopefully!)

– can buy good insects from mail order catalogues

– soapy water kills some bugs—or drives them away—doesn't hurt plants

– garlic water does too—*real* strong!

– slugs like beer—love to drown themselves in it

– praying mantises eat caterpillars and mites

– ladybugs devour tons of aphids

– can pick bugs off by hand (drown them in a jar) but takes *lots* of time

– milky spore disease kills Japanese beetles (according to article)

– <u>bacillus thuringiensus</u> (sp?) kills cabbage worms (same article)

– reflection from aluminum foil drives aphids nuts

– green lacewings eat mealy bugs

**FIGURE 1.1** *Brainstorming List*

## Clustering to Find Ideas

If you are not a linear thinker, you may want to work out your brainstorming in clusters rather than jotting your ideas down in a list. The process is the same. Type your topic or thesis in the middle of your screen, bold it or box it, start thinking, and let your ideas radiate out from there. You may wish to use your computer's draw or paint program for this kind of visual planning.

## Freewriting to Find Ideas

If freewriting worked for you in narrowing your subject, you can use it again to generate material. This time, type your thesis statement and continue writing as you think about that idea. Continue for ten minutes at least. Then, using the bold-face or highlight feature of your word processor, mark the lines containing information that you might want to incorporate into your paper. Finally, on a separate page, record everything that is useful, and you will have a list of ideas to choose from when you organize.

In Chapter 3 you will find detailed advice and a number of strategies for developing details.

## Exploring Ideas on a Computer

As we have suggested, most of the invention techniques discussed in this chapter can be done on the computer. You may find that you can brainstorm or freewrite more quickly and easily on a keyboard. To increase your concentration, turn down the brightness on the monitor so that you can write without seeing the screen. When you have finished, turn the brightness back up and view your freewriting on screen; then highlight points and details that seem valuable. As you develop more material, review it periodically and highlight the important points; then transfer these items to a separate page or file for later use. As mentioned above, if you have a draw or paint program, use it to do visual planning such as clustering.

### ■ EXERCISE 1.3: INVENTION

Using the thesis that you devised in Exercise 1.1, develop details for that thesis by brainstorming, clustering, or freewriting. Consider using all three techniques if you have trouble coming up with enough material to support the thesis.

### ■ PREWRITING CHECKLIST

Here is a list of questions that will help direct your thinking as you transform your brainstorming, freewriting, or clustering into an essay. Write out your response to each question.

1. What is my topic?
2. What is the main point I want to make about the topic?
3. Who is my primary audience? That is, what group of readers do I want to reach?
4. What is my specific purpose in regard to those readers?
5. What kinds of evidence am I going to use?

   Your responses will probably turn out something like these:

1. Topic: needle exchange programs to reduce spread of AIDS
2. Main point: needle exchange programs are an effective and relatively inexpensive means of reducing the spread of HIV among drug users.

3. Primary audience: readers who doubt or are unsure about value and usefulness of needle exchanges.

4. Specific purpose: to get doubters to reconsider their opinions—to understand why needle exchanges are effective, not detrimental.

5. Evidence: mainly reasons and explanations, but also summaries of several studies I have read about needle exchanges—a couple of quotations from columnist Clarence Page, who has written on this issue recently.

# Bringing Order Out of Chaos: Outlining

Finally, it is time to work out a plan—to arrange all this material into a sequence your readers can easily follow. You will need at least three or four main ideas to serve as the major points in your outline. In your paper about organic gardening, those major points will be methods of controlling insect pests.

## Sorting Out Main Ideas and Supporting Details

Examine the ideas you have generated, looking for patterns of similarity. Try first to determine which are the major ideas. These are the ones for which you can find *supporting details*—that is, the points and examples that explain, identify, illustrate, or qualify a major idea.

In the brainstorming list in Figure 1.1, for instance, "Some insects eat other insects!" is clearly a major idea. There are several examples to support it—praying mantises, ladybugs, and green lacewings; there are also the specific insects they control and the fact that all these useful insects can be purchased by mail. All represent natural remedies. That is plenty for one paragraph.

You may detect several supporting details that are similar but need to have a major heading added. Notice in the list that these items all share a common trait:

Putting out beer for slugs

Laying down aluminum foil to kill aphids

Squirting soapy water or garlic water on plants

These methods all use products usually found in the kitchen. By adding a heading, you can group these three under "Try safe and easy household remedies."

Two other items on the list clearly belong together: milky spore disease and *Bacillus thuringiensis.* (You discover such unusual remedies by reading articles or inquiring at your favourite garden store.) Since these biological techniques work by introducing diseases fatal to insects but harmless to plants and people, you might head this section "Introduce insect diseases to destroy pests."

Only two items in the brainstorming list remain unused: picking insects off by hand and encouraging birds to come to the garden. Probably picking bugs off by hand is too tiresome to be a practical suggestion. And enticing birds may hurt more than help. Birds eat bugs indiscriminately—the ladybugs along with the aphids—and are exceptionally fond of many succulent garden vegetables as well. You decide to let the idea of attracting birds go and mention in your conclusion that if all else fails, the fanatical gardener can always pick off the beastly bugs one by one.

## Arranging Your Major Points

After you finish choosing your main ideas and supporting details, the last step before the actual drafting involves deciding in what order to present the ideas. Since there is no chronology (time order) involved in presenting the material, you want to begin with an interesting point to grab your readers' attention. Most importantly, you need to end with your strongest point to leave your audience feeling it has read something worthwhile.

With this pest control outline, you could almost flip a coin. But with the household remedies being the most practical and the most entertaining to describe, you might want to begin there. Save the section on importing natural enemies for the end, since it sounds like a dramatic and surefire solution. A sample rough outline using this material appears in Figure 1.2.

---

**Thesis**: Fighting bugs organically allows home gardeners to avoid the many dangers of pesticides.

Introduction:
– Need to keep chemicals out of vegetables

(1) Try safe, easy home remedies
  – set out trays of beer to attract and drown slugs
  – spray soapy water or garlic water on plants
  – spread shiny aluminum foil under plants to disorient aphids, driving them to their doom

(2) Introduce insect diseases
  – milky spore disease kills Japanese beetles
  – bacillus thuringiensis is death to cabbage worms
  – both remedies available at garden stores
  – both harmless to plants and humans

(3) Bring in natural enemies
  – praying mantises eat caterpillars and mites
  – ladybugs eat their weight in aphids
  – green lacewings feed on mealy bugs
  – all can be ordered by mail

Conclusion:
  – If all else fails, pick bugs off by hand.

---

**FIGURE 1.2** *Rough Outline*

**NOTE:** In Chapter 3 you will find more help with organizing material and several more sample outlines.

## Outlining on a Computer

Using a computer to create an outline allows you to experiment with different ways of organizing your ideas. If you put the main headings in large, bold letters, they will keep the larger structure of your paper in view as you fill in subheadings and subpoints. You can add new points simply by moving the cursor and typing; you can shift details from one subheading to another by marking a line and hitting a few keys. Whole sections within your on-screen outline can be cut, renumbered, or rearranged.

If you did your prewriting on the computer, you can use the cut and paste functions to move key phrases and sentences from your freewriting or brainstorming into an informal outline. Most computer programs let you go back and forth between screens or windows, a feature that makes it easier to turn prewriting into an outline. Many word processors also have an outline feature that sets the levels within your outline for you; you can then use the outliner's collapse and expand functions to view your work at different levels of detail.

## EXERCISE 1.4: COLLABORATION

The following outline illustrates a number of weaknesses—supporting points that do not really support, minor points that pose as major points, major points that lack supporting points, and so on. With two or three classmates, discuss this sorry example until the group has revealed all its shortcomings; then, still working together, revise the material by adding, omitting, and rearranging ideas as necessary to produce what everyone agrees is a good outline.

**Thesis:** Studying in a student residence is impossible for anyone who lacks unswerving discipline.

1. Phones ringing and stereos playing
2. Friends drop by and keep me from studying
    a. Card playing and bull sessions
    b. Watching TV more fun than studying
3. Neighbours are forever partying
    a. Loud music, talking, and laughing distract me
4. Studying is really hard for me
    a. I fall asleep
    b. Chemistry 101 is beyond me

## EXERCISE 1.5: OUTLINING

Look over the material you generated in Exercise 1.3, and construct an outline for a short paper on that topic.

In the previous chapter we explained that all the choices you make about your writing—from selecting a topic to deciding how much material to include and how to arrange it—are determined by your purpose and your audience. You also need to consider how your readers will respond to the words you choose.

## Write as Naturally as You Speak

As a writer, how do you want to come across to your readers? Do you want to sound like an expert, lecturing the uninformed? Or like an old friend, informally discussing your thoughts and opinions? Do you want to seem serious or playful, warm or distant, excited or detached? The approach you choose determines the *voice* that your readers will hear when they read your writing.

Lewis Lapham, editor of *Harper's* magazine, complains that "few writers learn to speak in the human voice, that most of them make use of alien codes (academic, political, literary, bureaucratic, technical)." Many people think they are supposed to sound grand and impressive when they write, so they try to produce a form of language they would never use in speaking.

### Use First Person

You should strive for a human voice when you write—preferably your own. Those "alien codes" that Lapham speaks of are usually stuffy and pretentious and often sound like this:

> One can appreciate the health benefits of high school athletics for the ones who participate as well as the entertainment value for the ones who observe.

Put that sentence into plain English and you get:

> I think high school athletics can be healthy for the players and enjoyable for the fans.

Good writers usually prefer *I* or *we* instead of *one*, and many address their readers as *you*. On rare occasions the use of *one* is still required—in scientific writing, for instance, and in some theses and dissertations. We will explain later how to handle *one* gracefully, just in case you have to write on a very formal level. You should also know that the first person will make your writing sound too familiar and chummy for some readers; university professors, college instructors, and business publications may prefer that you use the first person sparingly. The key is to know your audience and its expectations.

**T I P !**

**Avoid the indefinite *you*.**

The words *you* and *your* should always refer to the readers. You may draw an unexpected laugh if you are explaining how to prune a tree and write, "Grasp your diseased limb firmly and saw it off above the joint."

## ▦ EXERCISE 2.1: REVISING

Translate these sentences into clear, straightforward English. You may have to guess at the meaning sometimes, but do your best. We have rewritten the first one to help you start.

1. One could conclude that the primary cause of her poverty was the number of offspring she possesses.

   *Translation:* I think she is poor because she has too many children.

2. This writer's report enjoyed a not unfavourable reception by the management.

3. The unacceptability of one's lifestyle can result in the termination of one's employment in some companies.

4. In colonial times, you had to depend on wood for fuel.

5. It was with no little enthusiasm that one's peers inflicted various contusions and lacerations on members of the opposing affinity group.

6. It is the feeling of this committee that the established priorities in management–employee relations are in need of realignment.

## Adjust Your Tone

You may sometimes want to make your audience angry—about injustice, poverty, bigotry—but you always want to avoid making them angry at you. You need to adopt a tone that will appeal to your readers. *Tone* means the attitude a writer conveys toward the subject matter and the audience. The language you use will tell your readers if you are serious, humorous, interested, bored, cynical, confident, defensive, irritated, enthusiastic, and so on. You have to understand that your writing will have a tone, whether you consciously think about it or not. So you might as well think about it.

The English language offers you a number of ways of saying the same message, depending on tone. You can word the simplest request to express subtle variations in your meaning:

> Lend me ten dollars.
>
> Please send me ten dollars.
>
> Can you spare ten dollars?
>
> I need ten dollars. I'll pay you back tomorrow.
>
> I'd like you to give me ten dollars.

The tone you use should reflect your understanding of the needs and feelings of your readers. It is difficult to make generalizations about tone, but you should avoid talking down to your readers by stating the obvious or talking over their heads by using words and phrases they will not understand. You also do not want to be falsely enthusiastic: readers can usually tell when you are not sincere. Also resist the temptation to be dogmatic, abusive, or overly sarcastic. Mark Twain supposedly never published a line or mailed a letter until his gentle wife Olivia had approved it. His famous letter to the gas company shows you why:

Hartford
February 12, 1891

Dear Sirs:

Some day you will move me almost to the verge of irritation by your chuckled-headed goddam fashion of shutting your goddam gas off without giving notice to your goddam parishioners. Several times you have come within an ace of smothering half of this household in their beds and blowing up the other half by this idiotic, not to say criminal, custom of yours. And it has happened again to-day. Haven't you a telephone?

Ys
S L Clemens

**TIP!**

**Imagine your readers reacting to what you have written.**

If you think your readers might get the wrong impression or have the wrong reaction, edit your tone accordingly.

Needless to say, Livy did not let this one pass. Twain revised his correspondence daily as his rage subsided, until he finally produced a temperate version that would not invite a libel suit. Try to do the same with your own writing.

## Choose an Appropriate Level of Language

The tone of your writing will reflect just how formal you want to be. As always, audience and purpose will dictate the level of language you decide to use. Although these levels overlap, you have three main forms from which to choose: *formal, informal,* and *familiar* (or slang). You need different levels of language for different writing occasions, just as you sometimes need formal attire for banquets and weddings, informal clothes for dates and shopping, and your grubbies for around the house.

---

**Formal:**      One should not admit defeat too quickly. I shall not admit defeat too quickly.

**Informal:**    We should not give up too quickly. I'll not give up too quickly.

**Familiar:**    I'm not throwing in the towel too quick.

| *Formal* | *Informal* | *Familiar (slang)* |
|---|---|---|
| automobile | car | wheels |
| comprehend | understand | dig |
| depart | leave | split |
| residence | home | crib |
| odious | offensive | gross |
| debilitated | exhausted | wasted |
| morose | sad | bummed out |

---

FIGURE 2.1 *Levels of Language for All Occasions*

The level of language that you choose will depend on your relationship with the topic and the audience. If you are writing to a close friend or family member about something personal, you will probably use familiar language. For less chummy or intimate writing, you will use informal or formal language. Figure 2.1 provides an illustration of these language levels.

## Formal Writing

You use formal language when your purpose is serious and you want to keep some distance between yourself and your audience. Many textbooks are written in formal English, as are most scholarly articles and books and some magazines. Business writing still observes many of the conventions of formal usage, but nowadays the use of *I* or *we* has generally replaced the strictly formal third-person approach. Here are the main features of formal writing:

1. No contractions or slang.

2. Third-person approach (*one, he, she, it, they*); do not address the readers directly as *you*.

3. No sentence fragments.

4. A serious or neutral tone.

> **T I P !**
> Use formal language when you want to downplay your personal involvement and emphasize the factual content of your writing.

## EXERCISE 2.2: TONE

Rewrite each sentence to make the tone consistent and more appropriate for the subject. We will show you how with the first one.

1. Many students who matriculate in a curriculum leading toward medical school really dig biology.

   *Revised:* Many premedical students like to major in biology.

2. People who want to improve physically can undertake several schemes to shed poundage and acquire robustness.

3. I think Desdemona is such a wimp; she just lies down and dies.

4. When running for office, a candidate can always try to make the other guy look like a doofus.

5. The very people who bug one the most are often those who most want to please one.

6. We must suppose, then, that the figures cited are okay.

7. You cannot help expressing yourself, unless one resides in a vacuum.

8. If you want to hold the attention of your reader, you should cultivate a bitchin' style.

9. Scientists have recommended that one strategy for alleviating the threat of global warming is to cut way back on car fumes.

10. The premier explained his reform proposal at length, but the audience was clearly tuned out and just didn't get it.

## Informal Writing

The formality or informality of language is a matter of degree. Little writing is exclusively formal or completely informal. Most of the writing you will be called on to do will probably be informal, although most professors and employers may insist on a more formal approach. Here are the guidelines for informal language:

1. Use contractions, if you want to.

2. Use slang *only* if it is appropriate for your audience.

3. Write in the first person; address your readers as *you,* if you wish.

4. Use an occasional sentence fragment for stylistic effect.

5. Adopt any tone that is appropriate for the purpose and audience.

**T I P !**

Use a familiar tone only when you are completely sure that your readers will enjoy and approve of this style of writing.

## Familiar Writing

This is the language found in personal letters, journals, and diaries. You use it when you feel close to your readers and can assume they will understand the context of your writing. It also comes in handy for reproducing the feel of an actual person's speech in an essay that is otherwise more formal. In this kind of writing contractions are expected, slang is fine, the first person *(I)* and second person *(you)* are typical, sentence fragments are acceptable, and the tone is often light or even humorous.

## Colloquialisms and Slang

Colloquialisms are expressions used in conversation and found primarily in familiar writing. You might talk about "hanging out" with your friends or "getting even" with someone who "ripped you off," but you would probably *write* that you "spent time" with your friends and "retaliated" against someone who "cheated" you. Colloquialisms also include shortened versions of words, like *prof* for *professor, lab* for *laboratory, grads* for *graduates.* Called clipped forms, these give a conversational tone to informal prose but are not appropriate for more formal writing.

Slang is extremely informal language; it is often imprecise and understandable only to a certain age group or social set. Terms like *blog, geek, chill, dis,* and *phat* and phrases like *schizzed out, trunky monkey,* and *really doe* can be lively and colourful, but they go out of style quickly. You run the risk of not being understood or of not being taken seriously if you use slang and colloquialisms in your writing. Some readers will object to its use on any level.

### EXERCISE 2.3: WRITING

Compose a brief paragraph in which you try to persuade the members of your household that they should conserve electricity or gasoline or natural gas. Then rewrite the paragraph twice more, choosing a suitable level of language to address each of the groups below. You will end up with three paragraphs. Be prepared to explain the differences in your three versions.

1. The Lost Souls Motorcycle Club
2. The local chapter of the Canadian Association of University Women

## Use Jargon Carefully

The term *jargon* has several meanings. Sir Arthur Quiller-Couch defined the term in his famous essay "On Jargon" as vague and "woolly" speech or writing that consists of abstract words, elegant variations, and "circumlocution rather than short straight speech." This kind of language, which is used to make thoughts and ideas sound more important than they are, is almost always ineffective because it sets up a barrier to communication with the reader.

Jargon can also refer to the technical vocabulary used within a trade, profession, or field of interest. This language is understood perfectly well by members of that specialized group but not by outsiders. Computer users mean something entirely different by *bit, mouse, crash, drive, disk, boot, worm,* and *virus* than non-users do.

Consider your audience and your purpose. If you know your readers will be familiar with the jargon, go ahead and use it. But the kind of jargon you should try to avoid includes those pretentious phrases that creep into the language from all sides—phrases like "increased propensity to actualize" (meaning "apt to happen"), "employee repositioning" (meaning "demoting and firing workers"), and "sociologically compatible behavioural parameters" (meaning who knows what).

### EXERCISE 2.4: WRITING

Think of some group you belong to or some activity you engage in, and make a list of its specialized words and phrases. Then write a paragraph to a general audience in which you define several of these terms. For instance, you might explain the basic shots in tennis—serve, ground stroke, volley, approach shot, lob, passing shot—for people who do not know what these terms mean.

## Use Gender-Free Language

In considering your audience, keep in mind that many of your readers may be displeased by gender-biased language—that is, words and phrases that unfairly ignore one sex or inaccurately call attention to gender. Fortunately, it is fairly easy to avoid sexist language. Here are some pointers to follow as you write and revise:

- Do not use the words *man* and *mankind* to refer to both men and women. Use the words *person, individual, human being, humankind, humanity,* or *the human race* instead. This advice also applies to words containing *man* or *men*:

| INSTEAD OF | USE |
|---|---|
| chairman | chairperson, moderator, chair |
| clergyman | minister, pastor |
| councilman | councillor |

| | |
|---|---|
| fireman | firefighter |
| foreman | supervisor |
| mailman | mail carrier, postal worker |
| manpower | personnel, workers, staff |
| policeman | police officer |
| salesman | salesperson, sales representative |
| weatherman | weather forecaster, meteorologist |
| workman | worker, labourer |

▨ Use parallel terms when referring to members of both sexes. If the males are *men*, then the females should be *women*, not *girls*. If you write about *ladies*, then also write about *gentlemen*.

▨ Do not mention gender when it is not necessary. Avoid such phrases as *male nurse, woman engineer, lady doctor, female architect.*

▨ Do not use the pronouns *he, him,* or *his* to refer to a singular noun that includes both genders. Instead of writing

Every writer should be careful with the pronouns he chooses.

Use the plural:

All writers should be aware of the pronouns *they* choose.

Or use *he or she,* if you can do it only once or twice:

Every writer should be careful with the pronouns *he or she* chooses.

Or eliminate the pronouns:

Every writer should be careful when choosing pronouns.

### ▨ EXERCISE 2.5: GENDERED LANGUAGE

See if you can eliminate all the gendered language from the following sentences without changing the meaning or causing awkwardness. We have rewritten the first one for you.

1. Man must work in order to eat.

   *Revised:*   People must work in order to eat. [or] Humans must work in order to eat.

2. Anyone with a brain in his head can see the dangers of using atomic reactors.

3. A homeowner can pay his taxes by mail, at the municipal offices, or at his bank.

4. The gregarious dog is man's best friend, but the aloof cat keeps his distance.

5. Girls outnumber the men on campus by almost two to one.

6. Deepa's mother is a computer repairman for the university.

7. The lady surgeon who performed Adrian's bypass operation got her medical degree from the University of Toronto.

8. The hippopotamus is happiest when he is half submerged in mud.

9. Canadian pioneers loaded up their wagons and moved their wives and children westward.

10. "As long as man is on earth, he's likely to cause problems. But the man at General Electric will keep trying to find answers." (advertisement for GE)

## Avoid Biased Language

You should avoid any derogatory language that is directed at a group, race, religion, or nationality. Identify all groups of people by their accepted proper names, and take care to avoid assigning stereotypical physical or behavioural characteristics to members of a particular group. Also, be aware that usage changes and that certain descriptive terms for groups of people may acquire unfavourable connotations. As a matter of respect for your readers, be sensitive to these details, and always use the terms that groups choose for themselves.

## To Say It or Not to Say It: Euphemisms

There may be times when you want to soften your language if you are writing about an unpleasant or emotionally loaded subject. In such cases you can employ linguistic smokescreens called *euphemisms,* most of which are quite innocent. Rather than bluntly saying "He died of cancer," you can say, "He passed away following a lingering illness." It takes the shudder out and cloaks the whole grim business of dying in a soothing phrase. Undertakers (or "funeral directors," as they prefer to be called) sometimes carry euphemism to grotesque extremes, like calling the room where the body lies the "slumber chamber." And in Victorian times, people would refer to the "white meat" of the chicken (instead of the "breast") and to the "second joint" (instead of the "thigh").

Such delicacy is quaint and amusing, but some people use euphemisms to evade the truth and conceal their meaning. In political discourse, this kind of language is often called *doublespeak.* The CIA, for example, substitutes the meaningless phrase "terminate with extreme prejudice" for the blunt word "murder." The military refers to lethal weapons as "antipersonnel implements" and civilian deaths may be glossed over as "collateral damage." Such transparent attempts to make human slaughter sound inoffensive are far from innocent.

This deceptive misuse of language has become widespread. Killing masses of people is called "ethnic cleansing." Police officers do not shoot to kill; they aim "to neutralize the adversary." An accident at a nuclear power plant is an "abnormal evolution" and an explosion is an "energetic disassembly." When the patient dies on the operating table, it is a "therapeutic misadventure" or "a negative patient-care outcome"; a death in the emergency room is "an adverse occurrence." Such euphemisms are deliberately misleading and border on being unethical.

You have to decide if innocent euphemisms are appropriate for your readers. Certainly you should never use deceptive ones. In most cases, your readers will probably want you to be honest and direct.

## EXERCISE 2.6: EUPHEMISMS

Translate these euphemisms into more direct language.

1. employee downsizing
2. pre-owned automobile
3. chemical dependency
4. adult entertainment
5. intelligence gathering
6. correctional facility
7. rest home
8. at-risk students
9. information specialists
10. revenue enhancement
11. substandard housing
12. encore telecast

Experienced writers employ a number of strategies for developing their ideas, usually without ever consciously thinking about how they are doing it. You may find your own planning and drafting easier if you become familiar with some of these techniques. Usually you will combine several strategies within one paper. For instance, you may include a narrative or a description or both while writing the explanation of a process.

We are going to present the basic strategies one by one here because that is the only way to explain them clearly. After each explanation, we will ask you to write an essay focusing primarily on that strategy to give you practice in using it.

## Strategies for Narratives

A *narrative* is simply a story, and *narration* involves telling a story. We use narrative frequently, both in everyday speech and in writing, because stories provide convincing examples, especially those about personal experiences. Stories can also be quite engaging, if skilfully told.

> **T I P !**
> Use a narrative when you want to illustrate a point or in your introduction to catch your readers' attention.

### Organizing a Narrative

Since a narrative recounts an event or an experience, you can simply arrange the details in the order in which they happened—that is, in *chronological order*. Sometimes, though, a *flashback* is effective. A jump into the past can reinforce a mood, explain someone's motivation, or give background to help readers understand the event. How do you decide whether such out-of-sequence material is a useful flashback or a tiresome digression? Keep your purpose firmly in mind. Ask yourself how much the proposed addition contributes to that goal, and give it space in proportion to its contribution.

Get your story straight by outlining before you begin—or else straighten it out when you revise. Eliminate any dull, unnecessary, or repetitious material, and then work hard to make it interesting by coming up with just the right examples and illustrations. All good writing is full of specific details, but a narrative will positively fall flat without them.

### Developing a Narrative

The process of deciding which details to include or exclude is critical to successful narrative writing. Give a lot of thought to these choices. No one wants to hear about the syllabus of your university or college philosophy course when the main point of the story has to do with the unusual way you disposed of the textbook when the class was over.

**T I P !**

**In writing a narrative essay, do not state your thesis in the introduction.** Put your thesis or purpose on your outline; then leave the main point implied in the paper itself. You do not want to take the edge off.

As in all good writing, you will want to make a point of some sort in your narrative, but avoid just tacking on a moral at the end. Nor does your point have to involve weighty revelations about the Meaning of Life or the Human Experience. Your purpose can be to tell an amusing, entertaining, exciting, unusual, or puzzling story. This kind of narrative can have a worthwhile point too. Just keep in mind that when you are describing a peaceful stroll on a perfect fall day, you may choose to ignore the squashed squirrel in the gutter.

## Pitfalls of Narrative Writing

Narratives are the easiest kind of writing to organize but probably the most difficult to write well. Ask someone reliable, preferably a classmate, to read your draft and help you figure out what needs improvement. It is hard to be objective about your own writing—hard to see what needs adding and what needs taking out.

With your helper, go over the following questions and take notes on any changes that should be made to your draft.

1. Is the point of the narrative clear? Can the reader tell why I am telling this story?

2. Are the events in order? Any gaps? Any flashbacks?

3. Are there enough details? Are these details specific and interesting? If not, which ones need improving?

4. Are there any details that are boring or unnecessary and should come out?

## Topics for Narrative Writing

Before you begin, think about who your audience is and what point you want to make in your narrative. (Refrain from including that point in the introduction, however.) After completing your first draft, find someone to help you evaluate what you have written and plan your strategies for revision.

Here are some possible topics for your narrative:

1. I learned _____ the hard way.

2. Think of a conflict situation between two people: teacher/student, parent/child, employer/employee, man/woman. Narrate the conflict first as though you were one person and then as though you were the other.

3. Write an account of your initiation into some element of the adult world that you were unaware of as a child: violence, hypocrisy, prejudice, sexuality, and so forth.

4. Write the story that your older relatives most often tell about something you did as a child.

5. Describe the first time you remember being punished at school (or at home).

6. Recount a situation in which you fortunately or mistakenly followed someone else's judgment rather than your own.

7. Narrate an experience that led you to a new realization about yourself (or someone else).

8. Tell the story of a tough ethical decision you once had to make and of what happened afterward.

9. Write a narrative to support or disprove some familiar proverb, like "Honesty is the best policy," "Nice guys finish last," or "Home is where the heart is."

10. To get some ideas for writing a narrative, visit a website like the StoryTellers Challenge *(http://storytellerschallenge.com)*, where you will find topics in the form of "challenges." Or look at the "Story of the Week" page at *www.Story teller.net*; it might spark some ideas.

## Strategies for Descriptions

Seldom will a description form the basis of an entire essay, unless you are writing for practice or pleasure. But you will probably use description in virtually everything you write—especially if you write creatively and interestingly.

### Organizing a Description

Writing specialists point out that most descriptions are organized spatially—top to bottom, left to right, near to far, back to front, and so on. True, you can describe your cat from nose to tail. But where do you include the texture of the fur, the stripes or spots, the colour of the paws, the way the cat moves? And what about the meow?

Good description involves working a number of carefully chosen details into some sort of spatial arrangement. There is no absolutely convenient way (like presenting details in chronological order) that will work with description. You have to tailor the arrangement of details to suit your subject.

### Developing a Description

First, consider your purpose. Do you want to arouse an emotional response in your readers? Or are you trying to convey a word picture, without emotion but sharp and clear as a photograph? Your choice of words and details will differ according to the effect you want.

> **T I P !**
> Try to put a picture in the reader's mind.

Before you begin to write, look—really *look*—at what you plan to describe. Maybe you will want to smell and taste and touch it as well. Then try to record your sense impressions—the exact shapes, the lights and shades, the textures, the tastes, the sounds, the smells. Do not include everything, of course, or you may overwhelm your readers. Carefully select the details that suit your purpose in order to give your readers an image of what you are describing. Then, as you revise what you have written, you can search for the precise words to let them see what you envision.

Notice in the following passage how Annie Dillard, through her selection of details and choice of words, allows us both to see and to hear the ocean:

> The white beach was a havoc of lava boulders black as clinkers, sleek with spray, and lambent as brass in the sinking sun. To our left a dozen sea lions were body-surfing in the long green combers that rose, translucent, half a mile offshore. When the combers broke, the shoreline boulders rolled. I could feel the roar in the rough rock on which I sat; I could hear the grate inside each long backsweeping sea, the rumble of a rolled million rocks muffled in splashes and the seethe before the next wave's heave.
>
> —"Innocence in the Galapagos"

## Pitfalls of Descriptive Writing

Remember that good descriptive details can clarify and enliven almost any kind of writing, but they are the very essence of descriptive writing. To include too few is fatal. Using tired, colourless words will also kill a description. Search your mind for lively verbs and choice descriptive words.

## Topics for Descriptive Writing

This assignment is designed to exercise your descriptive skills. You are not expected to produce a fully developed piece of writing, unless you happen to be so inspired.

1. Describe as thoroughly as possible two of the following: how soft rain feels, how hard wind feels, how modelling clay feels, how whipped cream tastes, how a snake moves, how a cat leaps, how your dog greets you—or how a vampire looks, or a werewolf, or a visitor from outer space.

2. With as much sensory detail as possible, describe a food you hate or love.

3. Describe something you know more about than most people.

4. Describe a place (like a classroom, a coffee shop, the local pool hall, a jail cell, a hospital room, your grandmother's kitchen, a professor's or instructor's office), and try to convey how you feel about it through your use of specific details. Avoid making an explicit statement of your feelings.

5. Describe a place in which you feel at peace—or one in which you feel ill at ease.

6. Describe a memorable vacation you took. Assume that your readers have not visited this place. Use the internet to refresh your memory and check the details of your description. If you vacationed in Nova Scotia, for example, you could browse the province's official tourism site at *www.explore.gov.ns.ca.*

# Strategies for Explaining a Process

One of the most practical kinds of writing tells readers how to do something. Being able to provide an accurate, step-by-step explanation of how something is done or will be done or how something works is an essential skill.

## Organizing Process Writing

Chronological, step-by-step structure is usually the best way to explain a process. No flashbacks here. If you suddenly remember a detail that you should have included earlier, you need to go back and insert that point where it belongs. You know how frustrating it is when someone giving you directions says at the end, "Oh, wait a minute! I forgot to tell you to hang a left at the courthouse." A rough outline will let you avoid such discouraging mishaps in writing.

Be careful to start at the actual beginning. Mention any necessary preparation, any gathering of supplies, any tips on how to get started. If, for instance, you are going to explain how to bathe a large reluctant dog, you will first want to suggest putting on old clothes or a bathing suit and proceed from there. Your outline might look something like this:

### Sample Process Outline

**Thesis:** How to wash a dog without losing your temper or frightening the washee.

1. What to wear
   a. In summer—old clothes or bathing suit
   b. In winter—next to nothing in the shower

2. Gathering the implements
   a. Mild soap or dog shampoo
   b. Lots of old towels
   c. Hand-held hairdryer, if winter

3. Where to do it
   a. In summer—on driveway or patio to avoid killing grass with soap
   b. In winter—in bathtub with shower curtain drawn
   c. If no shower curtain, wait till summer

4. Reassuring the animal
   a. Dog thinks you plot a drowning
   b. Talk continually in soothing tones

5. The actual washing
   a. Wet entire dog, apply soap or shampoo, work up lather
   b. Keep soap out of eyes and ears
   c. Don't forget the underside and tail
   d. Rinse very thoroughly—then stand back

6. Drying the dog
   a. Dog will shake, like it or not
   b. Rub damp-dry with towels
   c. If winter, finish with hairdryer

You might conclude that having a shiny, fragrant, flealess dog makes all this tribulation worthwhile. Or you might instead conclude that dog owners in their right minds who can afford the fee should pack the beast off to the groomer and let the experts do it.

There are, of course, other sorts of process papers that do not lend themselves to this easy chronological organization—topics like "How to choose a personal computer" or "How to care for an aquarium." For such subjects, you must fall back on classification, which is covered later in this chapter.

## Developing Process Writing

The process paper, although easy to organize, is difficult to make interesting. You might begin with a brief narrative introduction recounting your first failed attempt to wash your Labrador retriever. Best to leave out the swearing, but include as many descriptive words and lively verbs as you can without making the whole thing sound grotesque.

You may assume that if you are describing a technical process, such as how to clean a carburetor or how to replace a hard drive, your readers will follow out of a desire for enlightenment. There is no obligation to entertain. But instead, you must be doubly sure to identify all parts and to explain each and every step clearly in language your readers will be able to understand. Define any terms that you suspect your readers may not know.

> **T I P S !**
>
> **Do not forget the getting ready part.**
>
> **Include all the necessary steps—in order.**
>
> **Warn about any possible mishaps.**

Make your word choice precise and concrete. If you are explaining how to change a light switch, do not say "Strip a *short* piece of wire"; say, "Strip *three centimetres* of wire." If you are describing how to repair a toaster, label the parts (*A, B, C, D*) to help your readers visualize what fits where.

Include reasons whenever possible—especially if knowing the reason helps your readers understand the process. After you tell your readers to mix the dry yeast with lukewarm water, mention that cold water will not activate the yeast and hot water will kill it, and either way, the bread will not rise.

If your process has any foreseeable mishaps, like a wet, shaggy dog shaking in the bathtub, you should warn your readers in advance to pull the shower curtain. If a dangerous mistake is possible, use italics or capital letters: "Before sticking your fingers in the fuse box, TURN OFF THE ELECTRICITY BY PULLING OUT THE MAIN FUSE."

## Pitfalls of Process Writing

The problems you encounter in process writing often have their roots in understanding your audience. Give careful consideration to how much—or how little—your readers know before deciding where to start your explanations. You need to back up far enough so that you do not lose them at the outset.

Your best bet is to enlist the help of someone whose knowledge of the process is about the same as that of your intended audience. Ask this person to read your draft and respond to these questions:

1. Have I chosen the right starting point? Did I give too much background information? Too little?

2. Have I defined enough terms? If not, which ones need clarifying?

3. Have I been specific enough in the details? Was the explanation unclear at any point? If so, where? How can I make it easier to follow?

## Topics for Process Writing

Before you begin, think about who your audience is and how much (or how little) they already know about your topic.

1. How to train an animal (dog, parrot, turtle, cat, or such).

2. How to get rid of a bad habit: nail biting, smoking, interrupting others, procrastination, habitual lateness.

3. Find out and explain how some simple, familiar thing works (for example: soap, can opener, ballpoint pen, automatic pencil sharpener).

4. Think of some established process that could use improvement (registration, income tax, or courtship, for example). Describe how a preferable substitute system would work.

5. Think of an everyday operation that you would like to have automated. Describe in detail how a fantasy machine would perform this function.

6. Using a health website, such as Health Canada's *(www.hc-sc.gc.ca)*, gather information on diabetes, breast cancer, SARS, Alzheimer's, arthritis, AIDS, or any other chronic illness. Write a paper explaining the symptoms of the disease, options for treatment, and the outlook for new drugs and therapies.

## Strategies for Classifying and Analyzing

We classify and analyze things all the time with no struggle at all. We classify political candidates into Conservative, Liberal, NDP, Parti Québécois, and so on. We classify doughnuts into plain-glazed, chocolate-covered, and jelly-filled. We analyze whenever we try to figure out a friend's behaviour or decide the best way to store the potatoes. If you are an English major, you might classify people into those who like Tolstoy, those who like murder mysteries, those who like spy novels, and those who like Harlequin romances. If you then try to figure out why some readers choose Tolstoy while others favour romance novels, you are analyzing.

For much of the writing you will be doing in your life, classification provides an effective means of organizing. Also, breaking a subject down into categories facilitates critical thinking by enabling you to examine and analyze the relationship of the parts.

## Organizing Classification and Analysis Writing

To make an outline using classification, you devise a way to separate the material into categories—preferably into orderly, meaningful categories. For instance, in a paper for your child psychology class, you might classify various methods of disciplining five-year-olds this way: (1) scolding, (2) calling time-outs, (3) withdrawing privileges, and (4) spanking.

In deciding how to arrange your points, there are lots of choices: easiest to hardest, least effective to most useful, earliest to most recent, top to bottom, least complicated to most complex, smallest to largest, or even least annoying to most annoying. The trick is to find some reasonable kind of logical division that suits your material.

The following outline shows how journalist Florence King organized her analysis of a stereotype, the "Good Ole Boy."

### Sample Classification Outline

**Thesis:** The Good Ole Boy is a Southern WASP type easy to recognize but difficult to pin down.

Introduction

1. Physical characteristics
   a. Middle-aged, jowlish, beer belly
   b. Big buckle, white socks, ten-gallon hat

2. Dominant types
   a. Pearl, the playful masher
   b. Calhoun, the kindly fascist

3. Typical attitudes
   a. A lover of little dinky females
   b. Always searching for the oversexed Melanie
   c. A worshiper at Johnny's Cash 'n' Carry Tavern

Conclusion

## Developing Classification and Analysis Writing

Usually you will announce what you are classifying or analyzing in your introduction: four methods of disciplining five-year-olds, three unfair government subsidy programs, six signs of a troubled marriage, three types of stress, and so on. Each section could be a single paragraph or several, but the major sections should be fairly equal in length. If you write 150 words about one type of stress, you should use about the same number of words on each of the other two.

If the material is complex, you can do your readers a favour by using headings. Under each heading, include similar information and present it in the same order. For instance, in writing about three kinds of stress, you might give the first type a heading, such as "Stress on the Job," followed by a description, followed by examples. Then you would present the material about the other two kinds of stress in the same way. This parallel development helps readers process the information more easily and clarifies the distinctions between categories.

## Pitfalls of Classification Writing

Here are a couple of things to watch out for when you work with classification.

1. *Be careful not to shift the basis of your division.*

   If that sounds confusing, look at the following skimpy outline, and you will understand what we mean.

   > **Types of Aardvarks**
   >
   > **A.** The fuzzy aardvark
   >
   > **B.** The hairless aardvark
   >
   > **C.** The friendly aardvark

   The first two categories of aardvarks are based on physical characteristics, while the last type shifts to personality. You see the worry this causes: Can a hairless aardvark be friendly? Are fuzzy aardvarks ill-tempered? How much hair does a friendly aardvark have?

2. *Be careful not to shift the rank of your division.*

   This simple outline will show you what can go wrong.

   > **Types of Recorded Music**
   >
   > **A.** Classical
   >
   > **B.** Easy listening
   >
   > **C.** Marilyn Manson

Although Marilyn Manson represents a type of music quite distinct from classical or easy listening, the third category is not parallel, not equal in rank, to the first two. It is too narrow. It should be heavy metal or alternative, with Marilyn Manson used as an example.

> **T I P !**
> Check your outline for shifts in categories.

## Topics for Classification and Analysis Writing

Before you begin, think about who your audience is and what point you want to make. Analyze your material thoughtfully.

1. If you have ever been a salesperson, receptionist, or food server, analyze and classify your clientele.

2. Interview ten people to discover their attitudes toward the death penalty. Classify, then analyze their responses.

3. What types of TV shows are the most popular this season? Analyze the appeal of each type.

4. Study a magazine advertisement or an ad campaign (a series of related ads, like the "I Am Canadian" beer commercials). To what emotions or beliefs is this advertising designed to appeal?

5.  Divide into types and analyze any of these subjects: neighbourhoods, marriages, laughter, prisoners, automobiles, intelligence, dreams, teachers, students, tennis players, drinkers, pet owners, jokes, novels, bicycles.

6.  Write an essay classifying several different methods for managing money that you see among your friends and family. Give specific examples to identify each type of money manager you know. To develop this topic, locate some websites that give advice and information about managing finances; see what kinds of problems and approaches they mention.

# Strategies for Comparative Writing

One of the most common methods of development involves focusing on similarities and differences—or perhaps on one or the other—in order to make a point. Sometimes writers use a comparison to clarify. An effective way, for instance, to explain impressionism in literature is to compare it with impressionism in painting, which is visual and thus easier for many to grasp. Frequently writers employ a comparison to persuade; for example, by paralleling the failure of Prohibition in the 1920s with the ineffectiveness of the contemporary war on drugs. Remember, by definition, comparison considers both similarities and differences.

When focusing on differences, writers often seek to show that one category is somehow better than the other. You could, for example, establish a useful contrast between two products, focusing on their differences, in order to recommend one as a better buy than the other. You could contrast the campaign promises of two candidates to establish which would be the better choice for mayor. Or you could humorously contrast the differences between toads and snakes in order to contend that toads make better pets than snakes.

## Organizing a Comparison

Whether focusing on differences or similarities, you have two ways of organizing a piece of comparison writing.

## Using *Block* Organization

Especially handy for responding to essay examinations, this simple method of organization also serves perfectly to show how something has changed or developed: your earliest views about AIDS compared with your views now; North Americans' attitudes toward Communism in the 1950s compared with attitudes today; Robertson Davies's early novels compared with his later ones. In general, follow these steps to organize using the block plan:

1.  State your purpose.

2.  Present your points for the first part of the comparison.

3.  Provide a transition.

    (for contrasts: *on the other hand, but, however, yet, in contrast, contrary to, nevertheless, nonetheless*)

(for similarities: *similarly, also, likewise, in the same way, in a similar manner*)

**4.** Present similar points for the second part of the comparison.

**5.** Draw your conclusions.

If, for example, you were going to write a paper comparing the relative merits of airbeds and waterbeds for people contemplating a purchase, your block outline might look like the one below.

### Sample Block Comparison Outline

**Thesis:** Airbeds have several major advantages over waterbeds but cost a great deal more.

Introduction
  A. Features of a waterbed
     1. Fills with a hose
     2. Adjusting for comfort tricky
     3. Needs an electric heater
     4. Extremely heavy when full of water
     5. Reasonable in cost

  B. Transition

  C. Features of an airbed
     1. Inflates with a button
     2. Adjusting for comfort easy
     3. No need for a heater
     4. Light because just full of air
     5. Expensive to buy

Conclusion

## Using *Point-by-Point* Organization

A more precise way of showing a contrast involves setting it up point by point. This arrangement sharpens the contrast, but it also requires more planning because you have to classify your material thoroughly. You choose as your major points of comparison those ideas that best illustrate the similarities or differences. For instance, say you decide to write an essay contrasting married life without children and married life with children. After thinking of several important ways that parenthood alters lifestyle, you might come up with an outline like this one.

### Sample Point-by-Point Comparison Outline

**Thesis:** Having children causes life changes that bring major increases in responsibilities.

  1. Sleep—and lack of
     a. Before kids
     b. After kids

  2. Household chores
     a. Before kids
     b. After kids

  3. Expenses—present and future

      a. Before kids
      b. After kids

  4. Leisure time activities
      a. Before kids
      b. After kids

  5. Romance in the marriage
      a. Before kids
      b. After kids

Conclusion: Parenthood involves sacrifices as well as joys.

You could, of course, use exactly this same material in writing an essay in block organization. The choice depends on which arrangement best suits your purpose.

## Developing a Comparison

The introduction of your essay should disclose the subject and set it in context. Here is a summary of the purposes mentioned earlier for using comparison:

1. to clarify (explaining the unfamiliar by comparing with the familiar)

2. to persuade (showing that one element is better than another)

3. to inform (comparing past and present or by showing differences between similar elements)

You may want to mention one of these purposes in your opening paragraph. For example, here is an introduction written by a reviewer in a paper focusing on differences between similar events—in this case, two concerts by Elton John:

> Time changes everything, or so we are told. Over a period of time our looks, opinions, and viewpoints change. When I was a kid, I was a rabid fan of Elton John. I idolized Captain Fantastic when I saw him perform at McCormick Place in June of 1976. Still a devoted admirer, I recently attended another concert and was surprised by the differences in the two performances.
>
> —Debbie Brown

Using the block pattern, Debbie then went on in the body of her paper to describe her response to the first concert; then, after making a transition, she described her response to the second one, concluding with this paragraph, summarizing her changed impressions:

> As his third encore, he gave us "Your Song." I stood on that hillside, tears streaming down my face, once again listening to my favourite singer performing my favourite song. By now my initial disappointment at discovering that Captain Fantastic had turned into Reg Dwight was totally gone. Idolizing had changed to respect. Yes, time changes many things—but not everything.

Notice that the first sentence of her introduction is "Time changes everything, or so we are told." She neatly echoes that line in her final sentence, giving her essay a satisfying closing.

## Pitfalls of Comparison Writing

You can avoid one major pitfall by presenting the material in each category in the same order. Here are a couple of other mistakes to avoid.

1. *Do not use too many transitional words.*

   Point-by-point comparison writing naturally involves a lot of shifting back and forth between ideas. But you will not need to signal each one with a transitional word because your reader will become familiar with the pattern and will be expecting the shifts. If you use too many transitional words, your reader will become annoyed at being forcibly led rather than guided.

2. *Do not apologize in your conclusion.*

   After presenting a strong case for the superiority of one item over another, you may get to the conclusion and panic. You are tempted to write, "Of course, this is just my opinion; others might disagree." Do not do it. This modesty undercuts the effectiveness of your paper.

## Topics for Comparison Writing

Before you begin, think about your purpose, who your audience is, and what point you want to make.

1. Discuss one or more illusions that are presented as reality on television, and compare the illusion with the reality as you know it.

2. Compare two lifestyles you have experienced, two novels, two films, a film and the book it was based on, two television characters, two cars you have driven, two sports you have played.

3. Several extraterrestrial beings visit Earth. On their planet people are neither male nor female: each person is both. Using one of these beings as a first-person narrator, explain how their society is different from ours.

4. Write about a situation in which you expected one thing and got another—in other words, the expectation and the reality were different. Consider: your first day of school, your university roommate, your first date, your high school prom, your wedding day, dining in an expensive restaurant.

5. Find a typical magazine for men and one for women. Discuss three or four major differences that set these publications apart.

6. Visit two similar websites—two museums, two zoos, two cooking sites, or two music sites, for example. After exploring both of them, write an article that compares the sites on the basis of which is more interesting and worthwhile.

# Strategies for Explaining Causes and Effects

Human beings are naturally curious. We want to know why. Why will the lawnmower not start? Why does the computer keep giving me that error message when I have done nothing wrong? Why are some people better at math than others? This common human impulse to understand why things happen provides a powerful motive for reading and writing.

A lot of the writing done in college and university courses requires cause-and-effect thinking. Students are asked, for example, to explain the causes of the Northwest Rebellion, the origins of prejudice, the consequences of divorce on children, the effects of sleep deprivation on learning. As a bonus, once you learn to analyze causes and effects, you will become good at problem solving—a useful skill both on the job and in everyday life.

## Organizing Cause-and-Effect Writing

When you develop a piece of writing by analyzing causes, you are explaining to your readers why something happened. If you go on to explore the effects, you are analyzing what happened—the consequences. For example, if your topic is divorce and you write "Why Teenage Marriages Fail," that is primarily a cause paper. But if you write "What Divorce Does to Young Children," that is primarily an effect paper. You will probably stick to one purpose in a single essay, but you might take up both causes and effects if you have the time and the assignment allows.

## Focusing on Causes

Begin by describing a condition or result or problem (like having claustrophobia, failing your philosophy course, having your car's engine overheat), and then explain as fully as possible the causes or reasons.

Sometimes you may be able to use chronological organization. If, for instance, the problem is your claustrophobia, you could trace its development from the earliest cause at age five (getting locked in a broom closet), through another incident at age eleven (getting locked in a restroom), to the latest trauma at age twenty (getting locked in a stairwell).

More likely, though, your organization will fall into some logical pattern based on the relative importance of the causes—from least significant to most vital, from the most subtle to the most obvious, from local to nationwide. The following sample outline is arranged from the most understandable causes (poor reading and writing skills) to the least defensible one (missing class).

### Sample Outline Focusing on Causes

**Thesis:** I failed Philosophy 101 for several reasons, mostly the result of my own shortcomings.

A. I couldn't do the reading.
   1. Abstract material is especially hard for me.
   2. I couldn't follow the textbook.

B. I wasn't good at writing either.
   1. I couldn't express the complicated ideas asked for on exams.
   2. I put writing the papers off for so long that every one was turned in late.

   C. I was intimidated by the class discussion.
      1. Usually I could not answer when called on because I did not understand the ideas.
      2. Because I felt so stupid, I never asked questions that might have helped me.
   D. The class met at 8 a.m., so I often slept through it.
Conclusion: Because this class is required, I resolve to work harder next time.

## Focusing on Effects

You can start with some condition or event and explain the consequences. For example, you might begin by describing the breakup with your girlfriend and then go on to show how it affected you. Again, you can present the effects as they happened. At first you were depressed; then you began to spend more time with your friends. You also had more time to study, so your grades improved. Finally, you began to date again and found a much better girlfriend.

   More likely, though, you will want to sort your ideas into some logical arrangement that has more to do with the importance of the effects than simply with chronology, as we suggest above. In the following outline, the effects are classified into negative and positive. Because the writer wants to emphasize the positive effects, she puts them last.

**Sample Outline Focusing on Effects**

**Thesis:** My family has adjusted well to having Mom become a university student.
Introduction: After ten years as a housewife, I have gone back to university amid a chorus of whining.
   A. Negative effects
      1. My husband feels a bit intimidated.
      2. The children's clothes don't always get ironed.
      3. The house is not as clean as it used to be.
      4. I no longer have time to read for pleasure.
   B. Positive effects
      1. My husband is learning to know our children by sharing their care.
      2. The kids are learning to accept personal and family responsibilities.
      3. I enjoy a rewarding sense of accomplishment and have been freed from some boring housework.
Conclusion: The family has risen to the challenge, has accepted the changes, and now takes pride in my good grades.

## Developing Cause-and-Effect Writing

Since people are naturally curious about causes and effects, a good introduction will stimulate your readers to ask "Why?" For instance, if you are writing about what causes a hangover, you could begin by saying, "When you take two aspirins with a glass of water to cure a hangover, the water probably does you more good than the aspirin." Then you go on to explain in detail how alcohol dehydrates the cells, causing headache, dry mouth, and general malaise.

Another good way to begin is by making a prediction. Then in the body of the paper, you discuss the reasons that allow you to make such a statement. For example, you might begin an essay by declaring, "If you put radial tires on your car, you will probably save thirty-five dollars on gas next winter." Your readers will want to know how radial tires save gas, so you tell them.

In your conclusion, you can use any of the standard strategies—advise the reader, predict the future, or issue a call for action. Another strategy that works well in some cause-and-effect papers involves suggesting larger areas that your subject might branch into, leaving your reader with something additional to think about. If you are explaining how agricultural chemicals get into the grain fed to animals, for instance, you could close with an observation on the probable contamination also of drinking water and soil by herbicides and pesticides.

## Pitfalls of Cause-and-Effect Writing

An explanation of causes and effects will not be successful if your readers find your thinking fuzzy or flawed.

1. *Avoid oversimplifying.*

   Most conditions and events are complex, involving multiple causes and numerous effects. In a short essay, you may have to focus on only the primary reasons, so be sure to let your readers know that this is what you are doing.

2. *Be sure your causes are valid.*

   Just because you catch a cold after forgetting your sweater on a cold day does not mean that getting chilled caused the cold. More likely, someone sneezed on you. Before writing on causes, study "Jumping to Conclusions" in the section on logic in Chapter 7 (p. 94).

3. *Do not confuse the words* effect *and* affect.

   Check these words in Chapter 15 if you have a problem keeping them straight.

## Topics for Cause-and-Effect Writing

Before you begin, think about who your audience is and what point you want to make. After completing your outline, examine the logic of your causal analysis.

1. Discuss the probable causes of any situation, practice, law, or custom that strikes you as unfair.

2. Imagine that a close friend tells you that she/he is homosexual. The friend is the same sex as you. What are your reactions? Why would you have these reactions?

3. All school attendance has just been declared voluntary. How will this change the schools?

4. Explain the causes (or effects) of any drastic change of opinion, attitude, or behaviour you have undergone in your life.

5. Write a paper in which you explain what causes some natural phenomenon (for example, rain, dew, blue sky, twinkling stars, sweat, hiccups, the phases of the moon).

6. Does playing video games shape values and affect personality? Brainstorm to jumpstart your own thinking; then gather more information and ideas by browsing the internet. Look at sites where video games are advertised and played, as well as those where other points of view might be provided, such as sites created by parent–teacher associations.

# Composing Effective Paragraphs

Your writing will be made up of paragraphs: first, an effective introduction; then several interesting, unified, well-developed body paragraphs; and finally, a forceful, emphatic conclusion. Since the body paragraphs are the heart of any piece of writing, let us begin with them.

## Understanding the Basic Paragraph

If you are doing academic, business, or technical writing, the paragraphs that constitute the body of your paper should each have a topic sentence supported by plenty of concrete details. The average paragraph runs from about 100 to 150 words—somewhat longer in formal writing and considerably shorter in newspaper and magazine stories, where the small type in narrow columns requires frequent breaks to avoid eye strain and make for easier reading.

### Use a Topic Sentence

Every paragraph is going to be about something: it will describe something, question something, demand something, reject something, define something, explain something. That "something" can be identified in a topic sentence. Although narratives and descriptions may not include an explicit topic sentence, most informative writing does.

When writing reports, position papers, academic essays, summaries, and examinations, you will almost always place the topic sentence first. Like the thesis sentence for an essay, a topic sentence states the controlling idea for the paragraph. The ideas and details within the paragraph will support, elaborate, interpret, illustrate, or justify that idea. As you develop your thoughts in a paragraph, be sure that all the points and details pertain to the idea stated in the topic sentence. If, for instance, you decide to write a paragraph about the undeserved good reputation of dogs, you might begin with this topic sentence: "Far from being our best friends, dogs are slow-witted, servile, useless beasts that seldom deserve their board and keep." Then you trot out examples of slavish spaniels and doltish Great Danes you have known in order to convince your readers that dogs are more trouble than they are worth. But if you observe that "Cats are pretty contemptible, too," you need a new paragraph and a new topic sentence. Otherwise, toss that comment out as being beside the point, the point being whatever idea you committed yourself to in the topic sentence.

### Build on the Topic Sentence

The topic sentence states the main idea in each paragraph. You build on that idea by supplying facts, figures, examples, reasons, explanations, and specific details that relate to the topic sentence. A building strategy that works for some writers is based on the theory that each sentence in a paragraph stems directly from the sentence before it and in some way responds to it. Thus, adding material in a paragraph becomes a matter of expectation and response: each sentence responds to the one before it as well as providing the expectation (or idea) to which the next sentence will relate.

Let us look at a paragraph that begins with the following topic sentence:

The new McDonald's system was predicated on careful attention to detail.

As a reader, what do you expect from that sentence? You will probably want to know about that "attention to detail." So if the next sentence were something like

The McDonald brothers began their business in Chicago.

you might feel a slight confusion or a momentary letdown because you were expecting something else. As a matter of fact, the next sentence in the original paragraph does pick up on the expectation about attention to detail:

The McDonald brothers shortened the spindles on their Multi-Mixers so that shakes and malts could be made directly in paper cups.

Now, what do you expect from that sentence? You may want to know why that detail is important. So the writer explains with this next sentence:

There would be no metal mixing containers to wash, no wasted ingredients, no wasted motion.

The writer then adds a series of similar details, as you might expect, like this:

They developed dispensers that put the same amount of catsup or mustard on every bun. They installed a bank of infrared lamps to keep French fries hot. They used disposable paper goods instead of glassware and china. They installed a microphone to amplify the customer's voice and reduce misunderstandings about what was being ordered.

> **T I P !**
> **Stay focused on the main idea expressed in your topic sentence.**
> Make sure that whatever you put in a paragraph helps your readers understand that main idea.

After this series of examples, what do you expect next? You probably want to know what all this attention to detail adds up to, so the writer concludes with these statements that sum up the significance of the paragraph and bring it to a close:

By 1952 the McDonald brothers' employees, all men dressed neatly in white, were said to be capable of serving the customer a hamburger, a beverage, French fries, and ice cream in twenty seconds. Word of their proficiency began to spread through the restaurant industry.

—Philip Langdon, "Burgers! Shakes!" *Atlantic Monthly*

## EXERCISE 4.1: WRITING

Choose one of the topic sentences below and write a paragraph of about 150 words using the "expectation and response" strategy for paragraph development explained in the preceding section. Feel free to alter and adapt the topic sentence to fit your interests and experience.

1. My "bargain" used car caused me no end of trouble in my first week of ownership.
2. When I offered to build a fire at our campsite, I thought I could have it roaring in about five minutes.
3. I know that claustrophobia is all in the mind, but I still feel panic coming on when I'm in a closed space. [Substitute your own favourite phobia.]
4. If I am having trouble getting started writing, I go through a few familiar rituals.
5. Since I am by nature a night person, having to get up at six in the morning brings out the worst in me.

# Developing the Ideas Fully

Adequate and interesting development of material is crucial to writing effective paragraphs. Most experienced writers make their ideas clear and convincing by providing support for every observation or generalization. This supporting material may appear as descriptive details, factual items, illustrations and examples, or a combination of these varied modes of development.

## Use Descriptive Details

Descriptive details are usually intended to convey an impression—how something looked, smelled, tasted. They are especially effective in recounting personal experiences, detailing eyewitness accounts, and establishing ambience and mood—as in John Richardson's dramatic personification of the St. Lawrence River in *Wacousta*, a novel published in 1832:

> At the opposite extremity of this magnificent and sea-like lake, which is upwards of two hundred miles in circumference, the far-famed St. Lawrence takes her source; and after passing through a vast tract of country, whose elevated banks bear every trace of fertility and cultivation, connects itself with the Lake Champlain, celebrated, as well as Erie, for a signal defeat of our flotilla during the late contest with the Americans. Pushing her bold waters through this somewhat inferior lake, the St. Lawrence pursues her course seaward with impetuosity, until arrested near La Chine by rock-studded shallows, which produce those strong current and eddies, the dangers of which are so beautifully expressed in the Canadian Boat Song,—a composition that has rendered the "rapids" almost as familiar to the imagination of the European as the falls of Niagara themselves. Beyond La Chine the St. Lawrence gradually unfolds herself into greater majesty and expanse, and rolling past the busy commercial town of Montreal, is once more increased in volume by the insignificant lake of St. Peter's, nearly opposite to the settlement of Three Rivers, midway between Montreal and Quebec. From thence she pursues her course unfed, except by a few inferior streams, and gradually

widens as she rolls past the capital of the Canadas, whose tall and precipitous battlements, bristled with cannon, and frowning defiance from the clouds in which they appear half imbedded, might be taken by the imaginative enthusiast for the strong tower of the Spirit of those stupendous scenes. From this point the St. Lawrence increases in expanse, until, at length, after traversing a country where the traces of civilisation become gradually less and less visible, she finally merges in the gulf, from the centre of which the shores on either hand are often invisible to the naked eye; and in this manner is it imperceptibly lost in that misty ocean, so dangerous to mariners from its deceptive and almost perpetual fogs.

## EXERCISE 4.2: DESCRIPTION

Rewrite the following paragraph, adding as many descriptive details as you can to make this rural portrait more interesting and effective.

> The barn sat in the field. It had not been used for many years. The rail fences that had once enclosed its paddocks were gone. Weeds and shrubs grew around it. Its loft had caved in. As each winter came and went, the barn became more dilapidated. It was a symbol of what had happened to small farms in this area.

## Supply Factual Information

You can use facts and figures, if you have them, in developing your ideas. Note how the author of the following paragraph uses factual details to support the topic sentence at the beginning:

> No one change led to the virtual demise of the train robbery. A combination of stronger steel cars, modern law-enforcement techniques, and improved methods of transferring wealth made robbing trains too risky and unrewarding. Other forms of illegal activity in the 20th century occupied men (and a few women) who might have preyed on passenger trains fifty years ago. Bootlegging liquor, for example, seemed to be the 1930s equivalent of blowing up express cars.
>
> —John P. Hankey

This next paragraph is developed primarily by citing statistics:

> The linguist Michael Krauss says that as many as 3,000 languages, comprising half of all the words on earth, are doomed to silence in the next century. According to Krauss, who keeps count of dead and dying languages, 210 of the original 300 or more languages once spoken in the United States and Canada remain in use or in memory; 175 are spoken in the United States, including Alaska, and of these all but 20, perhaps fewer, cannot survive much longer. Only 250 languages in the entire world have at least a million speakers, considered the necessary safety level as globalization homogenizes every nation, every village, no matter how remote. Only languages with state sponsorship seem likely to survive: Spanish, French, English, Italian, etc. What of the more than 800 languages of Papua New Guinea? The 410 of Nigeria? The more than 300 in India?
>
> —Earl Shorris

## Provide Illustrations and Examples

Most of the time writers use illustrations and examples to flesh out paragraphs. Here is a paragraph that supports the claim in its topic sentence with one main example:

> The history of medicine is replete with accounts of drugs or modes of treatment that were in use for many years before it was recognized that they did more harm than good. For centuries, for example, doctors believed that drawing blood from patients was essential for rapid recovery from virtually every illness. Then, midway through the 19th century, it was discovered that bleeding served to weaken the patient. King Charles II's death is believed to have been caused in part by administered bleedings. George Washington's death was also hastened by the severe loss of blood resulting from this treatment.
>
> —Norman Cousins

In this next example the writer develops his paragraph by naming and describing the tests referred to in the topic sentence:

> Neurologists have a host of clinical tests that let them observe what a brain-damaged patient can and cannot do. They stroke his sole to test for a spinal reflex known as Babinski's sign or have her stand with her feet together and eyes closed to see if the ability to maintain posture is compromised. They ask him to repeat a set of seven random digits forward and four in reverse order, to spell *world* backward, to remember three specific words such as *barn* and *handsome* and *job* after a spell of unrelated conversations. A new laboratory technique . . . uses radioactively labeled oxygen or glucose that essentially lights up specific and different areas of the brain being used when a person speaks words or see words or hears words, revealing the organic location for areas of behavioral malfunction.
>
> —Floyd Skloot

## Be Specific and Concrete

Abstract words like *democracy, truth, justice, liberty,* and other familiar terms mean different things to different people. And sometimes they convey little meaning at all. Consider the following paragraph that purports to explain what a "democratic" education can do for a child:

> A democratic plan of education includes more than the mere transmission of the social heritage and an attempt to reproduce existing institutions in a static form. The purpose of democratic education is the development of well-integrated individuals who can live successfully in an ever-changing dynamic culture. The democratic school is also required to indoctrinate individuals with the democratic tradition which, in turn, is based on the agitative liberties of the individual and the needs of society.

If you can divine meaning from this paragraph, it is a vague, shadowy sort of understanding that cannot be pinned down precisely because of the numerous abstract words: *democratic, social heritage, well-integrated, dynamic culture*. And what *agitative liberties* are, only the writer knows. He does not provide a hint. The entire passage contains not a single concrete example to help us grasp the ideas.

You cannot avoid abstractions entirely, of course, but try to follow abstract words with concrete illustrations. For example, if you say that motorcycle riding can be *dangerous* (an abstract concept), mention the crushed noses, the dislocated limbs, the splintered teeth, the broken bones. Or provide some statistics about the high cost of insurance for motorcyclists and the frequency and severity of their accidents.

### ▓ EXERCISE 4.3: REVISING

Rewrite the following paragraph about first dates, adding specific details and concrete examples that will bring the material to life. Be as creative as you wish. Feel free to alter wording. Use first person (*I, me, my*) if that approach works best.

> A first date is always a risky occasion, with endless possibilities for disaster and disappointment. Sometimes both people realize at the very beginning of the date that it is a mistake. At other times they get to know each other a little before they see that their interests and personalities do not fit well at all. And frequently, only at the end of the date does the mismatch become clear.

### ▓ EXERCISE 4.4: WRITING

Think of a concept or an idea that is hard to explain to someone else. It might be a scientific principle, a belief about love or friendship, a political term, a formula for success. Write a paragraph about this concept, using examples and concrete details to help you clarify your thinking. Show your paragraph to several classmates; ask them if they understand what you mean. If they have trouble understanding, ask them to help you decide what changes or additions are needed to make your explanation clear.

## Keeping Your Readers with You: Unity and Coherence

As you are constructing paragraphs and putting them together to make a paper, remember that you want your readers to understand what you have written and to understand it easily on the first reading. You do not want them to get lost when you move from one idea to the next or when you change the direction of your ideas. The things you do to make your writing *unified* and *coherent*, to make it hang together, are fairly simple; yet they can often mean the difference between a first-rate paper and a merely passable one.

### Maintain Coherence Within Paragraphs

The first principle for writing a coherent paragraph is to make sure the sentences follow one another in a clear, logical sequence. Using the "expectation and response" strategy that we described earlier in this chapter will do a lot to ensure that your thoughts flow smoothly. But there still may be places where you need to provide signposts to guide your readers through your prose.

**REPEAT KEY WORDS.** One way to achieve coherence in a paragraph is to repeat key terms. Most of this repetition occurs naturally as you write, but being aware of the process will help you when you revise. In the following paragraph, observe how the sentences are held together by repeating the key word *choices* and the pronouns that refer to it (all italicized so you can notice them):

> Everyone makes *choices*, every day, although some of *these* are more crucial than *others*, and at every point where a *choice* is made, another *choice* is not, and if our life is defined by the *choices* we have made, it is also haunted, at least in moments of thoughtfulness, by *those* that weren't.
>
> —David Helwig

**SUPPLY CONNECTORS AND TRANSITIONS.** You can also use certain words and phrases to indicate the connections between details and ideas. These include coordinating conjunctions—*and, but, or, for, nor, yet,* and *so*—to link words, phrases, and clauses; subordinating conjunctions, such as *if, although, when, because, since,* and *unless,* which mark different levels of importance among ideas; conjunctive adverbs, such as *however, thus, therefore, indeed, furthermore,* and *consequently*; and transitional phrases such as *for example, in addition, on the other hand,* and *in fact.*

Figure 4.1 (p. 47) lists the most common shifts in thought that writers make (such as moving to a new point, adding an example, providing a contrast) and then offers a wide selection of words and phrases to fit each shift. Take note of the different types of transition illustrated; then tuck in a bookmark in case you get stuck and need a transition to help you over a rough spot.

In the following paragraph, biologist Stephen Jay Gould achieves coherence by skilfully blending transitional words and phrases, which we have italicized, with a series of repeated key terms *(brain, body, animal, large, small),* which we have put in boldface type:

> I don't wish to deny that the flattened, minuscule head of the **large bodied** "Stegosaurus" houses **little brain** from our subjective, top-heavy perspective, *but* I do wish to assert that we should not expect more of the beast. *First of all*, **large animals** have relatively **smaller brains** than related, **small animals.** The correlation on **brain** size among kindred **animals** (all reptiles, all mammals, *for example*) is remarkably regular. *As* we move from **small** to **large animals,** from mice to elephants *or* small lizards to Komodo dragons, **brain** size increases, *but* not so fast as **body** size. *In other words*, **bodies** grow faster than **brains,** *and* **large animals** have low ratios of **brain** weight to **body** weight. *In fact*, **brains** grow only about two-thirds as fast as **bodies.** *Since* we have no reason to believe that **large animals** are consistently stupider than their **smaller** relatives, we must conclude that **large animals** require relatively less **brain** to do as well as **smaller animals.** *If* we do not recognize this relationship, we are likely to underestimate the mental power of very **large animals,** dinosaurs in particular.
>
> —"Were Dinosaurs Dumb?" *The Panda's Thumb*

**To move to the next major point:**

| | | |
|---|---|---|
| *too* | *moreover* | *next* |
| *in the first place* | *second* | *third* |
| *again* | *besides* | *in addition* |
| *further* | *likewise* | *also* |
| *furthermore* | *beyond this* | *admittedly* |
| *like* | *eventually* | |

Examples:  We *also* can see that the quality of most television programs is abysmal.

*Furthermore*, the commercials constantly assault our taste and insult our intelligence.

**To add an example:**

| | | |
|---|---|---|
| *for example* | *for instance* | *such as* |
| *that is* | *in the following manner* | *namely* |
| *in this case* | *in the same manner* | *as an illustration* |
| *at the same time* | *in addition* | *incidentally* |

Examples:  The daytime game shows, *for instance*, openly appeal to human greed.

Soap operas, *in the same manner*, pander to many of our baser instincts.

**To emphasize a point:**

| | | |
|---|---|---|
| *especially* | *without doubt* | *ultimately* |
| *chiefly* | *actually* | *primarily* |
| *after all* | *as a matter of fact* | *otherwise* |
| *without question* | *even more* | *in fact* |
| *more important* | | |

Examples:  The constant violence depicted on television, *in fact*, poses a danger to society.

*Even more* offensive are deodorant commercials, *without question* the most tasteless on TV.

**To contrast a point:**

| | | |
|---|---|---|
| *but* | *still* | *on the other hand* |
| *on the contrary* | *nevertheless* | *contrary to* |
| *however* | *nonetheless* | *conversely* |
| *yet* | *although* | *in contrast* |
| *neither* | | |

Examples:  We abhor violence, *yet* we cannot approve of censorship.

*Although* commercials may enrage or sicken us, they do, *after all*, pay the bills.

**To qualify a point:**

| | | |
|---|---|---|
| *in some cases* | *admittedly* | *of course* |
| *granted that* | *no doubt* | *certainly* |

Examples:  There are, *of course*, fine educational programs on public television and some cable networks.

*Admittedly*, these shows enrich our culture; *in some cases*, they are inspiring and enlightening.

**To conclude or sum up a point:**

| | | |
|---|---|---|
| *consequently* | *therefore* | *so* |
| *accordingly* | *then* | *as a result* |
| *hence* | *in sum* | *in conclusion* |
| *in other words* | *thus* | *before* |
| *in short* | *finally* | *at last* |

Examples:  Soap operas *thus* contribute to the subtle erosion of moral values.

Commercials, *therefore*, are not worth the sacrifice of our integrity.

Television, *in short*, costs more than society should be willing to pay.

**FIGURE 4.1** *Useful Transitional Terms*

## Try Rhetorical Questions and Short Sentences

> He hath brought many captives home to Rome,
> Whose ransoms did the general coffers fill;
> Did this in Caesar seem ambitious?
>
> —Mark Antony in *Julius Caesar*, 3.2

The use of rhetorical questions, as in Mark Antony's famous speech, can be a very effective technique. Posing a question that you intend to answer, or a question in which the answer is already implied, may cleverly influence your readers and lead them into your next point, but you probably cannot get away with this technique too often in a short paper. You must have other devices in stock.

Like the rhetorical question, the short-sentence transition must not be used often, but it comes in handy when you need it. You simply state briefly and clearly what you intend to discuss next, like this:

> While stories can be read differently and analysed in various ways, most serious authors write for aesthetic readers. *Let me explain what I mean.* [Italics added.]
>
> —Don Gutteridge

The following paragraph uses a short-sentence question as a transition:

> I am convinced that Canada has a soul, and should get on better terms with it, because at the moment it is a sadly neglected aspect of our inheritance. And that is why I am sitting at this moment in St. James's Cathedral in Toronto, trying to bring my thoughts together in the hope of involving you in this neglected reality. *But how, and where, should we begin?* [Italics added.]
>
> —Robertson Davies

Molly Ivins uses both a question and a short sentence (together with several transitional expressions) to move her readers along in this paragraph:

> While we're meditating on Christmas gifts, let us consider who got coal and switches this year. According to the Center on Budget and Policy Priorities, 93 percent of all the entitlement reductions passed by Congress in the last two years were in cuts for programs for poor people. *This is an appropriately Dickensian plot for the season, don't you think?* Ninety-three percent of everything that's been done to balance the budget in this way is being taken out of the pittance of low-income people. *Of course, not all the news is bad.* CEO Michael Ovitz, for example, will receive at least $95 million in compensation for leaving the Disney Company after sixteen months of what is widely regarded as an unsatisfactory performance. [Italics added.]
>
> —"Early Christmas for Aerospace Giants"

## ■ EXERCISE 4.5: TRANSITIONS

In the paragraph below, we have removed the transitional terms and have inserted blanks in their place. Read each sentence carefully to determine which word or phrase from Figure 4.1 best conveys the meaning of the transition needed. Write your choice in the blank. Notice the punctuation so that you can tell when to use a capital letter.

Billy Bishop, a Canadian from Owen Sound, Ontario, was one of the most famous and successful of all Allied aces in World War I, _____ being credited with over seventy "confirmed victories," as they were termed, by the end of the war. _____, his escapades even included an encounter with the infamous Red Baron, from which, _____, both pilots flew away relatively unscathed. _____, Bishop rose to the rank of Marshal in the RCAF and, _____, was awarded the Croix de Guerre with Palm and the Victoria Cross. _____, Bishop's feats became a subject of controversy. Much of it revolved around certain uncorroborated combat reports that he submitted; _____, on June 2, 1917, he reported having engaged in a dogfight with four enemy aircraft over a heavily armed aerodrome, destroying all four. Although his deeds were acknowledged after nine weeks of investigation by the command authority, many of his colleagues felt that his account was pure fiction. The "Bishop Controversy," _____, has been refuelled in recent years with the publication of Brereton Greenhous's *The Making of Billy Bishop* and the National Film Board documentary *The Kid Who Couldn't Miss*, both of which challenge the authenticity of Bishop's description of his exploits. _____, other accounts, such as Dan McCaffery's *Billy Bishop: Canadian Hero* and David Bashow's chapter on Bishop in *Knights of the Air*, present different sides of the controversy. _____, just as he emerged from the battle-ravaged skies of World War I, so Billy Bishop remains today—larger than life in word and deed, a tantalizingly complex figure of wonder and mystery.

## Provide Transitions Between Paragraphs

You may sometimes need signposts for your readers when you change paragraphs. The indention for a new paragraph provides a visual clue that you are moving on to another main idea, but indention alone is not always helpful. Often you can use those same devices that you use when your thought changes direction or you want to add another example within the same paragraph: transitional expressions, rhetorical questions, and short transitional sentences. For instance, here are the opening sentences from several paragraphs of a student essay on fighting in hockey (the transitional words and phrases have been italicized).

*Ever since I was a kid*, watching a fight in a hockey game has seemed boring to me, paling by comparison with any real boxing match such as you might find in the Olympics.

*After the players glare at each other*, the actual conflict is usually a mix of flying gloves and aggressive tugging.

*Nevertheless*, for most fans these juvenile wrestling matches seem to be the highlight of the game.

*And* in the United States, this aspect of hockey seems to be the way the game is principally promoted.

*While* it is doubtful that fighting will ever be banned from the game, *even* the NHL has taken steps to curtail its role.

For many fans, *especially* those who enjoy the speed and skill and physical contact of the game, the outbreak of a fight is a good time to visit the concession stands, or, if they are watching on television, to head for the refrigerator.

### EXERCISE 4.6: WRITING

The student's organization and transitions are so effective that you can probably follow the development of her argument, even though you do not have the complete text of the essay. Write a paragraph in which you summarize the student's main ideas.

**USE ECHO TRANSITIONS.** An *echo transition* gives you a subtle way to move smoothly from one paragraph to the next. You manage this artful transition by "echoing" the last idea in one paragraph at the beginning of the next. You create the echo by repeating the same word or by using a word meaning the same thing, which thus "echoes" the idea. It is an effective technique and not difficult to perform once you see how it works. Here is an example from an essay by Northrop Frye in which he discusses the importance of the humanities in his life.

> Grammar taught me language as a *structure*. I even learned the elementary categories of philosophy from grammar, things like the concrete, the abstract, the particular and the universal.
>
> I think that a student often leaves high school today without any sense of language as a *structure*. He may also have the idea that reading and writing are elementary skills that he mastered in childhood, never having grasped the fact that there are differences in levels of reading and writing as there are in mathematics between short division and integral calculus. [Italics added.]
>
> —Northrop Frye

You can see how the repetition of the word *structure* in the opening sentence of the new paragraph forms a link to the previous paragraph and at the same time leads into Frye's next idea.

You do not have to repeat the very same word. You can, for instance, use a synonym or a related phrase, as in this next example, which gives you the final sentence from a paragraph about the destructive ice storm that hit Quebec and Ontario in 1998, followed by the opening sentence of the next paragraph which recounts some specific details of the storm. The transitional words are italicized.

> Nearly five days of freezing rain spread *a deadly sheet of ice* across Ontario and Quebec; as everything from trees and barns to hydro poles and power lines began to collapse, it became apparent that this was to be one of the greatest natural disasters in Canadian history.

> A *catastrophic frozen blanket* left thousands of communities in the dark and cold for days; some for over a month.

Finally, notice the easy transition from a paragraph describing negative human attitudes toward nature to the observation that, historically, humans have been intrinsically linked to nature. The contrast is dramatic; the transition, smooth and effective.

> Children learn attitudes and values very quickly and the lesson in cities is very clear—nature is an enemy, it's dirty, dangerous or a nuisance. *So youngsters learn to distance themselves* from nature and try to control it. I am astonished at the number of adults who loathe or are terrified by snakes, spiders, butterflies, worms, birds—the list seems endless.
>
> If you reflect on the history of humankind, you realize that for 99 per cent of our species' existence, *we were deeply embedded in and dependent on nature.* [Italics added.]
>
> —David Suzuki

### ▨ EXERCISE 4.7: COHERENCE

Locate an essay, article, or chapter of a book that uses a variety of strategies for achieving unity and coherence. Identify these strategies—transitional expressions, repeated words, rhetorical questions, short sentences, echo transitions—and comment on their effectiveness.

## Composing Special Paragraphs

Not all of your paragraphs are going to conform to the advice we have been giving you about the content and organization of typical paragraphs. Most notably, introductions and conclusions have special requirements that you need to consider.

### Advice About Introductions

You can draft the introduction to a paper at any point during the writing process. Some people like to write it first as a way of getting started; others wait till last so they can tailor it to fit the rest of the essay. Regardless of when you write the introduction, remember that because your audience reads it first, it should make a favourable impression.

**STATE YOUR THESIS.** Although getting your readers' attention is an important element of most introductions, the chief function is to let readers know what you are writing about. You will not always need a straightforward announcement of your central idea, but the more formal the writing, the more likely you are to need a clear thesis statement. In the following introduction the writer comes straight to the point:

> The main issue facing the Dene is not the proposed Mackenzie Valley pipeline or some such other colonial development. The issue facing us today is the same

> issue that has confronted us since the first non-Dene arrived in our land. The issue is recognition of our national rights, recognition of our right to be a self-governing people.
>
> —Georges Erasmus

This is point-blank as introductions go. Normally, you take several sentences to work up to your main idea, giving a little background information or making some fairly broad remarks about your subject, then narrowing the focus to the specific idea in your thesis. This method is used in the following introduction (thesis statements are italicized throughout this section):

> Like millions of other viewers, I watched the Barbara Walters interview with Monica Lewinsky. As I have been doing all my life, I watched television in order to gain a sense of the world I live in, to know the world. Through the years, I have read many texts, written some, spoken and listened to many more, and these texts have shaped my knowledge and knowing in ways I cannot even begin to spell out, but *no texts have shaped me more than the texts of television*.
>
> —Carl Leggo

The article then analyzes several critical perspectives on the effects of television viewing and explains certain skills that need to be developed to attain a degree of television literacy.

**CATCH YOUR READERS' ATTENTION.** Unless you are writing for readers who already have a professional interest in the topic of your paper, you need an introduction that will catch their attention and encourage them to continue reading. One good way involves putting a picture in their minds, as the writer does in this introduction:

> You know the couch potato: the flabby muscles and a generous waistline, one hand on the remote control and the other in a bag of chips. Medical research now has confirmed the aptness of this depiction. *Long hours in front of the tube and obesity, it turns out, go together like* Monday Night Football *and beer nuts.*
>
> —Elizabeth Stark

**FIND FASCINATING FACTS.** Another way to hook your readers is to begin with some interesting facts and figures, as in this introduction:

> Canada's 2004 federal election boasted a whopping twelve registered or eligible political parties, each trying to elect its candidates as members of Parliament. More than 1800 hopefuls ran in 308 electoral districts, with over 21 million Canadians eligible to vote. Competing for seats, of course, were representatives of the parties that traditionally dominate the voting: the Liberals, NDP, Bloc Québécois, and Conservatives. But appearing proudly alongside the usual suspects on our ballots were no less than eight minority parties: the Canadian Action Party, the Christian Heritage Party of Canada, the Communist Party of Canada, the Green Party of Canada, the Marijuana Party, the Marxist-Leninist Party of Canada, the Libertarian Party, and the Progressive Canadian Party. Still more parties, such as the Na-

tional Alternative Party of Canada, The Ontario Party of Canada, and the Absolutely Absurd Party of Canada, having lost their eligibility, were disqualified from fielding candidates. But how, you might wonder, do those lesser parties that manage to make the ballot even get that far? *Minority parties make their mark by standing for a specific set of beliefs that offer clear alternatives to the voting public.*

**SELECT A QUOTATION.** Sometimes a relevant and interesting quotation provides an effective way to introduce your main idea. In the following introduction from an essay on crime statistics, the author uses dialogue from a popular film to set up his main idea:

> One of the great comedic scenes of modern times takes place in the 1977 Woody Allen movie *Annie Hall*, in which Allen and Diane Keaton play an embattled couple who tell their shrinks how often they have sex. "Constantly!" says Keaton's character. "I'd say three times a week." On the other hand, says Allen's character: "Hardly ever. Maybe three times a week." In the language of shrinks, that kind of situation is known as "desire discrepancy": the two sides agree on the numbers, but extrapolate entirely different conclusions. *The same thing applies to the way we look at crime-related issues in Canada.*
>
> —Anthony Wilson-Smith, *Maclean's*

**TRY A DEFINITION.** Another useful way to get started is by defining your subject, like this:

> Tennyson called it a "flying game." Benjamin Franklin termed it a "sudden and terrible mischief." In Roman mythology, the god Jupiter used spiky thunderbolts as letters to the editor when he chose to show displeasure with the poor mortals below. *By whatever name, lightning is a spectacular natural event.*
>
> —Michael Cluston

**AVOID MINDLESS GENERALIZATIONS.** In your effort to begin with a general observation and narrow that down to a thesis statement, you want to avoid obvious generalizations like these:

Life can be very interesting.

People are funny sometimes.

If you begin with such clichéd comments, your readers may never get beyond the opening sentence.

> **T I P !**
>
> **Do not expect to write the perfect introduction on the first try. Refine your introduction and your thesis as you work through your draft and your revisions.**

## EXERCISE 4.8: REVISING

Find a paper you have written recently, and look at the introduction. How can you improve it? Write two more versions of the introduction, using the strategies described in this chapter.

## Advice About Conclusions

Like introductions, conclusions ought to be forceful and to the point. Work especially hard on your last paragraph, since its effectiveness will influence the way your readers react to the whole paper. If you trail off at the end, they will sigh and feel let down. Avoid any sort of apology or hedging at this point. You want an impressive ending.

**ECHO YOUR THESIS STATEMENT.** What you want in a conclusion is a tidy ending that reinforces the point you set out to make in the beginning. An echo of your thesis statement can be perfect. Consider the conclusion of Margaret Laurence's "Where the World Began," an essay in which she argues that her adult way of seeing the world, "my only real knowledge of the planet . . . my way of viewing," had its origins in the "small prairie town" in which she grew up:

> This is where my world began. A world which includes the ancestors—both my own and other people's ancestors who became mine. A world which formed me, and continues to do so, even while I fought it in some of its aspects, and continue to do so. A world which gave me my own lifework to do, because it was here that I learned the sight of my own particular eyes.

The conclusion implicitly echoes the thesis, restating it in slightly different terms and giving the essay an effective unity and satisfactory close.

**SUMMARIZE YOUR MAIN POINTS.** If your essay is long and complex, your readers may appreciate a summary of the major ideas. You want to be careful, however, not to write an ending that sounds forced and that simply repeats your introduction. It is a good idea to combine your summary with another strategy. For example, the student author of an essay that examines the influence on children of television violence concludes with a brief summary of her methods and findings and a general call for action:

> Theories of social learning have proven to be helpful in illuminating and explaining the debate over whether television violence produces aggressive behaviour in children. That is, to understand the determinants of children's response to television violence it is necessary to look within the larger social context. Factors such as gender, socioeconomic status, prior socialization, and existing knowledge all contribute to children's television viewing experiences. While it is safe to say that television violence certainly has some effect on children's aggressive behaviour, it must be remembered that children also learn inappropriate behaviours from many sources. They are influenced daily by their contact with adults and friends, by experiences on the playground, and by the absorption of other media, including music, movies, books, and magazines. The effects of television violence may not be any more destructive than these many other influences. Children have the capacity to see through and read beyond the television screen, but in order for them to realize this potential, to become television and media literate, they need the help of caring parents, teachers, and friends. Discussion, insights, and experiences that adults can offer children will give them direction and guidance.

Time and involvement is what they need in order to differentiate between television and real life. Once today's children have grasped this distinction, they will have the power to acquire from television the many benefits it has to offer.

—Kavita Jandu

**SUGGEST SOLUTIONS.** If you are writing an analysis or a persuasive piece, a useful closing strategy involves offering suggestions—possible solutions for problems discussed in the paper. This approach is valid only if you can come up with some sound ideas for solving the problems. Here, for example, are the final words of Linda Frum's introduction to her *Guide to Canadian Universities*:

Above all, instead of trusting hearsay and the memory of your guidance counsellor, be sure to visit any school you're considering. You don't want to end up like the Calgarian who, having in mind the great night-life, applied to U of T and spent the summer looking forward to four years in swinging Etobicoke. Deciding on a school is a deeply intuitive and subjective business. Read this book. Gather all the information you can. Sleep on it, and trust your instincts.

**OFFER ENCOURAGEMENT.** Especially in process writing, in which you are explaining how to do something, it is constructive to close with a few words of encouragement. Tell your readers how delicious they will find the cheesecake if they follow your instructions carefully. Or tell them how rewarding they will find growing their own tomatoes, as the writer does in this conclusion:

When you shop for tomato seeds or plants this season, consider trying at least one new variety. There are hundreds to choose from and if you keep looking, one of them may find a home in your garden. Even if you find nothing to match your favorite, you'll have fun, and the pleasure of gardening is not just in the eating.

—Mark Kane

**SPECULATE ON THE FUTURE.** Think about the long-term implications of what you have said in your paper. You might want to conclude by warning of hazards or by suggesting possible benefits. In the next example, the writer does both, concluding his argument about crime in Canada:

No one is saying the war on crime is over, or ever will be. But it's possible to look at the upside. Despite all the forecasts that Canada's increasingly multicultural composition would lead to more conflict and unrest, there's little statistical evidence of that. It also wouldn't hurt to give cops some credit: maybe, contrary to the old line, there *is* one around more often than not when you need one. Finally, what happens if everyone keeps insisting the statistics are wrong, and we're descending into chaos? Who's best served if law-abiding people become so scared of life on the streets that they stay off them? Let that happen, and the bad guys *will* win.

—Anthony Wilson-Smith

**T I P !**
Treat your conclusion like your introduction: Think about it off and on while you are writing— during coffee breaks or whenever you pause to let your mind rest.

Conclusions are not really all that difficult. Often they turn out weak because we write them last, when our energy and inspiration are lagging.

### ■ EXERCISE 4.9: REVISING

The following conclusion is flat and does not leave much of an impression on the reader. Use one of the strategies just discussed to put more punch in this ending. Even though you did not write the essay, you should be able to improve this concluding paragraph. Work especially hard on crafting the final sentence.

University or college is a big change for thousands of students every year. As I have indicated, these students are expected to be fairly mature; they must develop independence and self-discipline; and they have to take more difficult tests and compete for grades. Almost everyone finds university or college more difficult than high school.

### ■ EXERCISE 4.10: WRITING

Using any of the strategies just described, write two additional conclusions for a paper you have written recently. Show these alternative endings to several friends or classmates, and ask them which one seems the most effective for your paper and if they have any suggestions for improvement.

CHAPTER

In order to perfect your paragraphs, you need to revise your sentences—to make them more clear perhaps, more vivid, more concise, more interesting, more forceful. Before any paragraph can be effective, the sentences within that paragraph must be both coherent and readable.

## Sentence Combining: Coordination and Subordination

One way to improve coherence is through skilful sentence combining, which involves placing ideas within each sentence according to their importance so that the readers' attention stays focused on your major points.

Perhaps you have noticed that when little children talk, they tend to string simple sentences together, like this:

> We got hats and balloons and Tranh got presents and Angie was late and we had cake with candles and ice cream and I blew my balloon up big and . . .

So it goes, on and on and on, with little variety, few modifiers, and no distinction between important events and passing details. That is *coordination*—linking ideas together—in its most primitive form. We learn to read and write with a similar simplicity. But by the time we progress to grade three, we become sophisticated and start putting sentences together in patterns that depend on subordination.

### Clauses Versus Phrases

*Subordination* involves tucking less important ideas into dependent (or subordinate) clauses and small details into phrases. Then, major ideas are elevated into independent (or main) clauses, where they receive proper emphasis. If you are hazy about the difference between phrases and clauses, remember that a clause has both a subject and a predicate, whereas a phrase has only one or the other. Notice the difference:

PHRASES:     having lost my head

               to lose my head

               after losing my head

CLAUSES:     after I lost my head (dependent)

               I lost my head (independent)

               that I lost my head (dependent)

An independent clause can be a complete sentence all by itself. Because a dependent clause begins with a subordinating word (see list on page 200), it must be attached to an independent clause in order to form a complete sentence.

## How Sentence Combining Works

Most of this subordinating—this stashing of details into phrases and clauses—we do automatically as we speak and write. But it helps to understand the process when you revise and want to combine ideas to improve your sentence structure. Here is how it is done.

### Subordinating in a Phrase

Say you want to incorporate the following ideas into a single sentence:

Garfield is a cat.

Garfield is orange.

Garfield is striped.

Garfield weighs seven kilograms.

Garfield is incorrigible.

Garfield is a glutton.

Garfield is a cartoon character.

You could combine several of those details into a phrase this way:

Garfield, an orange-striped, seven-kilogram cartoon cat, is an incorrigible glutton.

You have subordinated the colour, stripes, weight, and cartoon status of the cat in one fell swoop. But suppose you wanted to stress Garfield's being a cartoon cat rather than his gluttony. The sentence might come out this way:

Garfield, an incorrigibly gluttonous, seven-kilogram, orange-striped cat, is a cartoon character.

Same details, but see the difference in emphasis? Because English is a language depending on word order for meaning, the way you put a sentence together affects the sense as well as the style. In the first example, the key positions in the sentence are these:

| subject | bare predicate | complement |
|---------|----------------|------------|
| Garfield | is | incorrigible glutton |

In the second one

| subject | bare predicate | |
|---------|----------------|------------|
| Garfield | is | cartoon character |

## Subordinating in a Clause

Of course, a clause can also become the less important element in a sentence if you make it a subordinate clause, like this:

> Garfield, who weighs seven kilograms, is an orange-striped, incorrigibly gluttonous cartoon cat.

Or you could do it this way:

> Because he is an incorrigible glutton, Garfield, the orange-striped cartoon cat, weighs seven kilograms.

But you would not want to arrange the ideas this way:

> Because he is an incorrigible glutton, Garfield, who weighs seven kilograms, is an orange-striped cartoon cat.

**T I P !**

**When combining ideas, be sure to get your important ideas into the main clauses, not the subordinate clauses.**

That is called upside-down subordination, and you can see why. It makes no sense to say that because the cat eats too much he has orange stripes and appears in a cartoon. (See Chapter 11 for additional grammar details about the nature and variety of conjunctions.)

# When to Use Sentence Combining

1. *If you are writing a lot of short choppy sentences, consider combining some.*

   For example:

   > Maria became a doctor. She didn't become a regular doctor. She became a medical missionary.

   Combined:

   > Rather than becoming a regular doctor, Maria became a medical missionary.

2. *If you notice needless repetition of a word or phrase, consider combining.*

   For example:

   > Sonya judges all her friends severely. Sonya always judges according to her own rigid standards.

   Combined:

   > Sonya always judges all her friends severely according to her own rigid standards.

3. *When a sentence begins with "This is" or "It is," you may want to combine that sentence with the one ahead of it.*

   For example:

   > To Michael, his car establishes his place in society. It is a sleek, shiny, luxurious Jaguar.

Combined:

> To Michael, his car—a sleek, shiny, luxurious Jaguar—establishes his place in society.

## ▓ EXERCISE 5.1: SENTENCE COMBINING

Look at the last paper you wrote. Did you find a fair number of short choppy sentences? If so, this exercise may help you become more fluent.

If you need this practice, combine each group below into one easily understood sentence by subordinating the less important ideas. We have done the first one to show you the idea.

**1.** Fido is a dog.

Fido belongs to me.

Fido needs a bath.

Fido has muddy paws.

Fido has fleas.

(Combined) My dog Fido, who has muddy paws and fleas, needs a bath.

(Combined) Because he has fleas and muddy paws, my dog Fido needs a bath.

**2.** Uncle Zou is coming to visit.

He lives in Edmonton.

He drives a city bus there.

He is coming on the early train.

He will stay with us a week.

**3.** My garden is in the backyard.

Rabbits ate the lettuce.

Worms got the tomatoes.

The cucumbers got trampled.

Somebody stepped on them.

**4.** I get off work at 4:30.

I pick up the kids.

The kids are at daycare.

I fix dinner.

I wash the dishes.

I fall asleep in front of the TV.

**5.** All the characters in this bestseller are stereotypes.

Some of these stereotypes are the Idealistic Young Man, the Disillusioned Older Man, the Scheming Siren, and the Neglected Wife.

## EXERCISE 5.2: SENTENCE COMBINING

If you are a fairly fluent writer who wants to practise sentence combining to avoid wordiness and improve your sentence structure, try the following exercise. Combine the following pairs of sentences, all of which were written by students in one of our literature classes.

1. Flowers serve an important role in Cather's "Paul's Case." Therefore, they are worthy of closer examination.

2. The boy's illusion is conveyed even more clearly through Joyce's description of the girl. Joyce describes her as turning a silver bracelet on her wrist.

3. Edna was so happy that she shouted for joy. Learning to swim was a big achievement for Edna.

4. The similarities between Dr. Sloper and Morris Townsend are numerous. They can be seen throughout the book.

5. Dr. Sloper warns his daughter about the dangers of marrying Morris. He does this because he sees so many of his own weak points in his daughter's suitor.

## EXERCISE 5.3: SENTENCE COMBINING

Using coordination or subordination, combine each set of sentences into a single sentence:

1. "Boys and Girls" is by Alice Munro. It is a good example of a type of story. It is a story in which theme predominates.

2. It is not entirely a *character* story. It is not entirely an *action* story. In these the main character is usually faced with a critical decision. Munro's story places its main character in a situation. It is a situation that is beyond her control. It is a situation that is illuminating.

3. The main character must act the way she does. If she does not, she will be caught. She will be destroyed, as Flora is.

4. The main character begins to be aware of many new things. These are things about herself. These are things about the world in which she lives. The main character begins to be aware of a difference between herself and her family. The main character begins to understand the roles cast by society for girls and the roles cast for boys. The main character begins to understand the unfairness of society.

## EXERCISE 5.4: SENTENCE COMBINING

Find the last paper you wrote and read through it slowly, paragraph by paragraph. Look for short sentences, needlessly repeated words or phrases, and sentences beginning with "This is" or "It is." If you find any of these signals, combine sentences to improve your style.

## Cut Out Unnecessary Words

Try to make your writing clean, clear, and concise. We do not mean to deprive you of effective stylistic flourishes, but ineffective stylistic flourishes have to go. So does just plain lazy wordiness. It is far easier to be verbose than to be concise. As Blaise Pascal wrote, "I have made this letter longer than usual because I lack the time to make it shorter." And as Hugh Henry Breckenridge tellingly observed, "In order to speak short on any subject, think long." Nothing will annoy your readers more than having to plow through a cluttered paragraph because you neglected to spend time cleaning it up.

You must diligently prune your prose. Sentences like the following may drive even a gentle reader around the bend:

> It is believed by a number of persons in this country that the young people of today do not assume as much responsibility for their actions as it might be hoped that they would. (34 words)

You can say the same thing more clearly with fewer words:

> Many people believe that young people today assume too little responsibility for their actions. (14 words)

### EXERCISE 5.5: CONCISENESS

If you have trouble saying things succinctly, practise by tidying the following wordy sentences. Keep the same meaning but eliminate the extra words. We have revised the first one.

1. The male-gendered style used online in ListServ communications is characterized by an adversarial attitude.

   (revised) The male style used in communications on ListServ is adversarial.

2. It is my desire to be called Ishmael.

3. In my opinion there are many diverse elements about this problem that one probably ought to at least think about before arriving at an opinion on the matter.

4. The obnoxious child was seldom corrected or reprimanded because its baffled and adoring parents thought its objectionable behaviour was normal and acceptable.

5. There came a time when, based on what I had been reading, I arrived at the feeling that the food we buy at the supermarkets to eat is sometimes, perhaps often, bad for us.

## Use Mostly Active Voice

If your writing is somewhat lifeless, the passive voice may be part of the problem. In the passive (which always involves some form of the verb *to be* plus a past participle) the subject is acted upon instead of doing the acting. Notice the difference between active and passive:

> **(active)**    The guard fed the prisoner.
>
> **(passive)**    The prisoner was fed by the guard.

As you can see, it takes more words to express an idea with a passive verb—unless you leave out the performer of the action. Thus a passive sentence like this one,

> A decision on the matter has been made by the court.

takes longer to read and process than the active version,

> The court decided the matter.

## The Devious Passive

Notice that the passive allows us to leave out information. You do not have to mention who fed the prisoner; you can just say "The prisoner was fed." That is not a misleading sentence because probably nobody was perishing to know who fed the prisoner anyway. But consider the same sentence with the verb changed:

> **(passive)**     The prisoner was beaten.

Now we want to know *by whom*? By the sheriff? By one of the deputies? By a guard? By a fellow prisoner? There is no way to tell from the passive construction. As Richard Gambino, an authority on doublespeak, observes, "The effect of the habitual use of the passive is to create a world where events have lives, wills, motives, and actions of their own without any human being responsible for them."

## The Appropriate Passive

Notice that it is the *habitual* use of the passive that is questionable. We do not mean that you should never employ the passive voice. Sometimes it can be the best way to convey information. You would likely choose the passive to announce that "The new government was elected by a comfortable majority," rather than using the active voice: "A comfortable majority elected the new government."

The passive is also a good choice when you want to stress the action or the receiver of the action:

> **(passive)**     The city hall was damaged by an earthquake.
>
> **(passive)**     My bicycle was demolished by a truck.
>
> **(passive)**     The candidate's credibility has been questioned by the media.

### ▨ EXERCISE 5.6: REVISING

If you have trouble distinguishing active from passive—or if you suspect that you use the passive too much—rewrite the following passive sentences in the active voice. We have done the first one to get you going.

**1.** Let our daily bread be given to us on this day.

> (revised)     Give us this day our daily bread.

**2.** The whistle was blown by the referee.

**3.** It was believed by the police that the child was kidnapped.

4. The day that he discovered sex was never forgotten by Cosmo.

5. Some basic human rights were violated by the officers.

6. Bribes were accepted frequently by the city engineer.

## Practise the Passive

Despite all these warnings against habitual use of the passive, we are aware that writers in a number of jobs and in some academic disciplines are expected—even required—to use the passive voice. If you are taking courses in education, corrections, or some sciences (chemistry, biology, physics, and the like), you may be required to learn how to write gracefully in the passive voice. It can be done, but you may need to practise to get the hang of it.

Proceeding from the pen of an accomplished writer, the passive voice is not in the least objectionable. Jessica Mitford, for one, employs the passive so skilfully that you never notice its presence:

> Today, family members who might wish to be in attendance would certainly be dissuaded by the funeral director.

That sentence is not noticeably improved by making it active voice:

> Today, the funeral director would certainly dissuade family members who might wish to be in attendance.

In order to help you perfect your use of the passive, we have collected some useful and fairly simple sentences as models. If you would like to learn to use the passive skilfully, try the following exercise.

### ■ EXERCISE 5.7: SENTENCE MODELLING

Copy each sentence carefully. Then, choosing subject matter from your academic major, write five sentences imitating the passive structure of each of the originals. Pretending to be agriculture majors, we have revised the first one to show you how it is done.

1. Certain things were not mentioned. (Jane O'Reilly)

   (Imitations)

   > Synthetic fertilizers were not invented.
   >
   > Pesticides were not advised.
   >
   > Crop rotation was not used.
   >
   > Early harvesting was not recommended.
   >
   > Organic methods were not tried.

2. The SKIP option can be used in input and output statements. (J. S. Roper)

3. The poor are slated to take the brunt of the federal budget cuts. (Barbara Ehrenreich)

4. The emphasis is generally put on the right to speak. (Walter Lippmann)

5. All others are excluded by law from the preparation room. (Jessica Mitford)

6. Every dollar earned was wrestled from the earth, carved, blasted, crushed, melted down, and skimmed off. (Will Ferguson)

# Be Specific and Vivid

Paul Roberts once wrote that most subjects—except sex—are basically boring, so it is up to the writer to make the topic interesting. Since you cannot write about sex all the time, you need to incorporate some of the following suggestions aimed at keeping your readers awake.

## Choose Action Verbs

One way to liven up your writing is to use lively, specific words whenever possible. You cannot always avoid the lifeless *to be* verb *(am, is, are, was, were, been, being)*, but when given a chance, you can toss in an action verb. James Thurber writes of a "world made up of gadgets that *whir* and *whine* and *whiz* and *shriek* and sometimes *explode*." (Our italics.) The force of the verbs conveys the feeling of anxiety produced by machine-age living.

George Orwell describes a dog that "came *bounding* among us with a loud volley of barks, and *leapt* round us *wagging* its whole body with glee." (Our italics.) The italicized words and the descriptive detail about the barking allow us to visualize the excitement of the dog.

Thomas Heggen, in *Mister Roberts*, writes, "Surely an artillery shell fired at Hanover *ripples* the air here. Surely a bomb dropped on Okinawa *trembles* these bulkheads." (Our italics.) These verbs and the specific place names produce precisely the effect he wants: the suggestion of being touched, but only barely touched, by events far away.

There are, of course, other stylistic elements combining to make the above examples effective. But if your writing is colourless and vague, consider adding specific details and substituting more descriptive verbs for these limp ones: *is, are, was, were, has, have, had, get, go, come, make.* If you have written "We all got into the truck," try "All four of us piled into Billy Bob's rusty pickup." You can, of course, overdo the use of forceful verbs and specific details, but most writers err in the other direction.

> **T I P !**
> Avoid the overworked words *terrible, wonderful, very*. Find more precise terms, like *inept, skilful, excellent.*

## Find the Exact Word

Mark Twain once observed that the difference between the right word and almost the right word is the difference between the lightning and the lightning bug. Our language is full of synonyms; but synonyms have different shades of meaning. Also be careful not to confuse homonyms: words that sound alike but mean something entirely different. Do not write *ambiguous* if you really mean *ambivalent*, or *sensuous* if you really mean *sensual*. Do not write *forceful* when you mean *forcible*, or *apprise* if you really mean *appraise*. Do not write *disinterested* if you really mean *uninterested*. Do not write *elicit* when you mean *illicit*. (Refer to Chapter 15, "A User's Guide to Troublesome Words and Phrases.")

## Dust Off Your Dictionary

Any desk-size dictionary can enlighten you on these distinctions. But in order to get reliable help from your dictionary, you should first learn how to use it. Nobody has ever standardized the format for dictionaries, so they arrange their material in slightly different ways.

Many people believe that the first meaning listed for a word will be the one they want. Not necessarily true. The first meaning will often be the oldest meaning and thus the least used. The same is true of alternative spellings. Lots of people think the first spelling is preferred. But unless some usage label is inserted (like "also" or "variation of"), all spellings listed are acceptable.

In general, be consistent—that is, adopt one spelling system and use it throughout your essay or report. Most professors or instructors prefer the use of Canadian spelling, which is a unique mix of British and American usage; for example, we use British spelling (*-our*, not *-or*) in words such as *labour* and *colour*, and American spelling (*-ize/yze*, not *-ise/yse*) in words such as *criticize* and *analyze*. And while Canadians rarely use the British spellings for *gaol* and *tyre*, we also rarely use the American spellings for *check* and *dialog*. Canadian spelling is quite a mosaic, and so using a Canadian dictionary can make your life easier in this regard. (If you would like to test your skill as a Canadian speller, try Exercise 6.4 in the following chapter.)

To help you understand the breadth of information your dictionary provides, read the explanatory notes that are usually included at the beginning. This may not be lively reading, but it can be rewarding. You will find out, for instance, that in most dictionaries the principal parts of verbs, degrees of adjectives, and plurals of nouns are not listed unless irregular. You will find, if you persevere, explanations of various usage labels, which warn you about words that may not be acceptable in standard English (archaic, slang, substandard, etc.).

You may also, if you have an inquiring mind, discover interesting material in the back (or sometimes in the front) that you never suspected was there. Many dictionaries include lists of abbreviations, proofreader's marks, signs and symbols; rules for spelling, punctuation, and capitalization; and occasionally a list of all the universities and colleges (with locations) in Canada and the United States. Some dictionaries even offer lists of common first names and of words that rhyme.

> **T I P !**
>
> **Good writers keep a dictionary handy and consult it often.**
>
> Your word processor will have a spell checker, which can also be very useful. And although spell checkers are usually set for American spellings, some programs, such as Word and WordPerfect, enable you to change the setting to Canadian English.

## Trot Out Your Thesaurus

A thesaurus, which is a dictionary of synonyms, comes in handy for locating just the right word. Your word-processing program probably has one that is quick to consult. It may not be as good as the kind that comes in book form, but it is better than none and easier to use.

If you need a synonym, either because you think the word you have used is not the precise word or because you have used it three times already, call up that word on your word processor's thesaurus or look it up in the book version that you keep on your desk. Sometimes we use both if the electronic one fails to offer enough choices. Did you notice that we have used a form of the word *use* four times already in this paragraph? That is a signal to consult a thesaurus.

We just called up *use* on our popular word-processing program and found seven words—*employ, utilize, exercise, manipulate, apply, exploit, operate*—and only the first two fit our meaning. The word *consult*, which we thought up ourselves, was not even listed. So, we checked our pocketbook-size thesaurus and found almost a full page of synonyms arranged according to meaning and part of speech (verb, adjective, adverb, etc.), with a *See* at the end citing four other words we could look up to find additional meanings. Clearly, a backup for your electronic thesaurus is valuable if you want to discover all your verbal options.

> **T I P !**
> **Synonyms are not always interchangeable.**
> Never choose an unfamiliar word from your thesaurus. Look it up in your dictionary first.

## Exercise Your Imagination: Figures of Speech

Try to come up with a few lively figures of speech—analogies and other imaginative comparisons—to add interest and clarity to your writing. Michael Ondaatje, for example, writes that "Your voice sounds like a scorpion being pushed through a glass tube." And Ralph Waldo Emerson once remarked that "New York is a sucked orange." Now there's an observation full of meaning, phrased with great economy.

Such comparisons are a form of analogy, a useful method of comparing something *abstract* (like the quality of life in a city) to something *concrete* and visual (like a sucked orange). Here is an apt analogy from Sharon Begley: "The immune system is notorious for falling apart like a dishwasher past its warranty."

When Dorothy Parker declares, "His voice was as intimate as the rustle of sheets," her *simile* (a comparison stated with *like* or *as*) is more interesting than just telling us that the man was speaking seductively. Notice how forcefully Barbara Ehrenreich conveys the hazards of smoking when she asserts that the "medical case against smoking is as airtight as a steel casket." And Margaret Atwood gives a vivid action image when she writes, "She came whizzing down the stairs, thrown like a dart."

Brigid Brophy uses a *metaphor* (an implied comparison) to assert her belief that monogamy is too confining: "At present, monogamy is the corset into which we try to fit every married couple—a process which has on so many occasions split the seams that we have had to modify the corset."

### Make Your Metaphors Meaningful

In writing expository prose (the kind we are focusing on in this text), your figures of speech should clarify your meaning. The cardinal rule here is Thou Shalt Not Puzzle Thy Readers. Better no metaphors at all than one that is confusing or mixed up. A *mixed metaphor* runs two metaphors together in an illogical way, like this gem: "The wheels of justice are coming apart at the seams." Just try to visualize that image, and you will see why it is a mistake. Lapses like that may bring, not admiration for your fine turn of phrase, but an unwanted chuckle from your bemused readers.

**T I P !**

The simple word *fine* is preferable to the tarnished phrase *worth its weight in gold.*

## Avoid Clichés

Be sure your figures of speech really *are* lively. Do not settle for the first phrase that comes to mind, as it will likely be a cliché—an expression people pick up because it sounds good and then tend to use over and over until it loses its force, like these chestnuts:

| | |
|---|---|
| bottom line | ballpark figure |
| burning questions | high and mighty |
| crystal clear | last but not least |
| few and far between | pretty as a picture |
| first and foremost | untimely death |
| at this point in time | have a nice day |

### ▨ EXERCISE 5.8: REVISING

To limber up your imagination, rewrite the following correct but lacklustre sentences. Add details and substitute action verbs and descriptive words wherever appropriate. Here is how we would revise the first one.

1. She was up late last night trying to finish typing her term paper.

   (revised)  Selina sat hunched over her typewriter, pecking away doggedly until three o'clock in the morning, trying to finish her term paper.

2. Alec left his office, walked to a store, and made a purchase.

3. The person I went out with last night was a character.

4. She came into the room, took off her shoes, and sat down.

5. Some person had removed the article I needed from the magazine in the library.

### ▨ EXERCISE 5.9: REVISING

Drag out your last paper, and revise the word choice as you go through it, sentence by sentence, replacing or eliminating overworked, tired words and images with more precise, colourful language.

## Constructing Impressive Sentences

Another way to make your prose effective involves writing an occasional forceful or unusual sentence. If every sentence built to a climax, the technique would lose its effectiveness, so do not work at it too hard. But in a key position—such as at the beginning or end of a paragraph or as the last line in your essay—a carefully constructed and forceful sentence is worth the time it takes to compose it.

### Save the Clincher for the End: Periodic Structure

Most of the time we do not deliberate about our sentence structure. We string ideas together, automatically subordinating the less important ones, until we come to the end of the thought, where we put a period and start in on the next one. These everyday sentences—like the one we just wrote—are called *cumulative* and constitute the bulk of our writing. If, however, you need a striking or particularly effective sentence, you either consciously plan it or rearrange it when you revise. You want to order the details to build to a big finish, so you do not disclose your main idea until just before the period, where it gains emphasis. These sentences are called *periodic*. Notice the difference in these examples:

| | |
|---|---|
| **cumulative:** | Sylvester made the honour roll while holding down a part-time job and playing the lead in *Hamlet*. |
| **periodic:** | While holding down a part-time job and playing the lead in *Hamlet*, Sylvester made the honour roll. |
| **cumulative:** | Our first consideration is the preservation of our environment, even though preventing pollution costs money. |
| **periodic:** | Even though preventing pollution costs money, our first consideration is the preservation of our environment. |

If you have a feel for prose, you probably already write periodic sentences when you need them without being aware that you are doing it. If, on the other hand, you are not long on style, you can develop some by cinching up a few of your sentences. Here are a few more useful strategies.

## Try a Short Sentence for Variety, Emphasis, or Transition

The short-short sentence is easier to handle than the periodic sentence and is remarkably effective—as long as you do not overdo it. Often short-short sentences appear at the beginning or at the end of a paragraph, since these are the most emphatic positions. But you can lob one in any time if you want to vary your sentence structure. Remember, though, not to overdo it. You cannot use short-short sentences often or you will lose the effect; your writing will merely seem choppy.

Notice the emphasis achieved in the following examples by the brief sentence preceding or following one of normal length:

This is our hope. This is the faith with which I return to the South to hew out of the mountain of despair a stone of hope.

—Dr. Martin Luther King, Jr.

Webster's dictionaries and the endless multiplication of handbooks and courses in English composition represent a desperate effort to prevent class distinction from revealing itself in language. And, of course, it has failed.

—John Hurt Fisher

What, therefore is the prognosis of our terminally ill planet? It is gloomy.

—Helen Caldicott

The short sentence also functions effectively as a transitional device between paragraphs (our italics):

> Economics, foreign policy, the split in the party as it relates to racial equality, and some resulting questions of political style all require a special word. *To these matters I now turn.*
>
> —John Kenneth Galbraith

## Experiment with the Dash

Since the end of a sentence is an emphatic position, you can use a dash there to good advantage, as in this common traffic reminder:

> Fasten your seatbelts—it's the law.

The dash can be used to tack on an afterthought, but you will find it more impressive for reinforcing a point or for elaboration, like this:

> Hollywood offered the public yet another marvel—talking films.

> This was the year of the big spectaculars—Biblical extravaganzas spiced with sex and filmed in glorious Technicolor.

The dash, like the short sentence, cannot retain its effect if overused. In fact, a flurry of dashes often produces a weak and ineffective style.

# Use Parallel Structure

Another way to keep your ideas clear and make your sentences impressive is to use parallel structure. This technique depends on deliberate repetition—sometimes of the same words, always of the same grammatical structures (phrases, clauses). Virginia Woolf repeats the same adverb *(well),* changing the verb each time to achieve this elegant sentence:

> One cannot think well, love well, sleep well, if one has not dined well.

The famous opening paragraph of Charles Dickens's *A Tale of Two Cities* is an effective example of parallel construction:

> It was the best of times, it was the worst of times, it was the age of wisdom, it was the age of foolishness, it was the epoch of belief, it was the epoch of incredulity, it was the season of Light, it was the season of Darkness, it was the spring of hope, it was the winter of despair, we had everything before us, we had nothing before us, we were all going direct to Heaven, we were all going direct the other way—in short, the period was so far like the present period, that some of its noisiest authorities insisted on its being received, for good or for evil, in the superlative degree of comparison only.

## For Everyday Writing

While parallel structure lends itself particularly well to emphatic sentences, the technique is fundamental to all good writing. If you by chance put together a sentence involving two similar elements or a series of them, your readers expect these similar parts to be balanced using parallel structure. Whenever you join parts of a sentence with a coordinating conjunction *(and, but, or, for, nor, yet, so)*, you need to make those parts parallel.

Consider the problem caused by lack of parallelism in this first simple example:

Clyde likes *to smoke* and *drinking*.

Your readers expect those italicized parts to sound and look alike—to be parallel in construction, like this:

Clyde likes to *smoke* and *drink*.

Or you could revise it this way:

Clyde likes *smoking* and *drinking*.

A more typical example is the kind of sentence you might write in a first draft and should make parallel in structure when you revise:

Politicians today face the difficult tasks of *solving urban problems* and *how to find the money* without raising taxes.

You need to match the two parts connected by *and*. The easiest way is to make *how to find* sound and look like *solving*—that is, use *finding*:

Politicians face the difficult task of *solving urban problems* and *finding the money* without raising taxes.

## For Effective Climactic Sentences

Once you become adept at constructing parallel sentences, you will find the technique perfect for composing splendid climactic sentences—the kind you need to summarize key points, to conclude paragraphs, and to bring your essays to a resounding finish. Martin Luther King, Jr., learned from the Bible how to repeat parallel phrases with ringing effect:

With this faith we will be able to work together, to pray together, to struggle together, to go to jail together, to stand up for freedom together, knowing that we will be free one day.

Here is Chief Dan George acknowledging the spiritual power of his relationship with the natural world:

The beauty of the trees, the softness of the air, the fragrance of the grass, speaks to me. The summit of the mountain, the thunder of the sky, speaks to me. The faintness of the stars, the trail of the sun, the strength of fire and the life that never goes away, they speak to me. And my heart soars.

**T I P !**

There is no better strategy than parallel structure to deliver so many ideas so clearly in so readable a way.

Parallel structure also provides the most effective way to compress a number of ideas into a single sentence with perfect clarity and easy readability. Notice how many ideas T. E. Kalem packs into this nicely balanced comment on one of George Bernard Shaw's plays:

> Shaw steadily sounds his pet themes: the chicanery of politics, the corruptive power of money, the degrading stench of poverty, the servile dependencies of marriage and family, the charlatanism of medicine, the fossilization of learning, the tyranny of the state, the stupidity of the military, and the bigoted, sanctimonious zeal of the church.

You can also use parallel structure to good effect in separate sentences by repeating key words in the same grammatical structure. Because the technique involves building to a climax, you cannot use it often, but the effect is impressive when well done. Notice how Reverend Martin Niemoeller, a Lutheran minister, achieves eloquence by using simple, parallel sentences to explain how he ended up in a Nazi concentration camp during World War II:

> In Germany, the Nazis first came for the Communists, and I didn't speak up because I wasn't a Communist. Then they came for the Jews, and I didn't speak up because I wasn't a Jew. Then they came for the trade unionists, and I didn't speak up because I wasn't a trade unionist. Then they came for the Catholics, and I didn't speak up because I was a Protestant. Then they came for me, and by that time there was no one left to speak for me.

## EXERCISE 5.10: REVISING

The following sentences were written by students whose grasp of parallel structure was less than perfect. We want you to restore the parallelism. Do not aim for impressive or emphatic sentences in this exercise. Just try to produce good, clear, everyday sentences.

First, read each sentence and decide which parts need to be made parallel. Look for elements in series or connected by coordinating conjunctions *(and, but, or, for, nor, yet, so)*. Then change the part that is irregular so that it matches the other part or parts.

Often you can find several equally good ways to revise such sentences. Here is how we would do the first one:

**1.** The plan is not workable; it delegates too much power to the provinces and because it is unconstitutional.

That sentence consists of three clauses in series. All three should be parallel. The first two are independent:

> The plan is not workable
>
> it delegates too much power to the provinces

Fine so far. The clauses do not have to be precisely parallel as long as the basic structure is the same. The trouble comes with the third clause, which is not independent but dependent (beginning with the subordinating word *because*):

> because it is unconstitutional.

Probably the easiest way to revise the sentence is to make all three clauses independent by dropping the subordinating word *because*:

> The plan is not workable, it delegates too much power to the provinces, and it is unconstitutional.

Or you could make the last two clauses both dependent, like this:

> The plan is not workable because it delegates too much power to the provinces and because it is unconstitutional.

Now have a go at revising these sentences:

2. The final step involves making a ninety-degree kick-turn and to start the pattern over from the beginning.

3. European trains are frequent, punctual, having easy connections, and travel at high speeds.

4. In the movies college men are portrayed as single, driving a nice car, well-off financially, good looks, and wearing cool clothes.

5. Progressive education aims to teach children to be open-minded, thinking with logic, know how to make wise choices, having self-discipline, and self-control.

6. This proposal would alert society to the fact that sexual assault is a prevalent crime and also only a few convictions are made each year.

## EXERCISE 5.11: REVISING

Look at that last paper again. Do you find any sentences that are out of kilter—that need parallel structure? If so, whip them into shape.

Have you written an emphatic closing sentence? If not, write an impressive sentence using parallel structure.

## Use Repetition Wisely

Deliberate repetition, such as you observed in many of those impressive parallel sentences, can be one of your most effective rhetorical devices. But needless repetition will probably irritate your readers because they can tell it stems from lack of thought and inadequate revision, as in this student's sentence:

> Walking up to the door, I came upon the skeleton head of a cow placed next to the door.

That is too many *to the door* phrases. Just changing the first one solves the problem:

> Walking up to the house, I came upon the skeleton head of a cow placed next to the door.

You need to eliminate any word or phrase that has been needlessly used twice:

> Clarence found the challenge of trying to make the honour roll a great challenge.

**T I P !**
A deliberately repeated word or phrase can reinforce a key idea.

When you revise, just eliminate the first challenge:

Clarence found trying to make the honour roll a great challenge.

*Deliberate repetition* can be powerful, as you saw in many of the examples of parallel sentences. Another way to achieve the same clarity and emphasis is to repeat a key term deliberately, as Katherine Anne Porter does in this sentence describing the execution of Sacco and Vanzetti (our italics):

They were put to death in the electric chair at Charleston Prison at *midnight*, a desolate dark *midnight*, a *night* for perpetual mourning.

You see the difference between well-executed deliberate repetition and careless repeating of the same word. Porter's *midnight* tolls like a bell, reinforcing the darkness of the deed.

## Straightening Out Screwed-Up Sentences

Some sentence problems are impossible to categorize as other than messed up. And these are the worst kind because the sentences make no sense and are likely to drive readers to drink—or induce them to quit reading.

### The Confusion of Mixed Constructions

The sorry sentences known, for want of a better term, as *mixed constructions* apparently result when a writer begins to say something one way, loses track in the middle, and finishes another way because the brain is faster than the fingers. That is our guess, anyway. The people who write them are more surprised than anyone when confronted with these prodigies.

These are the kinds of sentences that make readers do a double take. We shake our heads, rub our eyes, and read them again, hoping for a better connection next time. But we never get it from mix-ups like these:

When students have no time for study or moral training also breeds a decadent society.

The first planned crime will tell how well a boy has learned whether or not he is caught to become a juvenile delinquent.

Now those are pretty hopeless cases. They need to be scrapped. You will lose more time trying to revise sentences like these than you will by backing off and starting a different way. Take that last example. It needs a totally new beginning, perhaps like this:

Whether or not he is caught in his first planned crime may determine whether a boy will become a juvenile delinquent.

Occasionally a screwed-up sentence can be easily revised, like this one:

When frequently opening and closing the oven door, it can cause a soufflé to fall.

All you need to do to correct that one is scratch out the *when,* the *it,* and the comma:

> Frequently opening and closing the oven door can cause a soufflé to fall.

Nobody will hold you accountable if you accidentally write a mixed-up sentence in a first draft, but it is your job to catch and correct the problem when you revise.

## The Problem of Faulty Predication

We can describe what goes wrong in a sentence to produce faulty predication: the subject does not match the predicate. Apparently the writer loses track of the subject when supplying the predicate, so that the sentence ends up not quite making sense, like this:

> The excuse for earning money offers Koushik the job of ushering at Massey Hall.

Everybody knows that *excuses* do not *offer jobs,* so the statement has a lapse in logic.

Some faulty predication problems are easy to fix, like this one:

> Your first big city is an event that changes your whole outlook if you grew up in a small town.

Clearly, a *big city* is not an *event,* but we can set this one to rights just by adding a new subject:

> Your first trip to a big city is an event that changes your whole outlook if you grew up in a small town.

### EXERCISE 5.12: REVISING

Straighten out the following sentences, written by students. Some are mixed constructions; some suffer from faulty predication. If a sentence cannot be easily revised, consider backing off and beginning a different way.

1. The Rites of Spring Festival has been postponed because of too many students are sick with the flu.
2. Illegal parking is towed away at the owner's expense.
3. In time of crisis must be handled with cool judgment.
4. The second qualification for my ideal roommate would have to be easygoing.
5. Whether a person makes the choice to go to college or not has both its problems and rewards.
6. Miss Brill tries to convince herself that she really is a significant contribution to society.
7. By no means is the novel to glorifying war.
8. No matter if she is loved or not, did not matter any more.

9. Mrs. Pontellier carried herself in a way that people thought she would only be the mother of strong, gallant sons.

10. The importance of remaining married is essential in Edna's society.

11. Containers breeding mosquitoes may be carriers of disease.

12. The school busing controversy was intended to correct inequalities in educational opportunities.

## ▣ EXERCISE 5.13: CONSTRUCTING SENTENCES

Construct each of the following sentences in three different ways:

1. Carol smelled smoke, and running into the kitchen, she rushed to the stove.

2. When Kelly reached the blueline and saw her right-winger breaking into the clear, she fired the puck across the ice.

## ▣ EXERCISE 5.14: CORRECTING SENTENCES

Correct or improve each of the following sentences:

1. He drove into town and he purchased the supplies he needed and he drove home.

2. A grand profit of twenty-two cents was all the students' council made.

3. The employees will obey a company's orders that they like.

4. The woman was clever and she wrote editorials.

5. Last Sunday we went to the mall and our aunt from Edmonton visited.

6. The weather was cold, our dog was recovering from surgery, the car had a flat tire, and the Open House was cancelled.

7. The tornado ripped through the trailer park that happened last night.

8. For their March vacation they would like to golf in South Carolina or go skiing in Banff.

9. Sally did not want to serve on the committee and she did not wish to have her opinion ignored.

10. The team could not go neither by plane nor by train.

A common misconception about writing is that good writers get it right the first time. The truth is that good writers almost never say what they want to on the first try; they nearly always plan on revising. Teacher and writer Anne Lamott says that every piece of writing should go through at least three drafts. The first draft she calls "the down draft—you just get it down"; the second draft is "the up draft—you fix it up"; and the last draft is "the dental draft, where you check every tooth, to see if it's loose or cramped or decayed, or even, God help us, healthy."

We agree that these drafts are essential, but we call them the rough draft, the revision draft, and the editing draft. If you do not work through those last two, you will not achieve the best results, no matter how good you think your first draft is.

## Revising Your First Draft

Revision involves more than just tidying up your prose. The process of correcting your spelling, punctuation, and mechanics is called *editing,* but your paper is not ready for that yet. First you need *re-vision*—seeing again—to discover ways of making your writing more effective.

While a draft is still warm from the writing, you cannot look at it objectively. And looking at it objectively is the basis of productive revision. Your fondness for a well-turned sentence should not prevent you from cutting it when, in the cold light of morning, you realize that it does not relate to your thesis.

> **T I P !**
> Schedule your time so that you are able to put the rough draft aside at least overnight before attempting to revise it.

### Revise from the Top Down

Not all revising is the same. One kind of revision involves large-scale changes that significantly affect the content and structure of your paper. Such changes might include enlarging or narrowing your thesis, adding more examples or cutting irrelevant ones, and reorganizing points to improve logic or gain emphasis. A second kind of revision focuses on improving style: checking paragraph unity, strengthening transitions, combining and refining sentences, finding more effective words, adjusting tone. We recommend that you take a top-down approach to revising by starting with the large-scale issues and working down to the smaller elements.

Tackling the simple problems first may seem reasonable, but you will find that dealing with a major difficulty may eliminate some minor problems at the same time—or change the

> **T I P !**
> Distinguish between larger problems (like content and organization) and smaller ones (like sentence structure and word choice). Work on the large problems first.

way you approach them. If you try to do the fine-tuning and polishing first, you may also burn up valuable time and energy and never get around to the main problems.

## Outline the Draft

To be sure that your discussion is unified and complete, you should briefly outline your rough draft. This kind of after-the-fact outlining is not a waste of time, as it allows you to detect flaws in your organization and to review the development of your main ideas at the same time. First, write down your thesis statement; then add the topic sentence of each paragraph along with your important supporting ideas. Do not bother with complete sentences; short phrases are easier to check and evaluate.

After completing this outline, you should use it to check your paper for unity and completeness by considering these points:

1. Make sure that the topic sentence in every paragraph relates directly to your thesis.

2. Consider whether your support is adequate. Sometimes a paragraph can be developed with a single extensive example, but more often you will want at least three or four examples, details, or reasons. If you fail to find adequate support for a topic sentence, perhaps you need to rethink it, omit it, or combine it with another main idea.

3. Examine your supporting details to see if any are irrelevant or overlapping and need to be cut.

4. Look at the order of your paragraphs and the order of the supporting details in each paragraph. Your sentences and paragraphs should follow one after the other with no breaks and no confusion.

5. Make sure you have tied your sentences and paragraphs together with transitional hooks and signposts. For a useful list of transitional terms, see Chapter 4, Figure 4.1 (p. 47).

## Add Headings to Highlight Your Points

Contemporary writers use headings in all kinds of publications to highlight main ideas and to indicate shifts in topics, making the text easier to follow. Headings have always been appropriate in technical writing and business reports. Textbook authors also use them to focus attention on key concepts, provide greater clarity, and make the material easy to review. You will notice headings in newspaper and magazine articles. Whenever you present complex material that your readers might have difficulty following, consider inserting meaningful headings to signal your major points.

Word-processing programs make using headings a snap. With a single command, you can centre them. Or you can set them flush left and boldface them. You can also indent material to set it off and thus call attention to it. If you glance at the formatting of this book, you will see a number of options for breaking up blocks of type, adding emphasis, and thus achieving greater readability. You can perform every one of them with your word processor.

Remember, though, the essential factor in making a text easy to follow is having it clearly and logically organized. All the formatting in the world is not going to save a paper that is not unified or that lacks continuity.

## Revise for Style

Once you are satisfied that your ideas are developed fully and proceed smoothly and logically, you need to consider the shape of each sentence. Is any phrasing wordy or repetitious? Does the writing sound natural and interesting? Are the sentences forceful and varied? Rewrite those sentences that carry key ideas to make them elegant and emphatic. Work particularly hard on the opening and closing sentences—especially that last one. Do not let your otherwise fine essay trail off limply at the end because you ran out of steam.

Now is also the time to look up word meanings and use your thesaurus, if necessary, to find just the right words. Also make sure that the tone and language level are suitable for your purpose and audience. (See Chapter 2 for guidance about tone and language levels, Chapter 5 for specific direction about words and sentences, and Chapter 7 for a brief review of logic.)

## Get Feedback: Peer Review

Writers routinely seek the help of potential readers to find out what is and is not working in their drafts. Even professional writers ask for suggestions from editors, reviewers, teachers, and friends. In university or college, your English professor or writing instructor may divide your class into small groups to review one another's papers and provide suggestions for improvement. In the workplace, much of the writing you do will be passed around, with various writers adding their sections and making suggestions about yours.

Someone else can often see places where you *thought* you were being clear but were actually filling in details in your head, not on the page. You can help people who are reviewing your paper by assuring them that you want honest critical responses. Here are some guidelines to follow when asking for help with your revision:

1. *Specify the kind of help you want.*

   If you already know that the spelling needs to be checked, ask your readers to ignore those errors and focus on other elements in the draft. If you want suggestions about the thesis or the introduction or the tone or the organization or the examples or the style, ask questions about those features.

2. *Ask productive questions.*

   Be sure to pose questions that require more than a yes or no answer. Ask readers to tell you in detail what *they* see. You can use the questions in the Revising Checklist (Figure 6.1, p. 81) to help you in soliciting feedback.

3. *Do not get defensive.*

   Listen carefully to what your reviewers have to say, and interrupt only when you do not understand their comments. Above all, do not argue with your readers. If something confused them, it confused them. You want to see the writing through *their* eyes, not browbeat them into seeing it the way you do.

4. *Make your own decisions.*

   Remember that this is your paper; you are responsible for accepting or rejecting the feedback you get. If you do not agree with the suggestions that are offered, then do not follow them. But also keep in mind that your peer reviewers are likely to be more objective about your writing than you are.

# Revising on a Word Processor

Revision is much easier if you are using a word processor. Probably the biggest advantage of word processing is that it helps you see that writing is *changeable.* You can consider every word, sentence, or paragraph as just one possible choice among many. Because you can delete, move, and save the text in different files, the word processor invites you to explore alternatives. You can try a change and see how it reads; if the revision flops, you can easily restore the original draft.

Computer software can also help with sentence-level revisions. Most word-processing programs have spell checkers that identify questionable spellings and suggest possible correctly spelled alternatives. Of course, a spell checker does not understand your text and cannot determine if its suggestions are appropriate or even plausible, but it can focus your attention on words that you may need to change. Other programs, called *text analyzers* or *style or grammar checkers,* will give you information about word choice, sentence length, potential grammatical errors, and other features of style and structure. These programs can only point out *possible* problems, such as a long sentence or a weak verb; you have to decide whether the verb is effective or the sentence really is too long.

## Avoid Computer Pitfalls

There are some disadvantages to revising on a computer. Early versions of your essay are lost as you revise. In most cases, this loss is no problem, but if you make big changes you need to stop and print out old drafts as you go. They may contain work that can be retrieved later and used elsewhere. We encourage you to print your rough draft even when you know it is due for a major rewrite.

In addition, certain problems are easier to see on a printed copy than on the computer screen. For example, you see more paragraphs at a time on the page. On the screen, you may not notice that you have used the same transitional phrase at the beginning of several paragraphs, or that the paragraph lengths are wildly unbalanced. And when you revise sentences on the screen, you are much more likely to neglect to delete the old version or perhaps a word or two of it, leaving you with a garbled sentence.

A final caution about revising on computers: instructors expect clean, neat, correct final copy. Some allow for tidy corrections done in ink, but others insist on a new printout when you find an error. Your instructor may be righteously indignant over a misspelling that should have been flagged by the spell checker, attributing the error to your laziness or haste.

## Setting a Revision Agenda

Your revision will be easier and more efficient if you establish some priorities to guide your rethinking, rearranging, and rewriting. Not all revisions require the same amount of time and energy. You need to consider how much time you have and how effective your first draft is. If you have left enough time for your writing to evolve, you may not need a wholesale revision. On the other hand, a hurried first draft will need more thorough reworking.

The list of questions in Figure 6.1 will help you set up your own revising agenda. This checklist focuses on general questions first and takes up smaller matters later.

---

1. Does the paper meet the assignment and make the point I set out to make?
2. Is the thesis clear and intelligent?
3. Is the main idea of each paragraph directly related to the thesis?
4. Are the paragraphs fully developed with examples and details?
5. Do the ideas flow coherently? Are the transitions easy to follow?
6. Are the sentences clear and effectively structured?
7. Does the introduction capture the reader's attention and make the main point of the paper clear?
8. Does the conclusion provide an intelligent closing for the paper?

---

**FIGURE 6.1** *Revising Checklist*

## EXERCISE 6.1: REVISION

Revise each of the following to improve its clarity and effectiveness.

1. Tell me the name of the author and where she was born.

2. He knew neither the meaning of the word nor how to spell it.

3. Many adults believe that to be wealthy is successful.

4. The blackflies had not only stung my father but my sister and me also.

5. The success of a television program depends on how well the program has been promoted, the actors taking part, and is it a distinct genre.

6. I knew both the boys when they were young, their father owned the grocery store at the corner of our street.

7. Hamburgers were served to all of the guests smothered in onions.

8. Duddy felt that success in life depended on one's owning of property and he tries to purchase land using whatever means necessary.

9. Ophelia was reported to have said to the Queen these are the flowers, I gather.

10. It has been said that there are only two indigenous Canadian art forms. Native pictographs and Inuit carvings.

## EXERCISE 6.2: REVISION

Revise each of the following passages to improve its clarity and style. You may need to combine or separate some sentences and add, delete, and/or change certain details.

1. The main character in the story was a farmer. He was just barely making a living. His family was nearly starving. His mule died after a short illness. The owner of the land demanded his rent in advance. The man stared at the sunset not knowing what to do.

2. He had seen men blinded and smashed to pieces in the war. He had seen prisoners tortured and killed. He had held the hand of his closest friend and watched him die by inches. He could not understand how during this war any part of his nation at home could still carry on doing the same things, thinking similar thoughts, watching the old television programs, to find time to complain about the little problems that they always did and he thought that, truly, he never would be able to go home again.

3. Men and women blessed with political freedom, willing to work and able to find work, rich enough maintaining their families and educating their children, content with their lot in life and friends with their neighbours, defend themselves to the utmost but never consent to take up arms for an unjust war of conquest.

4. To give you an example of rationalizing, I have said to myself that I made a good grade on an examination that I know deep in my heart that I did not make a good grade, but finally I convince myself that I did make a good grade, then that is rationalizing.

5. The quality of merchandise sold is not always the best, because all enterprises are always looking for ways and means to manufacture their product at a lower cost and therefore be able to sell to the consumer at a slightly lower price than that of their competitors, and this leads to inferiority, in many cases, of the products.

## Editing the Final Draft

After you have finished your revisions, you must force yourself—or someone completely trustworthy—to read the paper yet one more time to pick up any careless mistakes or typos. Jessica Mitford rightly says that "failure to proofread is like preparing a magnificent dinner and forgetting to set the table." So, be thorough—proofread and then correct any errors. This correcting is called the editing process.

Careless errors can be unintentionally funny, like these from the real-life job applications of people who apparently did not edit their copy:

I am a rabid typist and have a proven ability to track down and correct erors.

I was instrumental in ruining the entire operation of a Midwest chain store.

Thank you for your consideration. I hope to hear from you shorty.

Do you suppose any of those applicants got the job?

Many careless errors are just plain witless and annoying—like repeating a word needlessly ("and and") or leaving off an -s and producing an illiteracy:

> The protester were arrested and herded off to jail.

Such errors do nothing to encourage your readers to admire the brilliance of your ideas—no matter how keen they are. So watch the little things. Do not write "probable" for "probably," or "use to" for "used to" or "you're" for "your" or "then" for "than." Check possessives to be sure the apostrophes are there—or not there in the case of "its." Figure 6.2 gives you some other points to keep in mind as you edit your draft.

---

1. Make sure that each sentence really is a sentence, not a fragment—especially those beginning with *because, since, which, that, although, as, when,* or *what* and those beginning with words ending in -*ing*.
2. Make sure that independent clauses joined by *indeed, moreover, however, nevertheless, thus,* and *hence* have a semicolon before those words, not just a comma.
3. Make sure that every modifying phrase or clause is close to the word it modifies.
4. Check your manuscript form to be sure it is acceptable. Have you placed the appropriate number of spaces between the title and the first line of the essay? Did you double-space throughout? Did you leave at least 2.5-centimetre (one-inch) margins on all sides, including top and bottom? Did you prepare a title page, if requested to do so? Did you staple the pages together?

---

**FIGURE 6.2** *Editing Checklist*

## Proofreading Advice

Most of us have difficulty proofreading our own writing because we know what we wanted to say and thus do not notice that we have not said it flawlessly. We become caught up in the content and fail to see the errors. If you have this trouble, try reading the sentences from the bottom of the page to the top, out of order, so that you cannot become interested in what you are saying because it will not make sense. Try to read slowly, word by word. Figure 6.3 gives you a list of points to check for when you proofread.

---

Pay no attention to content. Read only for errors to make certain that you have

1. no words left out or carelessly repeated.
2. no words misspelled—or carelessly spelled (*use to* for *used to*).
3. no plurals left off.
4. no apostrophes omitted in possessives or in contractions.
5. no periods, dashes, commas, colons, or quotation marks left out.
6. no confusion of *to/too, their/they're/there, its/it's, then/than, your/you're.*

---

**FIGURE 6.3** *Proofreading Checklist*

## A Word of Encouragement About Spelling

In the past, people were considerably more relaxed about correct spelling than we are today. William Shakespeare, demonstrating his boundless creativity, spelled his own last name at least thirteen different ways. John Donne wrote "sun," "sonne," or "sunne," just as it struck his fancy. But along about the eighteenth century, Dr. Samuel Johnson decided orthography was out of hand. He took it upon himself to establish a standard for the less learned and brought out his famous dictionary. Of course, the language refused to hold still—even for the stern-minded Dr. Johnson—and his followers have been trying to make it do so ever since.

Today educated people are expected to be able to spell according to the accepted standard. Nobody encourages a lot of creativity in this area. So, if you did not learn to spell back in elementary school, you may need help.

**USE YOUR SPELL CHECKER.** Help with spelling is easy to come by if you write on a word processor. You just need to run your spell checker after you finish revising and make the necessary corrections. But remember that your spell checker will not flag those troublesome words that are easy to confuse—*its/it's, to/too/two, then/than, there/they're/their, altogether/all together, choose/chose, effect/affect,* and all those other homonyms or sound-alike words—because you are not misspelling them. You are just using the wrong one. And remember, if your word processor uses only an American spell checker, you will need to double-check for accepted Canadian spellings. So, even with such helpful electronic assistance, you will still need to proofread carefully in case you have accidentally typed the wrong word.

**KEEP A LIST AND STUDY IT.** If you have serious trouble with spelling, you need to keep a list of the words you get wrong and learn how to spell them. Start now. Add to it whenever you discover you have misspelled a word. If you keep adding the same word—especially an easy, often-used word, like "writing" or "coming"—make a point of *remembering* that you cannot spell it so you can look it up or choose a synonym that you *can* spell. Everyone can become an accurate speller, but it may take more work and attention for some than for others.

**FIND A FRIEND TO HELP.** If you are fortunate enough to have a friend or relative who can help with your spelling, you are in luck. Beg or bribe this individual to check your papers for misspelled words.

### EXERCISE 6.3: SPELLING

The following passage contains forty-four spelling errors. Correct all of them.

> In Febuary the quite nurse surprised evrybody and gave up her profesion. She had finlly decided to try a diffrent busyness. What could she do? The anwser, she thoght, was to study grammer and become a editor. That wood shurely be more intresting then medacine.
>
> She seperated herself from her freinds and spent her time at the liberary, amoung books. She spent hours evry day with usually only ten minutes for a lite

lunch. It was definately hard work. She worked untill her head was filed with opinnions.

At last she was ready. She drove acrost the country looking for an exellent editting oppertunity, but she did'nt succede. She was completly dissappointed and embarassed. Everywhere, people had become sensible and had learnt to edit there own writting. Therefor, she changed jobs agen.

### ☐ EXERCISE 6.4: CANADIAN VERSUS AMERICAN SPELLING

Noah Webster introduced what he considered to be a simplified form of spelling in the United States in 1828. While Canadians have adopted some of the American spellings, we have also held on to many British spellings, and have invented some of our own. Test your knowledge of preferred Canadian spellings by completing the following. We have done the first one for you. If you are unsure as to which variation to use, here or elsewhere, check a reliable Canadian dictionary.

| AMERICAN SPELLING | CANADIAN SPELLING |
| --- | --- |
| analog | analogue |
| color | |
| behavior | |
| canceled | |
| catalog | |
| center | |
| fiber | |
| fulfill | |
| gray | |
| honor | |
| defense | |
| kilometer | |
| practice (v.) | |
| liter | |
| theater | |

# Three Drafts of a Student Paragraph

The stages of the revision process discussed in this chapter are illustrated in the following drafts of a concluding paragraph taken from the second sample student essay in Chapter 9. Following the first and second draft is a list of some revising and editing concerns. By recognizing these weaknesses and then making the required changes, the student develops her writing from one stage to the next. Of course, this process will likely require many more changes and modifications than can possibly be illustrated here, but these drafts will give you an idea of the kinds of issues involved.

## THE ROUGH DRAFT

There is no escaping the fact that in society today, women are not equally represented in the newsmedia. It is important to note that this phenomenon is a worldwide occurrence that must be faced in many countries throughout the world. Even if these changes to the media could be easily made, it is very difficult to say whether they actually would take place. It is clear that "the media trends we see are symbolic in our society" (Mediawatch, 2003), in other words, the things emphasized in the media reflect what society sees as being important. It is very difficult to say that a change in the newsmedia's portrayal of women would be possible without a corresponding shift in societal thought. As a societal whole it is necessary that a concious decision be made to include the experience of women. Without this, the way we view society through media is biased and misleading. These changes must not only occur in the newsmedia but in all forms of media if we are to see an improved representation of women.

- opening sentence is bland; needs to be more effective, more powerful (perhaps find a quotation)
- need to add some specific solutions
- does it really sum up what I have said in the rest of the essay (double-check)?
- use Mediawatch information in more detail
- paragraph does not seem to progress very far—seems to say the same thing over and over

## THE REVISION DRAFT

"I am woman. Hear me roar." There is no escaping the fact that in society today women are not equally represented in the newsmedia—we do not hear women's voices roaring very often. As Mediawatch suggests, the newsmedia must become more active on this front by forming advisory commitees to consult on gender issues, employing balanced reporting that includes feature stories delving into broader societal contexts, using female news sources, seeking a gender balance in reporting, covering women's issues with more regularity, and encouraging more editorial participation by women. In general, women must be given a place to stand, a place where our voices can be heard, a place to roar. As always, the individual in our society—you and I—must speak out; we must develop proactive strategies. As a society, the concious decision must be made to include the experience of women. Without this, the potential for women in society may never be fully realized.

- quotation seems to trivialize what I want to say; find another or delete altogether
- content seems to originate entirely from researched source—needs some of *my own ideas*?
- check spelling and documentation

- strengthen content—flow seems choppy
- improve logical development (include a general statement about representation of women; add specific ideas about change and improvement; insert a generalization to conclude)
- use "the experience of women" as opening; make direct connection with opening paragraph and thesis
- get my study partner to give it a read before I print the final

## THE EDITED DRAFT

As a society, a conscious decision must be made to include the experience of women. As Mediawatch suggests, the news media must become more active on this front by forming advisory committees to consult on gender issues, employing balanced reporting that includes feature stories delving into broader societal contexts, using female news sources and equal opportunity hiring, seeking a gender balance in programming and reporting, covering women's issues with more regularity, and encouraging more editorial participation by women ("Women Strike Out"). In general, women must be given a place to stand, a place where their voice can be heard. As always, the individual in our society—you and I—must speak out: we must write letters of observation and complaint to media outlets, insist on extensive media education and literacy programs within our schools, provide gender awareness and sensitivity programs for men and women, young and old, insist on programs of social justice within our schools and communities, be involved in our world—these are proactive strategies that must be put into practice, these are feasible practices that must become our strategies. In this way, we can make that world of "silence and slow time" come to life. Without this, without changing the real and represented roles of women in the media, the potential for women in society may never be fully realized.

# Logically

The most important element in the writing process is the critical thinking that produces what you write. Most of the knowledge and many of the insights you use in writing are acquired through reading. As you read, you will be exposed to ideas, theories, and opinions as well as facts. Reading, discussing, and synthesizing all this new information constitutes a large part of becoming educated.

## Cultivate a Questioning Attitude

The educational process bogs down if you do not keep an open mind. You should not reject a new idea just because it conflicts with an opinion you presently treasure. Because you have heard and accepted a statement all your life does not make that statement true. As Oscar Wilde once observed, "The pure and simple truth is rarely pure and never simple."

You should be willing to consider new ideas, examine them, think about them critically, and decide on the basis of the available evidence what is and is not valid. You will be bombarded by facts and opinions from all sides. Much of what we read and observe is designed to sway our opinions or sell us something—or both. Just consider the barrage of messages we are subjected to daily from advertising alone—in magazines and newspapers, on television, at the movies, on billboards and computer screens, and even on clothing. Not to mention all the misinformation that flows from local, provincial, and federal governments. In order to avoid being manipulated or deceived, you must try to distinguish the truth from the tripe. Truth may be mighty, but it does not always prevail.

> **T I P !**
>
> **Adopt a questioning mindset.**
>
> Look for the unstated assumption that often underlies apparently objective statements.

## Be Suspicious of Slogans

As you form the habit of questioning statements, the first ones to examine are those that come in the form of *epigrams* or *slogans*. These prepackaged ideas are neat and tidy, easy to remember, pleasant to the ear. They include such nuggets as Benjamin Franklin's "A stitch in time saves nine" and Winston Churchill's "Give us the tools, and we will finish the job." Epigrams usually state a simple truth, but often they cleverly disguise opinion as fact. For instance, you have heard that "Home is where the heart is," but George Bernard Shaw rewrote it as "Home is the girl's prison and the woman's workhouse." Clearly, the truth of either statement is debatable and may lie somewhere in between.

A slogan is a catch phrase or motto designed to rally people to vote for a certain party, buy a certain product, or agree with a certain group. During the 1995 provincial election in Ontario, for example, the Progressive Conservative party put forward a platform promising spending cuts and government responsibility which they labelled the "Common Sense Revolution." While this slogan captivated the imagination of the electorate—the Conservatives swept to victory—it was by no means a logical or feasible approach to governing. Governments have to solve complex problems and make difficult decisions that require something more than mere common sense, something more than the simple lay knowledge of the average person in the street. Governing is a complicated matter and must be dealt with by a variety of people with expertise in a variety of areas. So, slogans may sound inspiring, and most certainly serve various purposes, but do not mistake them for reasoned ideas. Your job as a reader, and as a writer, is to question such statements. Demand evidence and decide rationally, not emotionally, which opinions are valid, which are propaganda, and which are a mixture of both.

### ▓ Exercise 7.1: SLOGANS

Choose five popular advertising slogans (such as those used by Nike, McDonald's, DeBoers, Red Rose), and, in a sentence or two, explain the message implied in each.

## Detecting Slanted Writing

More difficult to detect than the bias of slogans is the subtle persuasion of *slanted writing*. Once you become aware of the emotional quality of many words, you will not likely be taken in by slanted writing.

### Be Cautious About Connotations

Words are symbols that can have both a *denotative* meaning (the actual meaning) and a *connotative* meaning (the emotional response to the word). The term *mother*, for instance, denotes a female who gives birth, but the word typically connotes warmth, love, comfort, and apple pie. Most words have connotations in varying degrees—some so strong as to be considered *loaded* or *slanted*. Whether you call the prime minister a *statesman* or a *politician* may well reveal your political affiliation. Consider the connotations of these pairs of words with similar denotative meanings:

| | |
|---|---|
| egghead | intellectual |
| pornographic | erotic |
| jock | athlete |
| penny-pinching | thrifty |
| mob | crowd |
| cur | doggie |

Whether you choose from the negative words on the left or the favourable words on the right will reveal your attitude to an alert reader.

Do not get the impression that connotative language is necessarily bad. It is not. In fact, without the use of emotional words, writing would be fairly lifeless, but you need to become alert to connotations.

The tone of righteous conviction achieved in the following passage is admirable. The argument is eloquent, emphatic, and persuasive. But it also is pure hogwash—blatant propaganda. See if you can pick out the emotionally charged words on which the appeal rests:

> If we stand idly by, if we seek merely swollen, slothful ease and ignoble peace, then bolder and stronger peoples will pass us by, and will win for themselves the domination of the world.

Note that the writer says not just "stand by" but "stand idly by." He fears we may seek "ease"—but not a good rest earned by hard work. No, it is a *"swollen, slothful* ease." Certainly the word "peace" alone would not serve his purpose: he makes it an *"ignoble* peace." Notice, too, that those who will "pass us by" are *"bolder* and *stronger* peoples," implying that only wimps would let them go unchallenged, for they are clearly standing in the way of our rightful, glorious conquest of the world.

That sentence, written by Theodore Roosevelt, deserves high marks as effective propaganda. But you as reader must be able to detect that the chinks in his logic are effectively plugged with rhetoric. It is this kind of use of the language that gives rhetoric a bad name.

You will hear similar appeals every day, not just from politicians but from advertisers and special interest groups as well. Your best protection from slanted writing is your ability to think—to examine the language and the logic, to sort out the sound ideas from the sound effects.

## Exercise 7.2: CONNOTATION

Underline the particularly connotative words in each of the following sentences, indicate whether a positive or a negative connotation is suggested, and rewrite the sentence by changing the words to reverse the connotation.

1. The retarded child was placed in a special class.
2. The controversial sponsorship scandal rocked the government.
3. The film had a remarkable conclusion.
4. The aroma from the barbeque filled the neighbourhood.
5. Her ideas were well stated but naive.
6. The soldiers fled from the battle.
7. My grandmother wears some very colourful outfits.
8. The neon signs on the strip screeched out their messages.
9. My professor is ancient.
10. The department store was noted for selling bargain-priced goods.

## Consider the Source

According to the old cliché, "Don't believe everything you read." And there is some wisdom in this. You need to be aware that, in almost all cases, the sources you are reading are not objective. There are usually at least three sides to every story—as much as you can, you need to be aware of biases as you do your research and to let your readers know about them when you quote sources. Do not just report what you read at face value. Always consider the source of the source.

Some sources you would recognize as biased without even reading them. You would know to be suspicious of information on gun control published by the National Rifle Association, data about smoking from Imperial Tobacco, or views on the need to cap players' salaries by the NHL governors. You would also know not to read only *Le Devoir* if you are researching issues of Quebec sovereignty. But the bias in many other sources is far more subtle. In a discussion of consumer issues you would probably want to balance the viewpoint of an article in *Adbusters* magazine with that of a less liberal publication, perhaps *Canadian Business* or *MoneySense*.

You could probably scare up most of the facts from reading one unbiased source, but the problem is discovering which one that is. The only way to make sure is to read widely. After you have read opinions on all sides of the issue, you should be able to recognize the centre—if and when you find it.

## Keep an Open Mind

Do not make the mistake of embracing what you consider a reliable source and then placing your trust in it till death do you part. Too many of us do just this: we plight our troth to the Bible, to the *National Post*, to CNN, or to CBC Newsworld, and assume we never have to think again. You will discover writers and publications whose viewpoints are similar to yours. These will naturally strike you as the most astute, cogent, perceptive, well-informed, reliable sources to consult. But be careful that you do not fall into the comfortable habit of reading or viewing these sources exclusively.

## A Quick Look at Logic

Developing a logical mind is important for you, both as a reader and as a writer. Whenever you write—especially when you write to persuade—your aim is to convey your thoughts and ideas into the minds of your readers. To be convincing, these thoughts and ideas must be logical. You should know the important principles of logic so that you can apply them in your own thinking and writing—as well as in detecting slippery logic in the writing and arguments of others.

In your writing you should follow specific exploration strategies: conduct thorough and detailed research, ask questions, compile observations, cite definitions and examples, identify causes and their effects, and develop your own ideas and suppositions. Avoid fallacies in your reasoning, including the acceptance of so-called common or conventional knowledge. Organize your writing in a pattern that is reasoned and that makes sense, perhaps arranging your material in a chronological manner, or by reverse chronology, or by importance of information (either from least to most important or the other way around). Finally, use those transitional forms suggested in Chapter 4 to make one part of your writing connect with the next.

## Cite Valid Authorities

**T I P !**

**Be especially questioning about sources from the internet.**

You will find more extensive cautions about using electronic sources in Chapter 8.

You are probably going to cite authorities whenever you write on any controversial subject. But you need to be sure your authority is convincing to your audience. Some people think that once they have clinched a point with "The Bible says . . .," they have precluded any rebuttal. If your reader happens to be one of the Christian faithful, you will be on solid ground. But not everyone would agree with the upright citizen who wrote a letter to the editor of our local paper offering this solution for helping the poor:

> The only remedy against poverty is to worship God as God, honour His word and obey His doctrines, call upon Him and humble ourselves. Then He will hear and heal the land.

More practical-minded readers are not likely to accept an argument requiring divine intervention to solve social problems. Cite authorities, by all means, but try for impartial authorities—noted scholars and researchers, who have published on your subject and are accepted as experts by most educated people.

## Avoid Oversimplifying

Most of us have a tendency to like things reduced to orderly, easily grasped, either/or answers. The only problem is that things seldom are that simple. Be wary of arguments that offer no middle way—the "either we do away with affirmative action or else white males are going to go jobless" sort of reasoning.

## Avoid Stereotyping

Stereotypes involve set notions about the way different types of people behave. Professional athletes, according to the stereotype, are uneducated, overpaid, greedy individuals interested only in matters of self-interest and self-promotion, and in making more money. Such stereotypes rarely give a truthful picture of anyone in the group and could never accurately describe all members.

## Avoid Sweeping or Hasty Generalizations

You will do well to question easy solutions to complex problems. A faulty generalization (a general statement that is far too broad) can result from stating opinion as fact:

> Rap music causes serious social problems by creating defiant behaviour in its listeners.

That statement needs evidence to prove its claim, and such proof would be nearly impossible to come by.

Since you cannot avoid making generalizations, just be careful to avoid making them without sufficient evidence. At least, qualify your statements:

| **(faulty)** | All Siamese cats are noisy and nervous. |
|---|---|
| **(better)** | Many Siamese cats are noisy and nervous. |

Statements involving *all, none, everything, nobody,* and *always* are difficult to prove. Instead try *some, many, sometimes,* or *often*.

## Watch for Hidden Premises

Another sort of generalization that may prove deceptive involves a *hidden premise* (the basic idea underlying the main statement). The following observation, to those who accept information without questioning, may sound plausible:

> If those animal rights demonstrators had left when the police told them to, there would have been no trouble and no one would have been injured.

The hidden premise here assumes that all laws are just and fairly administered; that all actions of the government are honourable and in the best interest of all citizens. The statement presumes, in short, that the demonstrators had no right or reason to be there and hence were wrong not to leave when told to do so. Such a presumption overlooks the possibility that in a free country the demonstrators might legitimately protest the right of the police to make them move.

## Use Analogy with Care

An *analogy* involves taking two similar situations and claiming that what holds true for one holds true for the other. For instance, psychologist Naomi Weisstein, in her article "Woman as Nigger," contends that women are conditioned with a slave mentality and exploited for the economic benefit of society just as African Americans were for centuries. As this example suggests, analogies can add interest and clarity to a persuasive paper, and they often illustrate points effectively. But conclusions derived from an analogy are not logical proof. Make certain your analogy is indeed convincing before giving it too much weight in your essay.

A *false analogy* occurs when the two situations are not comparable. For example, you often hear people say something like this:

> If we can put people on the moon, we should be able to find a cure for AIDS.

Although both of these situations involve solving a problem with scientific knowledge, the difficulties facing medical researchers are quite different from those solved by space engineers.

## Do Not Dodge the Issue

People employ a number of sneaky logical fallacies in order to sidestep a problem while appearing to pursue the point.

1. *Appealing to Emotion*

   Perhaps the most common—and the most underhanded—involves playing on the emotional reactions, prejudices, fears, and ignorance of the audience instead of directly addressing the issue, like this:

> If we allow condom distribution in the public schools, the moral fibre of the na-
> tion will be endangered.

That sentence, which contains no evidence to prove that condom distribu-
tion is either good or bad, merely attempts to make it sound scary.

2. *Attacking the Person (the* ad hominem *fallacy)*

Illogical thinkers and unprincipled people frequently attack the person they
are arguing against, rather than addressing the issue being argued. They may
call their opponents "effete, effeminate snobs," for example, and hope nobody notices that they have not actually said anything convincing.

3. *Employing Circular Reasoning*

People who use this dodge offer as evidence arguments that assume as true
the very thing they are trying to prove, as a devout person might do by
quoting the Bible to prove the divinity of Christ. Here is an example of circular
reasoning:

> If we want a society of people who devote their time to base and sensuous
> things, then pornography may be harmless. But if we want a society in which
> the noble side of humans is encouraged and mankind itself is elevated, then
> I submit that pornography is surely harmful.

That writer says, in effect, that pornography is evil because pornography is
evil. The statement might be true, but that does not make it logical or persuasive.

4. *Jumping to Conclusions*

A common problem in reasoning is called the *post hoc* fallacy (from the Latin
*post hoc, ergo propter hoc,* meaning "after this, therefore because of this"). This
fallacy assumes—without any concrete evidence—that because one event
follows another, the first is the cause of the second. Because we often employ cause-and-effect reasoning in attempting to make sense of our lives,
*post hoc* reasoning is common.

For example, suppose you have just read that the early symptoms of
mercury poisoning are restlessness, instability, and irritability. Since ecolo-
gists have warned that our waters are polluted with mercury in dangerous
amounts, and since everyone you know is restless, unstable, and irritable
these days, you conclude that the population is succumbing to mercury poisoning. And we may well be, for that matter, but if you expect to convince
anyone who was not already eager to make the same leap in logic, you will
need to gather more evidence—such as medical reports showing that human
beings (as well as fish and cattle) are actually ingesting dangerous amounts
of the poison.

# Think for Yourself

All of these techniques are frighteningly successful with untrained, unanalytical minds. Your best defence is critical thinking. Think while you are reading or listening, and think some more before you write. Be prepared to change your mind. Instead of hunting for facts to shore up your present opinions, let the facts you gather lead you to a conclusion.

And do not insist on a nice, tidy, clear-cut conclusion. Sometimes there is none. Your conclusion may well be that both sides for various reasons have a point. Simply work to discover what you honestly believe to be the truth of the matter, and set that down—as clearly and convincingly as you can.

# Use Effective Methods of Argument

There are many kinds of argument, ranging from formal, parliamentary-style debate to the informal rallying cry at a protest march. But whatever their form, effective methods of argument are based on principles of logic similar to those identified above and, of course, on many of the other writing strategies outlined in this text. Whether the form of the argument is a speech, a letter to an editor, a persuasive essay, or a political cartoon, you will need to consider the following:

- Be clear about your subject and your thesis.
- Understand your audience.
- Establish some common ground or area of concern, especially if you know that your audience may be opposed to your argument.
- Be specific in your facts and citation of statistics.
- Try to anticipate and counter opposing arguments.
- Be logical.
- Be confident and assertive but not too aggressive in your tone.
- Try to appeal to several aspects of your audience or readership—the heart as well as the head.
- Finish with your strongest point and an emphatic restatement of your thesis.

### Exercise 7.3: DISCUSSION

Find, photocopy, and bring to class four copies of an example of the use of faulty logic. Good places to look include TV or radio commercials (write a brief description and make copies), magazine ads, political speeches, letters to the editor, editorials, and opinion-page columnists. (Note: Advertising campaigns are quite notorious for their tendency to stretch logic through the use of testimonials, weasel words, fear tactics, pseudo-scientific or technical claims, slick slogans, intellectual flattery, and the like—see what examples you can find.) In a group with two or three fellow students, distribute and discuss everyone's examples. Identify the fallacies, and explain what makes the underlying thinking illogical.

## ▨ Exercise 7.4: REVISING

Examine the last paper you wrote that involved argument or persuasion. Jot down your main points and decide whether your logic was good or flawed. If you find flaws, figure out what went wrong and how to fix the problem.

## ▨ Exercise 7.5: WRITING

Think of a stereotype that you once believed in—for instance, the absent-minded professor, the dumb jock, the flighty blonde, the overbearing mother-in-law, the short-tempered redhead, the boring accountant, the greedy boss, the snobbish intellectual. Why did you believe this stereotype? How did you learn the stereotype was wrong? Write a paper in which you answer these questions.

## ▨ Exercise 7.6: ARGUMENT

Write a one-paragraph argument that completes one of the following:

1. I dislike people who . . .
2. The greatest technological invention in all human history is . . .
3. Canada should cut all ties with the monarchy because . . .
4. The best hockey team in Canada is . . .
5. The greatest Canadian of all time is . . .

## ▨ Exercise 7.7: ARGUMENT

Examine the following editorial and identify the techniques of argument used by the writer. Then, agreeing or disagreeing with the ideas expressed, write your own response.

### THE COST OF EDUCATION

There is an old saying that goes, "If you think education is expensive, try ignorance." That old saying has taken on a new and urgent credibility. A recent report by Statistics Canada forecasts a critical shortage of trained profession-als—doctors, lawyers, nurses, professors, and teachers—within the first decade of the millennium. Our particular concern here is the shortage of teachers, who rep-resent the foundation of all those other professions: "For want of a nail, the shoe was lost; for want of a shoe, the horse was lost." One thing leads to the next, in other words, and without the educational foundation that good teachers provide it naturally follows that other professions will suffer as well. Children who might have become doctors and nurses will not be inspired to do so, nor, perhaps, will they even have the opportunity.

A degree in education is an expensive proposition. Many students place them-selves in significant debt simply earning their undergraduate degree; to afford one more year is beyond their means. Consequently, the average age of students at most faculties of education is near thirty—many students leave university and come back sometime later to pick up their B.Ed. This too can be a costly en-deavour for students, many of whom have families that have to struggle to make ends meet while the student—who is often the principal breadwinner—completes the extra year. And this year spent as a student teacher also comes with unique expenses. Aside from tuition and books, student teachers must bear the additional cost of transportation to what are sometimes distant practice teaching assignments. As well, the typical wardrobe of an undergraduate will not do for the front of the classroom; new clothes must be bought. Add to this the fact that, even once they graduate and land a job, burnout and dropout rates are significantly high for beginning teachers. First-year teachers are often hired late, given demanding teaching assignments, offered little support, and shifted around regularly. One in five new teachers is asked to teach a subject for which she or he is not qualified. In all kinds of ways, then, the experiences gained by students during their B.Ed. year do not prepare them for the real world of teaching into which they are thrust. As a result, large numbers of fully trained teachers consider dropping out of the profession within the first few years. Combine this with high rates of retirement among experienced teachers, and a crisis is at hand.

As a society, we must make the preparation and retention of teachers our priority. Whether we provide tuition-free faculties of education, rebates for students who incur travelling costs to reach their assigned teaching schools, free mentoring and support programs for new teachers, semi-funded sabbaticals for all teachers, or improved pay and benefits, we must make tangible changes to the system or our entire culture will suffer. Those doctors who diagnose and operate on people to save their lives would not be practising without the teachers who guided them along that path. Put in that perspective, the cost of education does not seem that expensive after all.

# Writing a Research Paper

At some time you may be asked to write a paper that does not draw entirely on your own knowledge and experience. In fact, many kinds of writing involve the use of source materials. You may be required to do research: that is, to read fairly widely on a certain subject, to combine and organize this accumulated information, and then to present it in clear and coherent prose. Your preparation will involve a combination of *primary research*, which may include making personal observations, carrying out surveys, reading original materials such as novels or historical documents, or undertaking lab experiments, and *secondary research*, which will include an examination of articles, books, and research completed by other researchers and writers in your area of study.

Traditionally, research papers involve *argument*. You may be expected to choose a topic that is somewhat controversial, investigate the issues on both sides, and take a stand. Some of the strategies outlined in the previous chapter should help you in writing this argumentative kind of research paper. Alternatively, of course, you can engage in valuable and interesting research that simply involves finding and synthesizing information on any subject to increase your and your readers' knowledge.

In many ways, the writing process for a research paper is the same as for any other. You still need to narrow the subject to a topic that you can handle in the number of assigned pages, and you still have to come up with a thesis statement and outline or plan before you begin writing. But first you have to locate the material you are going to read; then you will have to take notes as you read so that you can give credit to your sources as you write the paper.

## Scheduling Your Research Paper

Writing a research paper is a time-consuming job. This is one paper that you simply cannot put off until the last minute. As usual, the writing will be better if you do it in stages. Dividing the project into units will allow you to keep the work under control.

### Setting Deadlines for Yourself

If your completed paper is due in, say, six weeks, you could put yourself on a schedule that looks something like this:

**1st week:** Locate your possible sources. Record all the necessary bibliographical information about them.

Try to narrow the topic to a workable thesis question to investigate.

**2nd week:** Read and take notes.

Settle on a preliminary thesis question.

| | Try to come up with a preliminary outline. |
|---|---|
| **3rd week:** | Continue reading and taking notes. |
| **4th week:** | Complete your reading and note-taking. |
| | Turn your thesis question into a statement. |
| | Arrange your notes and organize your ideas. |
| | Develop a complete, detailed outline. |
| **5th week:** | Write the first draft and let it cool. |
| | Begin revising and editing. |
| | Get someone reliable to read your second draft and tell you whether the paragraphs are coherent, the sentences are clear, and the quotations are effectively integrated. |
| **6th week:** | Polish the second draft or write a third one. |
| | Complete a final draft and let it rest at least overnight. |
| | Proofread this last draft carefully and make additional corrections as needed. If necessary, print a clean draft for submission. |

This is a fairly leisurely schedule. You can, of course, do the work in a shorter time if required. You will have to be more industrious about finding sources and taking notes. Some instructors deliberately ask students to complete the project within a month in order to prevent procrastination. Whatever your time limit, devise a schedule for yourself and stick to it.

## Finding a General Topic

If allowed to select your own topic, you can begin by looking for information about any subject that interests you. Start by identifying a general subject that appeals to you, one that you can refine and narrow as you work through the process. This is an opportunity to learn about some aspect of your academic major, to investigate a career, to explore a personal interest or hobby, or to pursue some interesting topic that has come up in conversation or in a course you are taking.

One way to locate a fresh subject is to skim though the table of contents of a magazine that interests you. Alternatively, surf the internet and use its many resources to look for a topic. You might join a chat group or look through some online periodicals. Using a browser, you can check out listings and websites in a range of subject areas: arts and humanities, business and the economy, computers, education, entertainment, government, health, news and media, recreation and sports, science, society and culture. A quick look under entertainment, for instance, reveals a long list of topics—everything from "amusement and theme parks" to "comics and animation," "performing arts," and "television." If you want to write about television, you can look under that heading to lead you to more specific ideas, such as public access television, ratings, TV violence, and the V-chip.

## Narrowing Your Topic

If you have an area of interest but no ideas about any way to limit that topic, you may wish to turn to the internet to shape some thoughts and to collect and narrow your information. More often than not, of course, these searches will give you far more information than you can use. If you would like to hone in on some aspect of tennis, for example, a quick Google search using "tennis" as the keyword provides nearly 24 million results. That kind of information overload, what David Shenk calls "data smog," will more than likely leave you scratching your head, more befuddled than before you began.

Alternatively, for some topics, do not underestimate the value of a good encyclopedia. An encyclopedia article on tennis will give you information about the origin and history of the game, the court and the equipment, strategy and techniques, outstanding players, professional tournaments, and the state of the sport today. As you read, you will run across the observation that improved equipment and increased physical training have changed the nature of the game in the last twenty years. Precisely how has the game changed? In what ways has the equipment been improved and how have the improvements affected play? Have these changes been positive or negative? All it takes is a sentence, a subtopic, or an example in a general encyclopedia article on your subject to provide you with a focus for your research. Then you might run another Google search and achieve a more focused result. Entering "tennis contemporary racket design and improvement," for instance, reduces the findings to about 2500 results.

# Topics for Researched Writing

If your mind remains a blank and your instructor will allow you to take one of our suggestions, here are some ideas that we think might be interesting to research.

## For Informative Writing

1. Research the history of a familiar product or object, such as Coca-Cola, Mickey Mouse, the dictionary, disposable diapers, the nectarine, the title *Ms.,* frozen yogurt, the typewriter.

2. Research and analyze a fad, craze, custom, or holiday: body piercing, tattoos, quick weight-loss diets, Beanie Babies, St. Patrick's Day, Mother's Day, Kwanzaa, Cinco de Mayo, Victoria Day, Hanukkah, Juneteenth.

3. Research how a troubled group of people can be helped: autistic children, alcoholics, sexual assault victims, anorexics, agoraphobics, battered women, people with HIV, nicotine addicts, steroid users.

4. Research the history of some feature of your hometown: a landmark, street names, architecture, an industry.

5. Research some hobby or job in order to inform someone unfamiliar with the activity.

## For Persuasion or Argumentation

After doing the appropriate research, defend either side of one of the following issues:

1. The use of animals in research should (should not) be allowed.

2. It should (should not) be harder than it is now for married people to get a divorce.

3. Today's toys often contribute (do not contribute) to violent behaviour in children.

4. Having a working mother does (does not) harm a child's welfare and development.

5. The fashion industry does (does not) exploit consumers. Or substitute another area of business: the cosmetics industry, the funeral business, car manufacturers, the oil industry.

6. Genetic screening of fetuses should (should not) be prohibited.

7. Sexual harassment is (is not) a serious problem in the workplace.

8. The government should (should not) cut welfare benefits for single parents.

9. News reporters should (should not) be required to reveal their sources in criminal cases.

10. English should (should not) be the only official language of Canada.

11. Affirmative action should (should not) be discontinued.

12. Homosexuals should (should not) be allowed to marry.

13. The profile of women working in the media needs (does not need) to be improved.

14. It is (is not) better for children if their incompatible parents get a divorce.

15. Teaching phonics would (would not) solve the literacy crisis in this country.

16. Laws restricting the use of pesticides should (should not) be repealed.

17. Free speech should (should not) be restricted on the internet.

18. Electronic music trading should (should not) be allowed.

## Organizing Your Search

Once you have narrowed your topic, you need a plan for efficiently tracking down your source materials. Think about how much time you have and what kinds of sources you will probably be using. A good strategy is to begin with sources that give a broad overview of the subject and then move to ones that provide more detailed information. If you were to write about electronic music trading, for example, given the relatively current nature of the topic, you might first look at a range of articles in contemporary web magazines such as *Barcode* or *Release,* and you might even visit an online discussion forum such as *liveDaily* for an update on the very latest news. By the end of your research you might turn to articles that are more technical or legalistic or reliable in nature, perhaps using the resources of Research Navigator (see p. 106) to peruse the databases of the *New York Times* or EBSCO.

In order to locate all the relevant information in the library, you may need to think of headings under which your subject might be indexed. The encyclopedia and general reference works might supply you with some clues. The *Library of Congress Subject Headings (LCSH)* can be very useful in providing terms or key words to search with, as well as additional terms that you might not have considered. Most of the entries in the *LCSH* give alternative terms listed as BT (broader topic), RT (related topic), and NT (narrower topic). For example, looking up "electronic music trading" provided "electronic music instruments" and "electronic music periodicals" as broader topics and "Napster, Inc.," "Shawn Fanning," and "Music Trade" as narrower topics. You can use these alternative terms as you search for sources about music trading.

## Some Suggestions for Using the Library

One of the first things you need to do is get acquainted with your library. Many universities and colleges offer orientation courses to show students how to find and use resources. Libraries have tours and guidebooks and brochures telling you where to find various materials. Taking one of these tours or studying the guidebook may save you many hours of aimless wandering.

> **T I P !**
> **If you fail to find what you need, ask for help.** Librarians are usually willing to answer questions and will often lead you to the material you want and give you valuable advice.

### Searching for Sources

In the old days, the first things you were likely to see upon entering a library were imposing rows of polished wood cabinets with small drawers: the card catalogue. In most libraries those cabinets have been replaced with row upon row of computers. It is almost certain that you will conduct your search for sources on a computer. Computer searches, online databases, and internet search engines vary in the way you can use them; they are being expanded and improved all the time. Here are some general instructions to help you find your way around the modern library. You will, of course, have to familiarize yourself with the unique features of your own library.

### The Online Catalogue

The computer version of the card catalogue is called a public access catalogue (PAC) or an online catalogue (OC). The PAC or OC terminal itself will tell you how to use it. The opening screen on the OC at the library we use shows that we can search by subject, title, and author, as well as by call number, shelf position, keyword, and international standard book number (ISBN). We can search for books, titles of journals, and other items owned by our library or by other libraries.

Using the online catalogue, we are directed to enter the keywords of our topic on the subject line and press "enter." We are also reminded that "You will achieve better results if you use a valid Library of Congress subject heading." Entering the topic gets us a list of related subject headings with the number of titles for each heading indicated in parentheses. We can view the detailed citations for these titles if we want to, or we can look down the list of more specific headings. "Napster, Inc.," for example, provides us with the titles of two monographs: *All the Rave: The Rise and Fall of Shawn Fanning's Napster* by Joseph Menn (2003) and *Sonic Boom: Napster, MP3 and the New Pioneers of Music* by John Alderman (2001). We write down the call numbers and library location of these two books and decide to search for articles in magazines and other periodicals.

## Article Indexes and Databases

Most libraries now subscribe to one or more computerized bibliographic utilities, such as *ProQuest* (which indexes articles from academic journals, corporations, government publications, and medical journals); EBSCO (which provides access to separate databases in the humanities, business, health, and the social and natural sciences); and Lexis-Nexis (an online commercial service that allows full-text access to a wide range of business, legal, medical, and political sources). If your library subscribes to one or more of these services, you will find them on the OC terminal. You may also be able to access many of these databases from your computer at home or in your residence room.

A specialized resource database such as Pearson's Research Navigator™ also offers an excellent way to expedite the research process. Research Navigator is a self-guided resource that provides extensive information and practical suggestions on all stages of the research and writing process. It also provides direct access to four reliable databases: EBSCO Academic Journal and Abstract Database, New York Times Search by Subject Archive, "Best of the Web" Link Library, and Financial Times Article Archive and Company Financials.

The terminals in our library allow us to move from the online catalogue to search more than eighty article indexes and specialized databases. These include general resources like Canadiana: The National Bibliography and WilsonSelect-Plus, both of which provide citations, abstracts, and complete articles for many subject areas. There are also a number of indexes that allow us to search specific fields, such as Early Canadiana, AIDS/Cancer, Business Abstracts, Contemporary Women's Issues, Public Agenda Online, Canadian Nursing, PsycInfo, and Social Sciences Abstracts.

In our search for information about electronic music trading, we first choose CBCA Current Events. This index features Canadian titles that focus on current events, including politics, business, the arts, sports, and most other kinds of news in Canada and abroad. After typing in the search term "music trading," we discover there are thirteen references, all for periodical articles or electronic references. Each citation gives us the article title, the name of the source, and the date and page number, when applicable; some contain abstracts of the articles. We mark the items that appear relevant and print out this list of possible sources.

Because CBCA Current Events is not a full-text database, we now need to track down the references we have recorded. Databases such as Alt-Press Watch, CPI (Canadian Periodicals Index), and Research Navigator include abstracts and many complete articles from both scholarly and general interest publications, and can be of great use. In our initial search, Alt-Press Watch provides five full-text articles, CPI comes up with seventy-eight, and Research Navigator offers more than eight hundred. Our search results also suggest a number of subdivisions we can look under, such as "analysis," "cases," "ethical aspects," "crimes against," "forecasts and trends," and "user statistics." We browse through these citations and find several to print out. Figure 8.1 shows the first page from one of these articles. We can also send the data from our searches to our home or residence computers by way of email.

## The New York Times
### ON THE WEB

### After a Tough Breakup, an East Sider Goes West

Published Sunday, October 19, 2003

TISHA KRESLER, 32, is one of the few women you'll meet who can look tidy and inspire awe dressed in a Ramones T-shirt. Brisk and direct, Ms. Kresler is director of media relations for a telecommunications company just recovering from a two-fisted punch: bankruptcy and the investigation of former executives. When her personal life took a similarly severe hit early last spring ? as she found herself newly alone, and suddenly without a home ? Ms. Kresler reacted with characteristic aplomb.

She decided that she would wipe clean the map of her past life in New York ? seven years on the Upper East Side with a variety of roommates, including her former boyfriend of five years ? and start fresh, in an entirely new environment. She would cross Central Park.

Her co-workers at her office in Florham Park, N.J., to which she drives 45 minutes and back each day, called her a City Elitist. "Move to New Jersey," they'd entreat, "we'll take care of you."

"But really," Ms. Kresler said, "how could I live in New Jersey? Manhattan is still the place to be if you're young and single and want to feel alive."

She bunked for a few weeks with her two best friends ? each has a studio, on West 74th and 78th Streets, respectively ? and toured a seemingly endless parade of grimy boxes for $2,000 a month, the extent of her budget. Her search was rewarded with a gem: a fairly ample one-bedroom on 85th Street just off Broadway with a renovated ? and actual ? kitchen, rather than a galley. The rent? $2,050 a month.

The 1920 apartment building was designed by Gronenberg and Leuchtag, a fairly undistinguished but prolific firm, said Andrew Alpern, the author of a number of books about Manhattan's apartment houses, including, most recently, "The New York Apartment Houses of Rosario Candela and James Carpenter" (Acanthus; 2001). The narrow building was one of many put up during an extraordinary boom time for Manhattan, at least for developers of speculative apartment buildings.

ITS lobby is a riot of sumptuous detail, with a black and white marble floor shined within an inch of itself, seemingly more gilt sconces than the Tuileries, a rococo marble fireplace and, improbably, a romantic piece of statuary, two cupids entwined on a pedestal. The elevator men, on 24 hours, sport gold braids on their shoulders.

**FIGURE 8.1** *Sample Page from an Online Article*

**T I P !**

**Remember that most libraries still hold almost all of this material in old-fashioned print.**

The *Readers' Guide to Periodical Literature*, for instance, still comes out in book form. If the computer terminals are crowded or not working—or if you simply want some peace and quiet while researching—your librarian can tell you where the references you seek are shelved.

# Electronic Publications

These are just the first few steps in our search for possible sources. Our library computers also allow us to access books, journals, and reference works online. The electronic reference materials are extensive. They include directories, dictionaries, thesauruses, encyclopedias, and almanacs, as well as materials and resources on careers, grammar and writing, the arts, business, education and psychology, health and medicine, news and current events, political and social science, and science and technology. Some of these sources can be accessed directly on screen; many others are available through links to the World Wide Web (see page 109).

In short, the library's computers provide an overwhelming number of sources and service options. With so many possibilities, you can see why it is important, if not crucial, to take that orientation course we were talking about earlier. You will also have to spend some time with these data systems to find out how they function and how useful they are for your work. But it is time well spent. Once you get the hang of it, you will be able to research your topic or any other with astonishing ease and thoroughness.

# Using the Internet

As you know, the internet links computers around the world; it is a vast storehouse of information that can be accessed in a number of ways. It is relatively easy to get on the internet. All you need is a computer, a modem, and a browser. If you do not have a computer at home, your university or college library will have a bank of computers that are hooked up to the net.

On the net you can find government documents and archives, newsgroups, online publications, texts of published materials, and databases provided by commercial servers such as Microsoft Canada, Prodigy, and Campus Networks.

It would take up too much space to give you detailed instructions for using the internet, but we can briefly describe three of the basic tools that are available there: electronic mail, newsgroups, and the World Wide Web. If you are interested in finding out more, consult a book like *E-research: Methods, Strategies and Issues* (Allyn & Bacon, 2003) by Terry Anderson and Heather Kanuka or *The Research Paper: A Guide to Library and Internet Research*, 3rd ed. (Prentice Hall, 2002) by Dawn Rodrigues and Raymond Rodrigues.

**T I P !**

**Evaluate the reliability of an email source in the same way you would judge any person you have interviewed.**

When referring to this source in your paper, provide background on the source and indicate why he or she is qualified to give information on your topic.

# Electronic Mail

You are undoubtedly familiar with electronic mail (email) as a way of communicating with friends and family. But email can be a valuable research tool as well. Many people participate in special-interest discussion groups via email; these groups are called *mailing lists,* and they use a *listserver* to send mail automatically to everyone on the list. Once you join a mailing list, the listserver will send you all messages on standard email.

The easiest way to find a listserver is to check one of the directories on the World Wide Web. Many are available. For instance, selected Canadian discussions for researchers can be found at the National Library of Canada's directory (*www.collections canada.ca/6/20/s20-220-e.html*), and sites such as Mailserve or Listserv can also be useful. These sites will provide you with simple instructions for searching and for subscribing to any list you might find useful.

## Newsgroups

A newsgroup is a kind of public bulletin board containing comments, questions, and responses on a particular topic. It is more extensive and more organized than an email listserv. Asking a question of a mailing list or a newsgroup is a great way to get information about sources and to find people who can help you with your research. The newsgroup message board keeps track of several discussions at once and organizes the messages and replies in groups called *threads*. A thread begins with the original message, or *posting,* and includes all replies made by every participant in the discussion.

A program called a *newsreader* is used to read newsgroups and follow the threads. If your college or university subscribes to a news feed (a central computer that stores all messages and feeds them to other providers), you will have access to a newsreader and will be able to locate a newsgroup to follow. Another way to access newsgroups is through an internet browser, although you may need to configure it to allow you to read the newsgroup. Once your system is appropriately configured, you might choose Netscape News, for example, from the browser menu to get a listing of the newsgroups to which your college or university subscribes.

## World Wide Web

The most popular tool for searching the internet is the World Wide Web. As you know, the web is a complex system for organizing and viewing information on the internet. The primary attraction of this system is that its documents, or *webpages,* are linked to other pages through *hypertext* (links that are usually underlined and in blue), which provide numerous cross-references and additional information. To navigate the web, you use a *browser* such as Netscape or Microsoft Internet Explorer. By way of example,

**T I P !**
**Use material gathered from a newsgroup with caution.**
Try to confirm from other sources the reliability of any information from a newsgroup that you want to use in a research paper.

**T I P !**
**The Library and Archives Canada website is an excellent resource for many things Canadian.**
An integration of the former National Library and National Archives sites, this site (shown in Figure 8.2) provides easy access to its own storehouse of resources and links to numerous other Canadian sites through a range of search tools, including Amicus and ArchiviaNet. We encourage you to use this national treasure in order to discover others.

Figure 8.2 shows the home page for Library and Archives Canada, viewed through Microsoft Internet Explorer.

Searching the web requires the use of one of many search engines, such as Netscape, Lynx, Copernic, or Microsoft Explorer, which search for the key terms you indicate and return a list of sites that include these key terms. A subject-directory engine, such as Research Navigator or Yahoo!, allows you to look for specific information about a general topic (such as sports or women in the media); a text-index engine, such as Google, Altavista, Hotbot, or Lycos, lets you look for specific words (such as *Yukon tundra*) and gives links to documents containing those words. Figure 8.3 illustrates the first page of results from a search for "women in the media" conducted using Research Navigator.

When searching the web, it is important to come up with a list of specific keywords as soon as possible. A single word like *cancer* will produce thousands

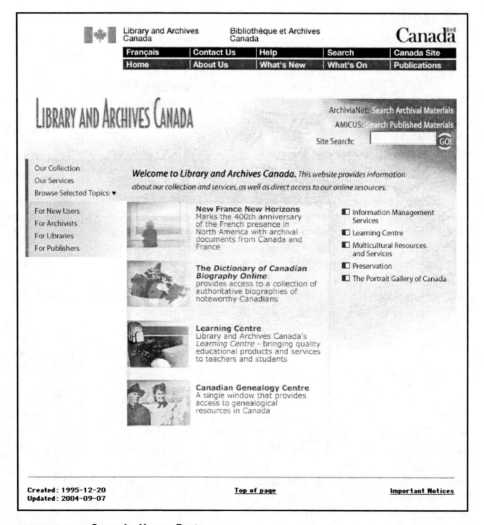

**FIGURE 8.2** *Sample Home Page*

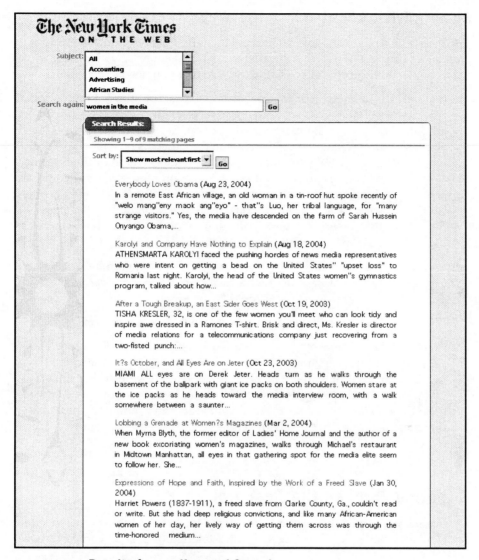

**FIGURE 8.3** *Results from a Keyword Search*

of documents; using a phrase like *pancreatic cancer in teenagers* will limit the results. You can also narrow your search by using AND (for example, *Shakespeare* AND *sonnet*), which causes the engine to find only sites that include all the keywords you specify. (Some engines require a plus sign rather than AND.) When the search engine shows a list of "top" sites, survey the list to identify the most promising and click on these. When you find a useful site, print or download its pages for later examination. If you are not satisfied with the first search results, try new search terms or a different search engine on your browser.

## Some Advice About Using the Web

The internet and the web give you access to a great deal of information that is often more current than anything available in printed sources. Nonetheless, there are a couple of serious pitfalls in using the web that you need to consider:

1. It is difficult to know how to judge the vast array of material that is available. Some websites are filled with useful facts and helpful advice, but others are full of propaganda, unsupported opinion, inaccurate information, and tasteless junk. Anyone can publish on the web; there is no editorial board to screen the material. So, you must apply sound judgment in evaluating each of your electronic sources, just as you would the print sources that you find in the library. Check the information against other sources, and carefully consider the credentials, and the biases, of the person or organization supplying the data. These sites give guidance on evaluating internet sources:

   Grassian, Esther. "Thinking Critically about World Wide Web Resources." *www.library.ucla.edu/libraries/college/help/critical/index.html*

   Kirk, Elizabeth E. "Evaluating Information Found on the Internet." *http://muse.mse.jhu.edu:8001/research/education/net.html*

> **TIP!**
>
> **Always record or store the address and references from an internet source.**
>
> You will need them later.

2. Searching can eat up a lot of valuable time. Because it is so easy to move from site to site through numerous interlinked sources, you can spend hours browsing the web. Your time might be better spent reading your source materials, taking notes, and writing your paper. To avoid wasting your time, always go to the web for specific purposes, skim the sites first, and note the size and downloading time of a document before printing it out. (Slow downloading can consume a lot of time.)

# Sweating Through the Research

Once you have located the sources—the books and articles that you will need to read and assimilate—you can begin reading, taking notes, and synthesizing the material.

## Get It All Down

Every time you consult a new source, copy all the information necessary for indicating your source to the reader. If you fail to record all the pertinent data, you may find yourself tracking down a book or article weeks later in order to look up an essential publication date or volume number that you neglected to record initially. The book may by this time be checked out, lost, or stolen, so get it all down the first time.

> **TIP!**
>
> **Always remember to get *all* the pertinent data about your sources!**

    The traditional method of keeping track of such information was to use note cards, but in this era of portable laptops and

PDAs, such record keeping is more likely to be done electronically. Accuracy is critical. Create a separate file for your list of sources and remember to keep the file up to date—never delete a citation until you are certain you will not be using that source. As an aid, you might refer to the section in Research Navigator called Research Process, which contains some excellent strategies for effective and accurate note-taking.

For whatever documentation system you are using, you will need to record the following information.

**FOR BOOKS:**

1. Title and author (or editor)

2. Publisher and place of publication

3. Date of publication (plus date of edition, if the book has more than one)

4. Pages read (if you do not read the entire book)

5. Library call number

**FOR ARTICLES:**

1. Author (or "no author")

2. Title

3. Name of magazine, newspaper, or journal

4. Volume number (if the journal uses them)

5. Date of the issue

6. Complete page numbers that the article covers

**FOR THE ELECTRONIC FORM OF EITHER BOOKS OR ARTICLES, YOU WILL ALSO NEED:**

7. Title of database (if relevant)

8. Medium (such as CD-ROM)

9. Name of the vendor or utility (like *FirstSearch* or *Research Navigator*—if relevant)

10. Electronic publication date

## On to the Reading

Using the list of sources you have developed so far, your next step is to locate all the materials that look promising and try to decide which ones will be genuinely useful. As you consider which articles and books to study thoroughly and which ones to eliminate at this stage, you need to give some thought to their reliability as well as their relevance to your thesis question.

**T I P !**

**Just because a statement appears in print, it is not necessarily honest or accurate.** You need to be wary as you read.

## Evaluate Your Sources

You might expect an unbiased analysis of an event from journalists who were there, but again you must stay alert because not all publications present—or even try to present—objective reporting. The conservative *Fraser Forum* will give a substantially different assessment of an event than the liberal *Canadian Forum*.

And in the United States, the *Congressional Record*, which sounds like an impeccable source, is actually one of the least reliable, since any member of Congress can read any foolishness whatsoever into the *Record*. You must consult several sources and sample a variety of authorities to weigh the issues and discount the prejudices.

**T I P !**

Look for sources that address the topic from different perspectives. Avoid relying too heavily on a single source.

The date of publication often makes a difference in its value or reliability. If you are doing a paper about the treatment of AIDS, an article from 1980 will be of little use. If, on the other hand, you are writing a paper on the *history* of treating AIDS, then a 1980 article could be quite important. In general, we place the highest value on recent sources simply because the latest scholar or scientist has the advantage of building on all that has gone before.

## Some Guidelines for Note-Taking

1. Record all the essential information about each source. If you get in the habit of documenting this information, there is less chance of forgetting an item or of having to waste time tracking down the source again.

2. In making your notes, record information on only one idea or point at a time. If the source offers several different ideas (and most useful sources do!), separate these in your note-taking.

3. Create subject headings for each of the notes you take—one or two words preceding what you have written to tell you what each note is about. If all works out well, these subject headings will probably correspond to sections of your outline and, ultimately, to subtopics of your essay.

4. Summarize the ideas in your own words. If you think you might want to quote directly from the source, copy the author's exact words and enclose them in quotation marks. If you are downloading information and ideas, be very careful to do the same. Taking notes effectively means that you will always give proper credit where credit is due and thus avoid plagiarism at all costs.

## The Printout/Photocopying Option

If the time you can spend in the library is limited, you might want to print out an online article or photocopy pertinent portions of books in order to have these materials available to study at your convenience. In fact, you might find it easier to take notes from a printout than from a computer screen. You can underline or highlight key ideas, and even colour code these highlighted passages to fit different subtopics in your paper. You can also write comments or cross-references to other sources in the margins.

## Constructing a Working Outline

At the same time as you are reading and taking notes, you should also be working on your outline. Chances are the best arrangement of points and ideas will not emerge until you are fairly well along with your research—possibly not until you are finished it. As you collect more and more information, see if the material can be arranged into three or four main categories to form the major headings of your outline. The sooner you can get one worked out, the more efficient your research becomes. You can see exactly what you are looking for and avoid research that is unnecessary and irrelevant.

If an idea recurs in your writing and gains significance, you may decide to add a section to your outline or to expand one of its sections. And later, at the organizing stage, if you have information that no longer seems to fit, you can let it go. Research and writing are recursive processes—sometimes ideas that you initially thought were central to the direction of your work prove to be ones that can be cast aside. Never ruin the focus and unity of your paper by trying to wedge in every single piece of information you have uncovered in your research.

Figure 8.4 illustrates how the first section of a Working Outline might look. In the next chapter you will find advice on synthesizing this diverse material into a unified, informative, well-documented research paper.

| First Section of Working Outline: *Women in the Media* |
| --- |
| *Section One: Underrepresentation of women—a problem?*<br>    A. Mediawatch—negative effects<br>    B. Health Canada report—statistics<br>    C. Mediawatch—portrayal of women in the media |
| A. Effects   —negative<br>            —"women strike out"<br>            —roles and images of women are often minimal and/or negative<br>            —media reflect values and beliefs of society<br>            —women are underrepresented |
| B. Statistics  —representation<br>            —interviewed and represented less often than men<br>            —national women news anchors—38%; as reporters 26%<br>            —local broadcasts—women as anchors 48%; as reporters 20% |
| C. Portrayal in the news<br>            —women are reported on less often than men—sports, business, news<br>            —focus on sports—WNBA as e.g.<br>            —exception—when a woman commits a serious crime |

**FIGURE 8.4** *Section of a Working Outline*

After you have read all the material you feel is necessary to cover your topic thoroughly, gather together your notes, your bibliographical documentation, your photocopied pages, your working outline, and anything else you need for writing your first draft. The actual drafting of the paper is a lot like writing any other paper, except that you will incorporate the material from your notes into your text (either in your own words or through direct quotations) and give credit to the original authors for information, ideas, and quotations that you gathered from them. The following sections will give you advice on how to take all this raw material and craft it into a smooth, readable research paper.

## Focusing the Thesis

You first need to refine the thesis question or idea that you devised before you started reading on the subject. The refined thesis should convey the point you want to make after studying your sources. If, for instance, you began by investigating the question "Do breakfast cereal ads manipulate and exploit children?" you might, after doing your research, end up with a thesis statement something like this one written by our student Barb Taylor:

> Advertisers use jingles, slogans, cartoon characters, incentives, and promises of athletic prowess to lure and mislead young consumers into getting their parents to buy sugary, low-nutrient cereals.

**T I P !**

**Your thesis may change as you work with your source material, but get a fairly clear idea of where you are going before you start your draft.**

### Imagine Your Readers

If your professor or instructor does not specify an audience for you, you will find it helpful to think of your readers as people who want to learn about your topic but do not know a lot about it. Your focus will be clearer if you have in mind a specific group of readers and perhaps a specific publication in which your writing could appear. For example, Barb Taylor's research essay could be directed at parents of small children and might appear in *Parents, Good Housekeeping,* or *Adbusters,* magazines that often criticize shoddy television fare and falsity in advertising.

## Organizing Your Notes

Once you have a clearly focused thesis and a strong sense of your target audience, go back and read through your notes. (We will assume at this point that you have collected your information using some form of note card system, whether electronic or paper.) Use the headings that you used while taking notes, and group similar ideas together. (If you photocopied most or all of your sources, write headings on the first page of the photocopy and sort the articles that way.) Then consult your working outline, and arrange your information in the order that the headings appear there. As you write, following this plan, you will have the information you need in front of you, ready to be incorporated into the first draft of your paper.

If your information does not match the outline but lies there in a confused, overlapping, mind-boggling mess, all is not lost. You can still bring order out of chaos. Here are a few methods:

1. *Tinker with your outline.* It may seem like a step backward, but now that you have new information from your research, the whole topic may look different. Look at the main headings and change any that do not seem to fit; add others that you have good material for but overlooked when you made the working outline.

2. *Cluster your research again.* This process may reveal an organizing strategy that you would not think of any other way.

3. *Put your notes aside and begin writing*—even if you begin in the middle of a thought. Force yourself, as in freewriting, to keep going, even if your paper seems repetitive, disorganized, and sketchy. Eventually, the writing will begin to take shape, giving you an idea about where to start your first draft.

4. *Find a key article on the topic, and examine its structure.* You may be able to find an organizational scheme that will work for your paper.

## Integrating Sources

One important difference between writing a paper using your own ideas and writing a paper incorporating research involves acknowledging your sources. Whether you are quoting directly or simply paraphrasing someone else's ideas and observations, you should always give credit in the text of your paper to the person from whom you are borrowing. Both the MLA and APA documentation styles require you to cite all sources *within* the paper. Many people who do researched writing make no attempt to work in direct quotations or provide complete citations in the first draft because pausing to do so interrupts the flow of their ideas. They just jot down the name of the person who has provided the information or idea; they go back later to fill in page numbers and integrate exact quotations.

### Structuring Your Documentation

Your reader needs to know where your own ideas stop and others' begin—and end. The following example from student Bob Harmon illustrates a clearly structured approach to documentation:

> Behaviour research has clearly shown that different types of music have different effects on different people. Music can increase or decrease anxiety, but its use in business to improve morale is questionable. In the *Journal of Marketing,*

**T I P !**

**Attribute sources (*According to Professor Charbonneau . . .*) in the text of your paper, not just in parenthetical citations.**

researcher John Milliman points out that past decisions to use music in the marketplace have been based on folklore or intuition rather than on empirical results (88). His study focused primarily on the experimental manipulations of no music, slow music, and fast music. The results indicate that music does control the speed with which subjects move through a store. Slow music results in subjects spending more time, and fast music means less time spent (Milliman 86–91). If music does affect the speed with which people move through a store, does it affect their perceptions of time? If fast music is used for music-on-hold, it may decrease people's sense of how long they are on hold; and slow music may expand the perceived length of time. Here again, proper selection is critical.

In this example, you see Harmon's transition from a preceding paragraph, his use of a paraphrase of the thesis of Milliman's article, then his summary of Milliman's research, and then his own application of the research. And you never confuse which is which, because the structured system of source citation makes clear where all the ideas come from.

## To Cite or Not to Cite

The main purpose of documentation—of citing sources used in a research paper—is to give credit for ideas, information, and actual phrasing that you borrow from other writers. You cite sources in order to be honest and to lend authority to your own writing. You also include citations to enable your readers to find more extensive information than your paper furnishes, in case they become engrossed in your subject and want to read some of your sources in full.

We are all unsure occasionally about when a citation is necessary. We can say with authority that you must include a citation for:

1. All direct quotations

2. All indirect quotations

3. All major ideas that are not your own

4. All essential facts, information, and statistics that are not general knowledge—especially anything controversial

**T I P !**

**It is better to bother your readers with too many citations than to have them question your integrity by having too few.**

The last category is the one that causes confusion. In general, the sort of information available in an encyclopedia does not need a citation. But statements interpreting, analyzing, or speculating on such information should be documented. If you write that Tim Horton died in an automobile accident, for example, you do not need a citation because that is a reasonably known and undisputed fact. If you write that Tim Horton and his partner opened their first doughnut and coffee store in Hamilton and that the company has since grown to be the largest such operation in Canada, most people would not feel the need for a citation because such information is part of a common knowledge base. If you write that Mrs. Horton sold her shares in the company shortly after her husband's death and was cheated by doing so at the time, you should cite your source. Because such information is not widely known and is also debatable, you need to identify your source so that your readers can judge the reliability of the claim. As well, they might want further enlightenment on the matter, and your citation will lead them to a more complete and informed discussion.

## Accuracy Is the Aim

Get the form of your citations correct every time, right down to the last comma, colon, and parenthesis. After years of being told to be original and to think for yourself, you are now being told—on this one matter, at least—to fall into line and slavishly follow the prescribed format. What you might consider a blessed bit of variety will not be appreciated in citing your source information. That information (date, publisher, place of publication) is located on the title page and copyright page of each book. For magazines you usually can find it all on the cover.

## When in Doubt, Use Common Sense

Keep in mind that the purpose of documentation is two-fold:

1. To give credit to your sources

2. To allow your readers to find your sources in case they want further information on the subject

If you are ever in doubt about documentation form (if you are citing something so unusual that you cannot find a similar entry in the samples here), use your common sense and give credit the way you think it logically should be done. Be as consistent as possible with other citations.

## To Quote or Not to Quote

Never quote directly unless (1) the material is authoritative and convincing evidence in support of your thesis, or (2) the statement is extremely well phrased, or (3) the idea is controversial and you want to assure your readers that you are not slanting or misinterpreting the source. You would probably quote an observation as well put as this one:

> Charles Darwin concluded that language ability is "an instinctive tendency to acquire an art."

There is no need, however, for the direct quotation in the following sentence:

> Transport Canada, in an effort to aid the rail industry, has asked for a "federal study of the need and means for preserving a national passenger service."

You could phrase that just as well yourself. But remember, even after you put the statement into your own words, you still have to indicate (in a parenthetical citation) where you got the point.

**T I P !**

**Too much quotation can suggest that you have too few ideas of your own.**

Use quotations to support your points, not to make them for you.

## Quoting Quotations

Sometimes in your reading you will come across a quotation that says precisely what you have been looking for and says it well. If the quotation is complete enough to serve your purpose, and if you honestly do not think you would benefit from tracking down the original, then do not bother. Instead, include that quotation in the usual way. But notice that your parenthetical citation will include "qtd. in" before the source and page number:

> Oscar Wilde once said about education, "It is well to remember from time to time that nothing that is worth knowing can be taught" (qtd. in Pinker 19).

## Working Quotations in Smoothly

If you want your research paper to read smoothly, you must take care when incorporating quotations into your writing. You will need to have a ready supply of introductory phrases to slide the quotations in gracefully—phrases like "As Banting discovered," "Professor Weber notes," and "According to Dr. Li." These attributions help your readers evaluate the source material as they read it and distinguish source material from your remarks about it. If you run through the examples in this section on quoting, you will find a generous assortment of these phrases. Borrow them with our blessing.

Notice, please, that the more famous the person, the less likely we are to use Mr., Miss, Mrs., or Ms. in front of the name. "Mr. Shakespeare" sounds quite droll. If the person has a title, you can use it or not, as you think appropriate: Dr. Pauling or Pauling, Mayor Feinstein or Feinstein, Prime Minister Trudeau or Trudeau.

### Lead into Your Quotations

Do not drop quotations in without preparing your readers. Provide clear lead-ins, usually including the author's name, to connect the quotation to your text:

> Many fluent native speakers of English will claim they do not understand grammar. As Professor David Crystal points out, "Millions of people believe they are failures at grammar, say that they have forgotten it, or deny they know any grammar at all—in each case using their grammar convincingly to make their point" (191).

For variety, you may want to place the connecting phrase in the middle every so often, this way:

> The fundamental purpose of language is to communicate intelligibly. "But if thought corrupts language," warns George Orwell, "language can also corrupt thought" (38).

You do not always have to quote full sentences from your sources. You can quote only the telling phrases or key ideas of your authority, like this:

Barbara Strang remarks that worrying about split infinitives is "one of the most tiresome pastimes" invented by nineteenth-century grammarians (95).

Or like this:

The play's effectiveness lies, as E. M. W. Tillyard points out, in "the utter artlessness of the language" (34).

The self-portraits of Frida Kahlo are bold and personal. Art critic Hayden Herrera describes them as "autobiography in paint" (xii).

But do introduce your quotations, please. Identifying the source before presenting the borrowed material helps your readers know which ideas are yours and which come from sources.

> **T I P !**
> If you have difficulty finding new ways to introduce your authorities in the text of your paper, perhaps you are using too many direct quotations.

## Make the Grammar Match

When you integrate a quotation into your own sentence, you are responsible for making sure that the entire sentence makes sense. You must adjust the way your sentence is worded so that the grammar comes out right. Read your quotations over carefully to be sure they do not end up like this one:

When children are born, their first reactions are "those stimuli which constitute their environment."

"Reactions" are not "stimuli." The sentence should read this way:

When children are born, their first reactions are to "those stimuli which constitute their environment."

What a difference a word makes—the difference here between sense and nonsense. Take particular care when you are adding someone else's words to your own; you get the blame if the words in the quotation do not make sense, because they *did* make sense before you lifted them out of context.

## Use Special Punctuation: Ellipsis Dots and Brackets

When you write a documented paper, you may need to use *ellipsis dots* and *brackets* to condense quotations and blend them in smoothly with your text.

To shorten a quoted passage, use *ellipsis dots* (three periods with spaces between) to show your readers that you have omitted some words. To distinguish between your ellipsis points and the spaced periods that sometimes appear in written works, put square brackets around any ellipsis dots that you add:

"The time has come [. . .] for us to examine ourselves," declares James Baldwin, "but we can only do this if we are willing to free ourselves from the myth of America and try to find out what is really happening here" (18).

Ellipsis dots are not needed if the omission occurs at the beginning or end of the sentence you are quoting. But if *your* sentence ends with quoted words that are not the end of the original quoted sentence, then use ellipsis dots:

Thoreau insisted that he received only one or two letters in his life "that were worth the postage" and commented summarily that "to a philosopher all news, as it is called, is gossip [. . .]."

That fourth dot is the period. If you include documentation, such as a page number, add the period after the parentheses:

"is gossip [. . .]" (27).

Use *brackets* to add words of your own to clarify the meaning or make the grammar match:

In her memoir, Jessica Mitford confirms that "In those days [the early 1940s] until postwar repression set in, the [Communist] Party was a strange mixture of openness and secrecy" (67).

## Handling Long Quotations

If you quote more than four typed lines of prose or more than three lines of poetry, you set the quotation off by indenting it 2.5 centimetres (one inch) or ten spaces. Introduce the quotation, usually with a complete sentence followed by a colon; begin the indented quotation on the next line; double-space the quotation and do not use quotation marks (since the indention signals that the material is quoted).

In 1892 George Bernard Shaw wrote to the editor of the London *Chronicle*, denouncing a columnist who had complained about split infinitives:

If you do not immediately suppress the person who takes it upon himself to lay down the law almost every day in your columns on the subject of literary composition, I will give up the *Chronicle* [. . .]. I ask you, Sir, to put this man out [. . .] without interfering with his perfect freedom of choice between "to suddenly go," "to go suddenly" and "suddenly to go." Set him adrift and try an intelligent Newfoundland dog in his place. (qtd. in Crystal, 195)

Notice that in an indented quotation, the page number is cited in parentheses *after* the period. The quotation marks within the indented material indicate that Shaw punctuated those phrases in that way.

## Using Graphics

An old advertising slogan, often misquoted, claims that "One picture is worth ten thousand words," and that may be true in your own writing as well. The use of graphics—charts, tables, figures, diagrams, graphs, technical drawings, pictorial illustrations, and other nontextual materials—can significantly enhance the effectiveness and clarity of the information you are discussing. While not all written projects will benefit from their use, in many cases graphics can offer a direct image that will simplify concepts, augment ideas, and intensify interest. A graph or drawing can instantly provide the big picture and create a strong intellectual and emotional impact.

Here are some suggestions for the effective use of graphics:

- Use the graphic format that most effectively suits your purpose. (See below for examples of the most commonly used types.)
- Introduce the graphic clearly and incorporate it smoothly into your text (just like quotations).
- The graphic should appear immediately after you introduce it in the text; instead of dividing a paragraph, however, it may be best to situate the image at the next paragraph break. If you make numerous references to the same graphic, or if the graphic contains only supplementary information, you may include it in an appendix at the end of your paper.
- Make the graphic as self-explanatory as possible, with appropriate labels, legends, numbers, keys, and so on.
- Number each graphic, and give it a brief title. After the title, identify its source.
- Try to position the graphic vertically so that your reader does not have to turn your paper sideways to view the image—that may lessen its effect.
- Make your graphic as clear and clean as possible; avoid images that are too dense or cluttered. Use lots of space—the graphic should clarify, not confuse.
- If feasible, and appropriate, use colour to enhance and dramatize your graphic.
- Most computer programs allow you to manipulate your graphic effects—to show them in 3D, to change angles, to separate and emphasize certain parts, to vary shadings and colours. Play with these effects until you get the most forceful results.

*Pie charts* effectively show the relationship between parts and the whole and are particularly effective in illustrating percentages and money. For clarity, limit the *number of slices* to ten or fewer, provide clear labels, and keep it simple.

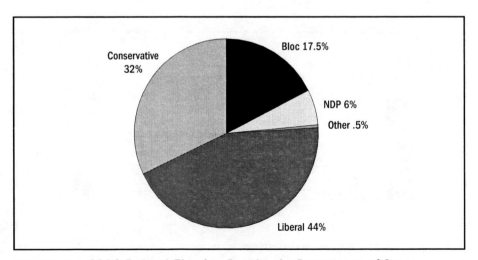

**FIGURE 9.1** *2004 Federal Election Results, by Percentage of Seats.*

*Bar charts* can provide more detail than pie charts and are particularly good for comparison. The lengths of the bars should vary and be arranged sequentially, but the bars should always be of equal width. Using a horizontal or a vertical display can alter the desired effect and accommodate more or less information, as shown in Figures 9.2 and 9.3.

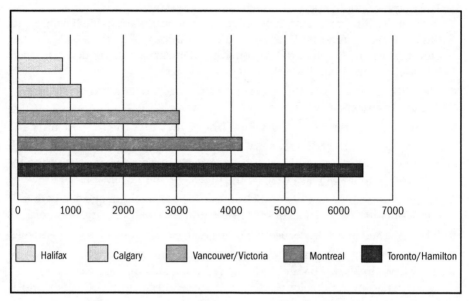

**FIGURE 9.2** *2002 Rankings by Population (000s) of Canadian Television Markets.*

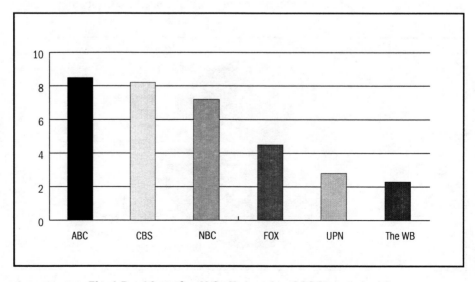

**FIGURE 9.3** *Final Rankings for U.S. Networks, 2004.*

*Line charts* are effective for indicating trends. In using both horizontal and vertical axes, the quantities of two different variables can provide very precise information. Always start numerical scales from zero and, if including multiple lines, use particular care to avoid confusion—never use too many lines.

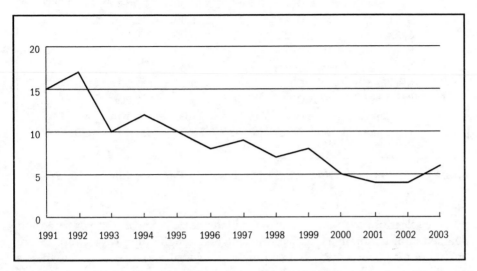

**FIGURE 9.4** *Average Percentage Increases in Tuition Fees at Canadian Universities.*

*Tables* are designed in the form of a grid (with labelled rows and columns). They are used to present a collection of data, and can convey a dense amount of information. The term *table* is usually reserved for numerical data; the generic term *chart* is often used when textual information is presented. When designing a table, use plenty of space, round off the numbers, use abbreviations (for example, $, £, kg, %), and include any necessary footnotes below the table.

| Year | Intake | Discharge | Consumption |
|------|--------|-----------|-------------|
| 1980 | 36 510 | 32 991 | 3 613 |
| 1985 | 41 246 | 38 005 | 3 734 |
| 1990 | 44 678 | 40 478 | 4 211 |
| 1995 | 44 457 | 39 773 | 4 656 |
| 2000 | 43 870 | 39 218 | 4 998 |

Note: All figures are indicated in million cubic metres.

**FIGURE 9.5** *The Industrial Use of Water in Canada.*

| Rank | Program | Outlet | Day | Start | End | Viewers |
|------|---------|--------|-----|-------|-----|---------|
| 1 | Stanley Cup Final | CBC | M | 20:00 | 23:50 | 5 202 000 |
| 2 | Canadian Idol 2 | CTV | W | 20:00 | 21:00 | 2 134 000 |
| 3 | C.S.I. | CTV | Th | 21:00 | 21:59 | 2 037 000 |
| 4 | Canadian Idol 2 | CTV | Th | 20:00 | 21:00 | 1 993 000 |
| 5 | Law & Order: SVU | CTV | T | 22:00 | 23:00 | 1 249 000 |
| 6 | CTV Evening News | CTV | F | 18:00 | 19:00 | 1 189 000 |
| 7 | NHL Pregame | CBC | M | 19:30 | 20:00 | 1 080 000 |
| 8 | Cold Case | CTV | Th | 20:00 | 21:00 | 1 049 000 |
| 9 | The Simple Life | CTV | W | 21:00 | 21:30 | 985 000 |
| 10 | The Simpsons | Global | Su | 20:00 | 20:30 | 895 000 |

**FIGURE 9.6** *Top Television Programs Viewed in Canada, June 7–13, 2004.*

The selective use of graphics can facilitate the delivery of complex ideas and detailed information in a creative, efficient, and enlightening way. Graphics are one more means by which you can make your written work as impressive as possible.

## Avoiding Plagiarism

Plagiarism means using somebody else's writing without giving proper credit. You can avoid this dishonesty by using a moderate amount of care in taking notes. Put quotation marks around any material—however brief—that you copy verbatim. As you are leafing through your notes trying to group them into categories, circle the quotation marks in red so that you cannot miss them, or else highlight the quoted material as a reminder.

You must also avoid the author's phrasing if you decide not to quote directly but to paraphrase. You naturally tend to write an idea down using the same language as your source, perhaps changing or omitting a few words. This close paraphrasing is still plagiarism. To avoid it, read the passage first, then look away from the original as you put the idea down in your own words. You will scarcely be able to fall into the original phrasing that way.

**T I P !**

When you summarize, try to condense several pages of reading into a single, short note.

Use of the internet has made plagiarism an especially easy and tempting practice in recent years. Avoid the temptation. Never download any passage or borrow any information or idea that you do not cite completely. The wages of plagiarism, intentional or otherwise, are usually dire, and rightfully so. It represents the worst form of academic cheating.

# Writing an Acceptable Paraphrase

Sometimes, of course, you must do fairly close paraphrasing of important ideas. Because plagiarism can occasionally be accidental, we will give you a couple of examples to show you exactly what unintentional plagiarism looks like. Here is a passage from *The Language Instinct* by Steven Pinker. Assume that you want to use this idea to make a point in your paper.

> Language is not a cultural artifact that we learn the way we learn to tell time or how the federal government works. Instead, it is a distinct piece of the biological makeup of our brains. Language is a complex, specialized skill, which develops in the child spontaneously, without conscious effort or formal instruction.

If you incorporate this material into your paper in the following way, you have plagiarized:

> **(wrong)**    Humans do not learn language the way we learn to tell time or how the federal government works. Language is a part of the biological makeup of our brains, a complex skill that a child develops spontaneously, without conscious effort or formal instruction (Pinker 18).

The fact that the source is cited suggests that this plagiarism perhaps resulted from ignorance rather than deception, but it is plagiarism nonetheless. Changing a few words or rearranging the phrases is not enough. Here is another version, somewhat less blatant but still plagiarism:

> **(wrong)**    Humans do not learn language in the way we learn to count or understand how a steam engine works. Language is part of our physical makeup, a complex, specialized skill that develops automatically, without conscious effort or formal instruction (Pinker 18).

There are still two phrases that are distinctly Pinker's: "a complex, specialized skill" and "without conscious effort or formal instruction." It is quite all right to use those phrases but *only if you put them in quotation marks*. You should also acknowledge your source in the text of your paper whenever possible, like this:

> **(right)**    According to linguist Steven Pinker, humans do not learn language in the way we learn to count or understand how a steam engine works. Language is part of our physical makeup, "a complex, specialized skill" that develops automatically, "without conscious effort or formal instruction" (18).

Notice, by the way, that the phrase "in the way we learn" and the words "makeup" and "develops" do not have quotation marks around them, even though they appear in the original. These words are so common, so frequently used that quotation marks are unnecessary. Here is another acceptable paraphrase in which none of the original phrasing is used:

> **(right)**    Linguist Steven Pinker claims that human beings do not learn language in the way that we learn to count or understand how a

steam engine works. Language is a part of our physical makeup; it is a sophisticated skill that children acquire automatically and effortlessly without explicit training (18).

## EXERCISE 9.1: WRITING

Write paraphrases of two of these paragraphs from Chapter 4: Floyd Skloot's paragraph on neurological tests (p. 44), Stephen Jay Gould's paragraph on dinosaurs (p. 46), and Anthony Wilson-Smith's paragraphs on crime in Canada (pp. 53 and 55). If you have the chance, compare your paraphrases with your classmates' to see how well you did at capturing the original meaning and avoiding plagiarism.

# Revising the Draft

Because a research paper requires the incorporation of other people's ideas and the acknowledgment of these sources, you need to take special care in revising. Consult the Revising Checklist for Researched Writing in Figure 9.7, below.

---

**Check the Usual Things**
1. Be sure the introduction states your thesis.
2. Be sure each paragraph is unified, coherent, and directly related to your thesis.
3. Be sure that the transitions between paragraphs are clear and effective.
4. Be sure your conclusion evaluates the results of your research. If the paper is argumentative, be sure the last sentence is emphatic.

**Check the Special Things**
1. Be sure that you have introduced direct quotations gracefully, using the name and, if appropriate, the title or occupation of the person quoted.
2. Be sure each citation is accurate.
3. Be sure that paraphrases are in your own words and that sources are clearly acknowledged.
4. Be sure that you have not relied too heavily on a single source.
5. Be sure that you have written most of the paper yourself; you need to examine, analyze, or explain the material, not just splice together a bunch of quotations and paraphrases.
6. Be sure always to separate quotations with some comment of your own.
7. Be sure to use ellipsis dots if you omit any words from a quotation; never leave out anything that alters the meaning of a sentence.
8. Be sure to use square brackets, not parentheses, if you add words in a quotation.
9. Be sure to underline the titles of books and magazines; put quotation marks around titles of articles and chapters in books.
10. Be sure to indent long quotations ten spaces without quotation marks.

---

**FIGURE 9.7** *Revising Checklist for Researched Writing*

## Preparing the Final Copy

Before you work on your final draft, give your entire attention to the following instructions on form.

1. Provide margins of at least 2.5 centimetres (one inch) at the top, bottom, and sides.

2. Double-space throughout.

3. Do not put the title of your own paper in quotation marks.

4. Put page numbers in the upper right-hand corner. Count all pages in the total as you number. Note correct page numbering on the sample student papers, which follow.

5. Proofread. You may well be close to exhaustion by the time you finish keyboarding the final copy, and the last thing you will feel like doing is rereading the blasted thing. But force yourself. Or entice somebody else to do it. But do not skip the proofreading.

6. Edit. If (or when) you find mistakes, make the necessary corrections—with word processing, such changes are relatively easy to do. The final draft you submit should be as perfect as you can possibly make it.

### EXERCISE 9.2: DISCUSSION

Interview someone who has written a successful research paper and find out what the person did to make the process work. Report back to your class on this interview, and discuss what advice and warnings you picked up.

## Sample Student Research Papers

The following two documented essays, written by undergraduate university students, provide practical examples of the style and format used in such papers. Annotations have been added to highlight some of the particular features of each. The first, by Mikiko Fukuda, follows the MLA (Modern Language Association) style of documentation commonly used in the humanities, and the second, by Amanda Phillips, follows the APA (American Psychological Association) style used in the social sciences. Further details about these and other styles of documentation can be found in Chapter 10. You should, of course, always use the format and documentation that your instructor requests. Never mix documentation styles in an essay. If you have any doubt about which style to use, ask.

Fukuda 1

Mikiko Fukuda

Professor Skylar

English 274E

May 27, 2004

Sound and Stone in Joy Kogawa's Obasan

Joy Kogawa once explained to a reporter that her novel is entitled Obasan because Obasan "is totally silent. . . . How does society stop oppressing those who never speak up?" (qtd. in Davidson 18).

The treatment of non-white immigrants, as well as non-white Canadian citizens, by white Canadians throughout history is deeply disturbing and is the germinal issue at the centre of Kogawa's work. Despite the nation's democratic reputation as a country where peoples of all races and nationalities can experience freedom from racial discrimination, extreme xenophobia by white Canadians has always been apparent to those who are less fair skinned. And the Japanese and Japanese Canadians, especially, felt the extremities of such attitudes, of such fear and hatred, during World War II.

In Obasan, Kogawa explores the dark side of silence within the Japanese community trapped in the internment camps along the West Coast during World War II. That internment has ended the world they once knew. As Suanne Kelman suggests: "With Naomi Nakane, the reader is forced to mourn the fragile beauty of a community and its delicate web of attachments, now never to be restored" (40). The culture clash that ensues between the first generation Japanese (Issei) and the

Canadians (including many <u>Nisei</u>, those second generation Japanese Canadians who were partially acculturated to white Canadian society) is represented in the contrast between the silence of Obasan and the vociferation of Aunt Emily. Even the names of the two women are representative of their metaphorical roles: Obasan translates to "aunt" in English; however, she is never addressed as "Aunt." Representative of the <u>Issei</u>, natives of Japan who rigorously adhere to Japanese traditions and culture, Obasan is the diametric opposite of Aunt Emily. Aunt Emily represents the <u>Nisei</u>, the North Americanized Japanese—thus her name is transposed into English, she is "Aunt" not "Obasan." She is Canadianized enough that the phenomenon of silence that is reflective of Japanese culture and that suits Obasan is not for Aunt Emily. The struggle between silence and vociferation in <u>Obasan</u> is exemplified in Aunt Emily's substantial amount of memorabilia, in the relationship between the protagonist, Naomi, and her aunt, and in the often conflicting use of language, both English and Japanese.

Aunt Emily's personality emerges, then, as quite the opposite of Obasan's. Her collection of newspaper clippings, journal entries, and letters represents her willingness to remember the past and keep it alive and her effort to try to stop discrimination against peoples of all races. She wants to make certain that such acts of discrimination, as occurred in Canada during the 1940s, never take place again. Early in the novel, as Naomi and Aunt Emily are having a discussion, Aunt Emily argues, "The past is the future" (Kogawa 45), and that opinion is embodied in her accumulation of documents pertaining to the internment and treatment of the Japanese and Japanese Canadians during the war years. Emily gives this package to Naomi, symbolically and tangibly, as a way for Naomi to become enlightened about her

*Your last name and page number are placed in a header one centimetre (one-half inch) from top of page.*

*Citation includes author's name and page number in parentheses.*

Fukuda 3

family's history during the war. The package containing government documents, newspaper articles, and Aunt Emily's journal replaces the voices of her family members—voices that refuse to recall painful memories of the past and that are silent, unwilling to tell their story to her. As Erika Gottlieb notes:

> Obasan is a book about silence. The narrator is an extraordinarily quiet child whose relatives often wonder if she is in fact mute. But this muteness is a deliberate withdrawal into silence. It is a child's resentful response to a world which has wounded her anonymously, impersonally, inexplicably [. . .] the little girl [. . .] is compelled to transform the silence of shame, hurt, and abandonment into words. (36)

The diary given to her by Aunt Emily becomes Naomi's only insight into the outcry of emotions expressed by a family member. The letters in the package, written on "blue-lined rice paper sheets" (Kogawa 48), are inscribed in Japanese, and Naomi cannot understand them. Nor does she know from whom they originate; however, as King-Kok Cheung suggests, "Naomi breathes life into the verbal knowledge transmitted by the letters [. . .] by means of a nonverbal mode of apprehension" (122). It is not a coincidence, of course, that the diary belongs to Aunt Emily, for her voice is the only one that speaks up and speaks out about the internment and treatment of the Japanese. She teaches others about that history by writing papers and giving lectures and speeches to inform and educate the nation, and she is the only character who does not excuse white Canadians for their behaviour. Naomi compares her own path to insight with a surgery and imagines her aunt as the surgeon: "Aunt Emily, are you a surgeon cutting at my scalp with your folders and your filing cards

---

*If you use more than four typed lines of direct quotation from a source, begin a new paragraph and indent all the lines ten spaces (or 2.5 centimetres) from the left margin. Do not use quotation marks around the indented material.*

*The "122" is the exact page number from which the quotation in the sentence came. Since this sentence tells us the name of the author, there is no need to include the name in the parentheses.*

Fukuda 4

and your insistence on knowing all? The memory drains down the sides of my face, but it isn't enough, is it?" (Kogawa 214).

Naomi is brought to understand and forced to accept and admit truths known and unknown prior to her "apprehension" of the letters and her reading of the diary and the newspaper clippings; she bluntly confronts herself and her previous views of her life: "Greed, selfishness, and hatred remain as constant as the human condition, do they not? Or are you thinking that through lobbying and legislation, speech-making and story-telling, we can extricate ourselves from our foolish ways? Is there evidence for optimism?" (Kogawa 219). As the package informs Naomi of untold stories, events, and feelings, as it unveils a history, a language, that she has never known or has never been allowed to know, Naomi begins to discover her own voice and come to terms with a new identity, and she begins to question Obasan and Uncle. The personal insight the package brings unfolds through the entirety of the novel as Naomi incessantly searches out the answer as to why her parents mysteriously vanished and never returned during the war.

The voice of Aunt Emily is consistent, loud and clear, and insists on telling the whole story; Obasan, however, is the complete opposite: "How different my two aunts are. One lives in sound, the other in stone. Obasan's language remains deeply underground but Aunt Emily, BA, MA, is a word warrior" (Kogawa 33). The quiet relationship between Naomi and Obasan is at times interrupted by speech; however, for the most part, conversation, communication, between the two is minimal, particularly when Naomi asks Obasan questions referring to the war and her family: "'Please tell me about Mother,' I would say as a child to Obasan. I was consumed by the question. Devoured alive. But Obasan gave me no answers" (26). Obasan avoids replying to Naomi when she

> Notice that there is no punctuation between the author's name and the page number—just a space. The same goes for an article title in your parenthetical citations.

> Notice that the quotation marks close the sentence, then the parenthetical citation appears, followed by the period to close the whole thing.

asks such questions, and Naomi is aware of this: "[Obasan] stares
steadily at the table. The greater my urgency to know, the thicker her
silences have always been. No prodding will elicit clues" (49). Obasan's
silence is the result of an urge to forget the past: "Didn't Obasan once
say, 'It is better to forget'? What purpose is served by hauling out the jar
of inedible food? If it is not seen, it does not horrify. What is past recall is
past pain" (48). While Aunt Emily is Canadian Japanese, Obasan is truly
Japanese Canadian; in personality, they are worlds apart, cultures apart.

The soundless relationship of Obasan and Naomi is a protective
tactic used by Obasan, in her mind, to keep Naomi from being hurt by the
events of the past, and, as well, to protect herself from her own
memories and feelings. Naomi's curiosity and constant questioning only
induce Obasan to reinforce and maintain her stony silence. When talk
does occur between the two, it is, at best, a fragmented affair, a mix of
Obasan speaking Japanese with some fragmented English words and
phrases and Naomi speaking English. It is, indeed, language of stone.

The significance of language in Obasan is remarkable for various
reasons, one being that language highlights the issue of cultures in
conflict. When Naomi remembers asking her Uncle about the North
American ideology of romantic love, he is confused: "I am thinking of the
time when I was a child and asked Uncle if he and Obasan were 'in love'.
My question was out of place. 'In ruv? What that?' Uncle asked. I've
never once seen them caressing" (Kogawa 6). The problem with language
in this instance is that the phrase "in love" does not exist in the
Japanese language, and in marriage in Japan, even today, compatibility is
often a happenstance of marriage. Thus, in numerous ways and on
numerous occasions in the novel, language underscores the fundamental
difference between the Japanese citizens and the Japanese Canadians—

Fukuda 6

it is the essence, symbol and reality, that forever divides the two, and it is inextricably linked to culture.

At one point, in considering this culture, Naomi wonders: Who is it that teaches her the Japanese belief "that in the language of the eyes a stare is an invasion and a reproach? Grandma Kato? Obasan? Uncle? Mother? Each one, raised in Japan, speaks the same language, but Aunt Emily and Father, born in and raised in Canada, are visually bilingual. I too learn the second language" (Kogawa 51). The Japanese cultural conduct of not staring is one of respect and considered to be very important; thus, Naomi separates her family members into the two camps. Those who were born and raised in Japan would instinctively understand the rule, and would be more apt to follow it. Although those born and raised in Canada would also know the rule, they would also be less likely to feel the inclination to obey it, for they have not and do not live in Japan.

Language can be, and often is, manipulated by the characters of the novel, and consequently what <u>is</u> being said becomes just as critical as what <u>is not</u> being said—sound and stone. When Aunt Emily presents a pamphlet to Naomi ". . . entitled 'Racial Discrimination by Orders-in-Council,'" Naomi notes that her aunt has crossed out the words "Japanese race" and written in their place the words "Canadian citizen" (Kogawa 34). Just as words can be muted and concealed, they can also be modified and revealed—and the truth about the history of the internment of Japanese Canadians in Canada during World War II can be unveiled.

Aunt Emily's character is the catalyst that brings to light the secrets that Naomi's family has kept from her, and reveals to her the horrible facts that have been concealed by white Canadians about the internment.

The use of ellipsis points indicates that words have been omitted from the original source.

If you quote from the same page of a work more than once in a paragraph, and no other quotation intervenes, only one reference after the final quotation is necessary.

Fukuda 7

Emily explains to Naomi: "'Now look at this one,' she said. 'Here's a man who was looking for the source of the problem in the use of language. You know those prisons they sent us to? The government called them "Interior Housing Projects!" With language like that you can disguise any crime'" (Kogawa 35–36). Aunt Emily in Kogawa's novel initiates the sound waves that pierce the silence of the Canadian government and of those Canadians disinclined to admit the wrongs done to Japanese and Japanese Canadians. And they pierce Obasan too.

The use of square brackets indicates an addition to the original.

Throughout Kogawa's novel, "The language of [Obasan's] grief is silence" and voice is the reason for, and method of, Aunt Emily's crusade. The cultural differences inherent in the voices of these two women collide. Aunt Emily's package of written documents, Naomi's bond with Obasan, and the role of language—all are a means for Kogawa to revive silent stories (Skylar qtd. in lecture). Kogawa pursues ways of verbalizing the injustices of the past and the problems of the present through finding and using voice and the written word. As Gary Willis notes, "[I]n <u>Obasan</u>, Kogawa has written the vision and made it plain: the book is an imaginative triumph over the forces that militate against expression of our inmost feelings" (249). Speaking history, singing it, acknowledging and coming to terms with it—this is Kogawa's reminder to people of all races that written history is merely muted voice transcribed onto paper; it is language. Aunt Emily writes in her journal during the war, "Strange how. . . protesters are so much more vehement about Canadian-born Japanese than they are about German-born Germans. I guess it's because we look different. What it boils down to is an undemocratic racial antagonism which is exactly what our democratic country is supposed to be fighting for" (Kogawa 88). Canada is a democratic nation, particularly if you are white; however, as Kogawa's novel finally suggests,

Fukuda 8

the many voices of minorities that exist in contemporary Canada may

achieve a deeper, more personal democracy, a true voice (one is tempted

to add <u>strong and free</u>), by refusing to be suppressed in voice or

language, by being sound that rejects being stone.

**Works Cited**

The Works Cited form for a book gives the name of the author or authors, the title, and the publication information, including city, publisher, and date. As long as the entire book has been read, no page numbers are included; if only an excerpt of the book has been read, indicate that in your citation.

In the Works Cited listing for a printed article, give the page numbers for the whole span of the article, even if you used material from only one or a few pages. The Gottlieb article spanned pages 34 to 53.

In general, the sources you cite in your Works Cited page should include only those works to which you have actually made reference in your essay.

The writer of this essay has used <u>underlining</u> to indicate the titles of books and periodicals. An alternative is to use *italics*, although since they sometimes distort the clarity of letters, some instructors may prefer underlining.

Cheung, King-Kok. "Attentive Silence in Joy Kogawa's

Obasan."

<u>Listening to Silences: New Essays in Feminist Criticism</u>. Eds.

Elaine Hedges and Shelley Fishkin. New York: Oxford,

1994. 113–129.

Davidson, Arnold. <u>Writing Against the Silence: Joy Kogawa's

Obasan</u>. Toronto: ECW, 1993.

Gottlieb, Erika. "Silence into Sound: The Riddle of Concentric

Worlds in <u>Obasan</u>." <u>Canadian Literature</u> Summer, 1986:

34–53.

Kelman, Suanne. "Impossible to Forgive." <u>The Canadian Forum</u>

Feb. 1982: 39–40.

Kogawa, Joy. <u>Obasan</u>. Toronto: Penguin, 1981.

Skylar, Thomas. "Joy Kowawa's <u>Obasan</u>." English 274E class

lecture. University of Western Ontario, London. 18 Mar.

2004.

Willis, Gary. "Speaking the Silence: Joy Kogawa's <u>Obasan</u>."

<u>Studies in Canadian Literature</u> 12 (1987): 239–49.

APA requires a title page with pagination beginning on the first page and an abbreviated title appearing as a header five spaces to the left of the page number.

The full title of your essay is placed in upper and lower case, double-spaced and centred in the top third of the page. Give your paper a title that suggests your topic and your point of view and try to make your title interesting so that your reader will want to read what you have to say.

Centred in the lower third of the page and double-spaced, include course name (and section number, if applicable), your instructor's name, and the submission date.

Women in the Media    1

Silence and Slow Time:

Women in the Media

Amanda Phillips

Your name, as author, is centred approximately in the middle of the page.

Communications 117E

Professor Wesley Terranian

December 15 2004

Silence and Slow Time: Women in the Media

If someone were to ask you to name two reporters or two TV news anchors, or even two athletes, chances are that most of the names you would be able to come up with would be male. This is not to say that women do not hold these positions—to the contrary, many women are wonderful reporters and superb athletes, but male examples leap to mind because they are far more prominently portrayed on television and radio and in the pages of magazines and newspapers. Some consider that the showcasing of males in the media is a natural state of affairs that simply mimics a cultural ideology that has existed throughout history, an ideology that sees women as being in some way *second* or *lesser*. This is a reality, of course, that is evident in a majority of cultures throughout the world. It follows, then, that this same phenomenon would be evident in the media, which in so many ways reflects the values and beliefs of society. In fact this is the very phenomenon we see in all aspects of media. It is quite evident that men are showcased and women tend to be underrepresented—and while this representation seems to have changed in recent years, in reality, it has not changed much. Like the frozen figures of John Keats's (1820) famous "Ode on a Grecian Urn," women seem trapped in a world of "silence and slow time" (p. 209). Through an examination of the representation of women in news and sports in radio, television, and print media over the last twenty years, it will be possible to qualify these inequities and to theorize workable solutions to this situation.

To begin with, a question needs to be asked. Is this under-representation of women in all facets of the media really a problem? Many people today would argue that it is indeed a significant problem.

Include your full title at the beginning of your essay; it should be centred.

The author's name has been indicated in the sentence, so only a page number is required; note that *p.* for *page* (or *pp.* for several pages) is used.

While the media to which we are exposed may invent or nurture certain selected ideas and thought processes—the "I Am Canadian" advertising campaign, for instance, certainly raises our sense of patriotism (perhaps our thirst for beer as well)—it is clear that the media also reflect the values and beliefs of society. The relationship between culture and the media is symbiotic. The portrayal, the status, of women seen in the media does influence the status of women in society. Major studies by Press (1991) and by Baehr and Dyer (1987) both indicate that the media, and television in particular, play a determining role in women's perception of their identity in terms of gender and class. A recent content analysis study by Mediawatch (2000) concludes that "women are significantly under-represented as professionals and as news sources" and, ultimately, such underrepresentation is influential and generally detrimental.

### Women in Television

We will begin looking at how women tend to be underrepresented in the news media by examining television newscasts. There seems to be a remarkable similarity among the news media in regard to how women are represented. According to a Health Canada Report, *Gender and Violence in the Mass Media* (1993), women are most often seen on television as anchors on the news; even there, the report states that in national TV newscasts women news anchors make up only 38 percent of all anchors and 26 percent of reporters (p. 14). As subjects of the news, women fare even worse, tending to be interviewed and reported about far less often than males. As such, women typically come across as *non-experts* and hold less authority than their male counterparts (p. 16). As reporters, women are often allocated to assignments that involve reporting on

Headings are used for purposes of clarification.

Women in the Media    4

topics of less significance, so-called entertainment or fashion or human interest stories. In local newscasts women have more equal representation, making up approximately 48 percent of anchors and 20 percent of reporters (p. 14). The reason for this difference between national and local newscasts may simply be that national reporters seem to have more responsibility and authority than local news reporters and, because of that, in a national news broadcast a male anchor is perceived to have more audience appeal and is presented as having more credibility as a voice of authority. While a full examination of female stereotypes per se is beyond the intent and scope of this study, it is useful to note that, as any quick perusal of national networks such as CNN or ABC or the like will reveal, of those women who do hold on-air positions as anchors and reporters, most are young, thin, and attractive. Well into the twenty-first century, it is still evident that just being female is not enough—a particular (stereo)type is still in demand.

Women are not only underrepresented in TV news as anchors and reporters, but also as sources of news. The majority of news stories covered by evening newscasts involve men, not women. According to Mediawatch (2000), the reason for this discrepancy may be that "the news is about power and influence. Few women hold these roles and are thus less likely to be reported." This is particularly evident in the area of sports, a large component of any television newscast. Despite a rise in the number of women participating in sports, the majority of sports reported and shown in the media are men's. According to Alina Bernstein (2002), men account for 93.8 percent of sports media coverage in the United States (p. 417). A similar conclusion was made regarding the U.K., where 90.2 percent of sports reported on BBC1 were men's and only 6.7 women's (Bernstein, 2002, p. 417). When women are found in

Dates are inserted in parentheses after the name of the author or source.

television sportscasts they tend to receive less air time than their male counterparts. For example, how much air time is given to a WNBA playoff game as compared with the NBA playoffs? How often are women's golf or hockey tournaments shown compared with men's? It was suggested that women tend to get more coverage in the news if they are involved in sports that are seen as being gender appropriate, such as tennis or gymnastics (Bernstein, 2002, p. 418). It is worth noting that one of the first of Canada's digital networks to go off the air was the Women's Sports Network, which failed in September of 2003, according to its parent company, because of a "lack of growth and revenue" (CTV, 2003). Without an established culture accustomed to the reporting and the viewing of women's sport, this network never had a chance.

This online article has no author byline. Use the article title in its entirety or shortened within the parentheses. Alphabetize in the References by the first main word of the title.

Not only are women athletes underrepresented in television sportscasts, but the way women are portrayed is significantly different from that of male athletes. Newscasters and announcers reinforce traditional roles of women by infantilizing women athletes, calling them "girls" or "young ladies." They refer to them by their first names 52 percent of the time, rather than by their last names as is traditionally done with male athletes, who are referred to by first names only 7.8 percent of the time (Bernstein, 2002, p. 420). Also, the media tend to emphasize appearance and attractiveness in women athletes much more so than with male athletes. A typical news story about a women's tennis match, for example, may emphasize how graceful the player was on the court, or her personality, rather than her actual skill as an athlete. This tends to devalue women's ability as not being worthy of mention in a broadcast. A perfect example is the media's portrayal of tennis star Anna Kournikova, who has yet to win a major singles title but is well represented in the media because of her appearance and charm (Bernstein, 2002, p. 420).

Bernstein argues that hypocrisy is involved when speaking about women in television news. Recently, broadcasters seem to want to increase the amount of representation women receive but, at the same time, they want the news coverage about women to be of a more positive nature and to ensure that it does not set some sort of double standard. Interestingly, according to Health Canada (1993), the way that the television news media portray women has not changed since the early 1990s, in spite of regulations that have tried to combat this discrepancy (p. 6).

The "p. 6" is the exact page number from which the information in the sentence came.

### Women in Newspapers

Newspapers seem to demonstrate an almost identical problem in representing women; according to Health Canada, there is nearly a 2:1 ratio of male to female images, and references to women were outnumbered in all sections except the lifestyle pages (p. 29). Health Canada's report concludes that, on average, references to women account for 17–19 percent of news stories, a very limited amount (p. 30). This is reinforced by Mediawatch (2000) research, which states "Women make up 15 percent of all newsmakers." While women are shown in more diverse roles in newsprint, which is an encouraging sign, the language used to describe these women is quite often sexist, focusing on appearance or other "feminine" characteristics (Health Canada Report, 1993, p. 29). As well, according to a Mediawatch (2000) survey of several of Canada's major newspapers, *The Globe and Mail, National Post* and *Toronto Sun*, females comprise only about 27 to 30 percent of all staff reporters (see Figure 1). As Gail Evans (2003) notes, gender inequality is a major problem because "[n]o press is truly free unless women share an equal voice." It has also been noted that the majority of

Women in the Media      7

For corporate authors
or organizations with
particularly long
names, the full name
is given in the first
reference with an
abbreviation in
square brackets; in
subsequent citations,
the abbreviation is
used.

the "hard news stories"; for example, those dealing with murder, politics,
etc., are filed by male reporters, leaving the women to report on less
sensational aspects (Health Canada Report, 1993, p. 16). According to
the results of a "Gender and Media Baseline Study" (International
Women's Media Federation [IWMF], 2003), this is a serious issue
because women are thus stereotyped into a certain type of reporting and
limited in opportunity for advancement in their careers.

Two very interesting case studies further illustrate the way women
are represented in television and in newspapers. One is an analysis of
the media coverage of male and female candidates in the United States
primary races for the Senate. This research was conducted by D. Strom
and T. Robertson (2001), and their main findings are quite informative.
They argue, for example, that women candidates in general received
slightly less coverage than their male counterparts, being mentioned in

The inclusion of a
graphic dramatically
reinforces the
information in the
text. Note that the
source of the graph is
documented in the
title line.

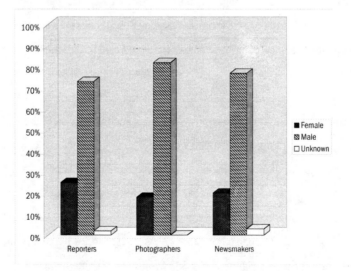

**FIGURE 1** *Percentage of Women Reporters, Photographers,
and Newsmakers at Canada's Newspapers.
(Source: Mediawatch.com.)*

42 percent of the 707 reports gathered for the study. Of this coverage,
women candidates were less likely to receive negative press (18.4
percent) than men (73.6 percent) (Strom & Robertson, 2001, p. 2000).
These findings underscore the patronizing attempt to encourage equal
involvement by women in a society that is used to holding men in
positions of power. While there does not seem to be a large gap in the
actual extent of media coverage given male and female candidates, the
type of coverage each received was very different. Strom and Robertson
indicate that the physical appearance of the women candidates mattered
much more than that of the male candidates, and that women were
asked many more personal questions during their campaign; significantly
fewer inquiries were directed toward the actual issues of the campaign
(p. 2000). Approximately 25 percent of the media coverage mentioned
the woman's marital status compared with 12.7 percent for male
candidates. If the female candidate had children, they were mentioned in
13.3 percent of the news coverage versus only 4.2 percent of the time
for male candidates. Only 31.7 percent of the news coverage on female
candidates talked about their viability as a senatorial representative
(Strom & Robertson, 2001, p. 2000). While some may feel that this
portrayal is helpful because it frames women as capable caregivers and
supporters, it is equally plausible to point out that this representation of
women candidates is detrimental because it puts viability, which should
be the major concern, second.

Another interesting case study of women in the news media was
conducted by Elizabeth Carll (2003). In this study, the researcher focused
on the portrayal of women and violence in the news. The author's main
concern is that the "media reinforces how women are seen as victims
and perpetrators of violent crimes" (Carll, 2003, p. 1601). The author

states that women are five to eight times more likely to be victimized by their partner. Carll argues that the media reinforces this by portraying women who commit crimes in a different light than men who commit similar crimes and, actually, by showing few women perpetrators in the news. Generally speaking, for male perpetrators of violent crimes, "news reports minimize the violence until there is enough pressure that action must be taken" (Carll, 2003, p. 1602). Women, on the other hand, if they commit a violent crime, become front-page news material. There is more media coverage for woman-as-perpetrator of crimes even if they are less violent than those committed by men (Carll, 2003, p. 1604). The overblown coverage of Martha Stewart's transgressions and trial is a case in point. And, according to Carll, when a woman does commit a heinous crime of violence, such as killing her husband or children, the media tend to become intent on looking at why the woman acted as she did. This concern is not generally present in the media coverage of male violence. For example, when a husband murders his wife or partner, the act is reported; why he committed the act is rarely explored (Carll, 2003, p. 1603). The way these incidents are handled by the media reinforces the belief that men acting violently is simply routine—"Just the facts, ma'am"—and no further investigation is needed.

### Women in Radio

While there is considerable research on women's roles in television news and newspapers, there is less information regarding women and radio broadcasting. The number of women employed as on-air radio announcers dramatically increased between 1984 and 1988. Today, approximately 22 percent of announcers are women as compared with only 12 percent in 1984 (Health Canada Report, 1993, p. 23). This is a very positive trend; however, there are still major strides to be made in terms of how women are employed and portrayed in this medium. In general, women still hold fewer jobs as radio reporters and interviewers. Most often women in radio are delegated to "music introduction" (32 percent), and less often to read the news (26 percent), report the weather (28 percent), and do sportscasts (8 percent) (Health Canada Report, 1993, p. 24). According to the Health Canada Report, women were mentioned on the radio only 7 percent of the time and were used less frequently for voiceovers in advertisements, and so on (p. 24). Again, in radio, women are typically delegated to roles that are seen as being gender appropriate rather than being given non-traditional gender roles. In this way, women can be, and often are, relegated to second place in the radio broadcasts both as messenger and message. Even when women and men share the microphone—many morning shows, for example, have a male and a female host—the man will speak more often on air.

   Through the examples of television news, newspapers, and radio discussed here, it is evident that the general trend is to underrepresent women in these media. Even more to the point is the fact that when women are presented, the way they are portrayed is quite often startlingly different and more limiting than is the portrayal allowed for men. John Fiske (1995) mentions the notion that these differences could be the result, in part at least, of the way certain genres of media have traditionally been seen, some as being "male" and some as "female" (p. 340). For example, soap operas and afternoon talk shows are considered "female"; news and sports are seen as "male." The process is circular, and exclusive. The male-dominated nature of the news media invariably discourages women from entering the profession and this, in turn, influences the type of reporting we see in the media. Because males dominate the field and make most of the decisions as to what and how reporting is done, the way women see and are seen in the news media is affected. And thus different forms of media continue to come across as being "male" or "female." According to Alvarado and Boyd-Barett (1992), these differences may also be reinforced by the media's efforts to tailor or shape content to their audience. When, for example, a newspaper knows its audience is mainly males who are interested in sports and business, it will emphasize the maleness of these sections by including fewer female figures and references (Alvarado & Barrett, 1992, p. 367). The females included may only be of the "Sunshine Girl" type. As Mediawatch (2000) concludes:

If you use more than four typed lines of direct quotation from a source, indent all the lines ten spaces (or 2.5 centimetres) from the left margin. Do not use quotation marks around the indented material.

> The media play an important role in shaping societal perspectives and influencing our priorities. Role models for young women are very important. If the media continue to focus on men rather than giving equal attention to activities of women, girls and young women will not envisage themselves as important players in society. A fair and equitable portrayal of women would build self-esteem in young women and encourage them to strive for success in all arenas.

With such deep-rooted foundations of inequality in these media, the question of what can be done becomes a challenging one. One line of thinking, simply put, is that we, as a society, need strong and plentiful representations of women in both traditional and non-traditional roles. Ironically, of course, in our contemporary world, the best way to disseminate such images is through the media itself. And, as Kathy Latrobe (1992) notes, this might occur if more women actually worked in the field and held positions of authority (p. 136). Women executives might be more inclined to reduce negative images and equalize gender representation, but women executives in the media are rare—that vicious circularity again.

As a society, a conscious decision must be made to include the experience of women. As Mediawatch (2000) suggests, the news media must become more active on this front by forming advisory committees to consult on gender issues, employing balanced reporting that includes feature stories delving into broader societal contexts, using female news sources and equal opportunity hiring, seeking a gender balance in programming and reporting, covering women's issues with more regularity, and encouraging more editorial participation by women. In general, women must be given a place to stand, a place where their voice can be heard. As always, the individual in our society—you and I—must speak out: we must write letters of observation and complaint to media outlets, insist on extensive media education and literacy programs within our schools, provide gender awareness and sensitivity programs for men and women, young and old, insist on programs of social justice within our schools and communities, be involved in our world—these are proactive strategies that must be put into practice, these are feasible practices that must become our strategies. In this way, we can make that world of "silence and slow time" come to life. Without this, without changing the real and represented roles of women in the media, the potential for women in society may never be fully realized.

Your list of works cited is entitled "References" and begins on a new page; the title is centred.

In general, the sources you cite i your References page should inclu only those works that you have actually made reference to in yo essay.

## References

Alvarado, M., & Boyd-Barett, O. (1992). *Media education: An introduction*. London: BEI Publishing.

Baehr, H., & Dyer, G. (1987). *Boxed in: Women and television*. London: Pandora.

Bernstein, A. (2002). Is it time for a victory pap? Changes in the media coverage of women in sport. *International Review for the Sociology of Sport 37*(3–4), 415–428.

Carll, E. (2003). News portrayal of violence and women. *American Behavioral Scientist 46*(12), 1601–1610.

CTV specialty to close WTSN. (2003, August). Retrieved May 16, 2004, from http://micro.newswire.ca/release.cgi?rkey= 1108295916&view=62877–0&Start=0

Evans, G. (2003, November). Quotation. International Woman's Media Foundation. Retrieved May 28, 2004, from http://www.iwmf.org/programs/8218

Fiske, J. (1995). Gendered television. In G. Dines (Ed.), *Gender, race and class in media* (pp. 469–475). London: Sage Publications.

Health Canada Report. (1993). *Gender and violence in the mass media*. Ottawa: Family Violence Prevention Division.

International Women's Media Foundation. (2003). Gender and media baseline study. Retrieved December 4, 2004, from http://www.genderlinks.org.za/docs/2003/ GMbaselinestudy/gmbs-full-text–1.htm

Keats, J. (1978). *Poetical Works*. London: Oxford.

Latrobe, K., & Laughlin, M. (1992). *Multicultural aspects of library media programs*. Englewood: Libraries Unlimited.

The writer of this essay has used *italics* to indicate the titles of books; no quotation marks are used for articles. For a book, provide the name of the author or authors, the date, the title, and the publication information, including city and publisher. As long as the entire book has been read, no page numbers are included; if only an excerpt of the book has been read, indicate that in your citation.

Date of retrieval i included for websites.

Mediawatch. (2000). Women strike out. Retrieved May 31, 2004,

from www.mediawatch.ca/research/strikeout/Default.asp?pg=2

Press, A. (1991). *Women watching television: Gender, class, and*

*generation in the American television experience*. Philadelphia: U

of Pennsylvania.

Strom, D., & Robertson, T. (2001). Framing the fight: An analysis of

media coverage of female and male candidates in primary races

for governor and US senate 2000. *American Behavioral Scientist,*

*44*(12), 1999–2013.

In the References listing for a printed article, give the page numbers for the whole span of the article, even if you used material from only one or a few pages. This article spanned pages 1999 to 2013.

In general, references are listed alphabetically by author's last name. Record by surname, using only first initials and ampersands to connect more than one author. If the author is unknown, include the reference alphabetically by title. All entries are double-spaced and subsequent lines are indented.

CHAPTER

In this chapter you will find complete instruction for documenting papers according to the two most widely used academic styles:

1. MLA (Modern Language Association) for the humanities.

2. APA (American Psychological Association) for the social sciences.

You will also find a list of sources for other styles. Different academic disciplines require the use of different styles of documentation, so if you are writing a paper using library sources and have any doubt as to which style to use, consult your instructor.

## The MLA Documentation Style for the Humanities

The Modern Language Association (MLA) recommends that source citations be given in the text of the paper, rather than in footnotes or endnotes. This in-text style of documentation involves parenthetical references. Throughout this chapter, titles of books and periodicals are underlined (a printer's mark to indicate words to be set in italic type). With italic lettering available on most word processors, you can use italics instead of underlining, as long as your instructor approves.

**A.** Normally you will introduce the cited material by mentioning the name of the author in your lead-in and giving the page number (or numbers) at the end in parentheses, like this:

Frank Davey tells us that the narrative line of Daphne Marlatt's work is "entirely

phenomenological" (193).

**B.** Your readers can identify this source by consulting your Works Cited at the end of your paper (see items H through K). The entry for the source cited above would appear like this:

Davey, Frank. <u>From There to Here</u>. Erin: Press Porcépic, 1974.

**C.** If you do not mention the author in your lead-in, then include his/her last name in parentheses along with the page number, like this:

The most powerful of Marlatt's books is the long prose poem, <u>Rings</u>. This work

is written from inside the eyes and mind of a woman whose marriage is becom-

ing increasingly strained and untenable and whose first child is about to be

born (Davey 194).

D. If you have to quote indirectly—something from another source not available to you—use "qtd. in" (for "quoted in") in your parenthetical reference. The following example refers to a book written by Donald Johanson and Maitland Edey.

Richard Leakey's wife, Maeve, told the paleoanthropologist David Johanson,

"We heard all about your bones on the radio last night" (qtd. in Johanson and

Edey 162).

E. If you are using a source written or edited by more than three people, use only the name of the first person listed, followed by "et al." (meaning "and others") in your lead-in:

Blair et al. observe that the fine arts were almost ignored by colonial writers (21).

F. If you refer to more than one work by the same author, include a shortened title in the parenthetical reference:

(Gould, Mismeasure 138).

G. If the author's name is not given, use a shortened title instead. Be sure to use at least the first word of the full title to send the reader to the proper alphabetized entry on your Works Cited page. The following is a reference to a press release entitled "Carmanah Wins National Environmental Award for Export Performance":

Canada's Environmental Leaders are celebrated at the 3rd Annual Globe

Awards for Environmental Excellence. Carmanah Technologies Corporation (TSX

Venture: CMH) is pleased to announce that it received the Industry Award for

Export Performance at the 2004 GLOBE Awards held in Vancouver, British Co-

lumbia on April 2, 2004 ("Carmanah").

H. On a separate page at the end of the paper, alphabetize your Works Cited list for all sources mentioned in your paper. Use *hanging indention*; that is, after the first line of each entry, indent the other lines five spaces.

I. Omit any mention of *page* or *pages* or *line* or *lines*. Do not even include abbreviations for these terms. Use numbers alone:

Granatstein, J. L., and Norman Hillmer. "Canadians Who Inspired the World"

Maclean's 4 Sept. 2000: 26–48.

J.  Shorten publishers' names: for example, use "Allyn" instead of "Allyn and Bacon, Inc." or "Norton" instead of "W. W. Norton and Co." or "Oxford UP" instead of "Oxford University Press" or "U of Toronto P" instead of "University of Toronto Press." See sample entries 1 through 14.

K.  Use regular (not roman) numerals throughout, even to indicate act and scene in plays: "In <u>Othello</u> 2.1, the scene shifts to Cyprus." Exceptions: Use *lowercase* roman numerals (ii, xiv) for citing page numbers from a preface, introduction, or table of contents; use roman numerals in names of monarchs (Elizabeth II).

L.  Use raised note numbers for *informational notes* only (that is, notes containing material pertinent to your discussion but not precisely to the point). Include these content notes at the end of your paper just before your Works Cited page, and use the heading "Notes."

M.  Abbreviate months and titles of magazines as shown in the sample entries.

## Sample Entries for a Works Cited List

The following models will help you write Works Cited entries for most of the sources you will use. If you use a source not illustrated in these examples, consult the more extensive list of sample entries found in the *MLA Handbook for Writers of Research Papers,* 6th ed., or ask your instructor for guidance.

### Books

1.  Book by one author

    Tooze, Sandra B. <u>The Canadian Writer's Market</u>. Toronto: McClelland and Stewart, 2003.

2.  Two or more books by the same author

    Atwood, Margaret. <u>Oryx and Crake</u>. Toronto: Seal, 2003.

    ———. <u>Negotiating with the Dead: A Writer on Writing</u>. Toronto: Anchor, 2002.

3.  Book by two or three authors

    Petracca, Michael, and Madeleine Sorapure. <u>Common Culture</u>. Upper Saddle River: Pearson, 2004.

    Barnet, Sylvan, William Burto, and William Cain. <u>An Introduction to Literature</u>. Toronto: Pearson, 2004.

**4.** Books by more than three authors

Hume, Karen, et al. <u>Sightlines 7</u>. Toronto: Prentice Hall Ginn, 1999.

[The phrase *et al.* is an abbreviation for *et alii,* meaning "and others."]

**5.** Book by an unknown author

<u>Children's Literature</u>. Toronto: Ontario Assessment Instrument Pool, 1990.

**6.** Book with an editor

Van Luven, Lynne, and Priscilla L. Walton, eds. <u>Pop Can: Popular Culture in</u>

    <u>Canada</u>. Scarborough: Prentice Hall, 1999.

[For a book with a single editor, use "ed."]

**7.** Book with an editor and an author

Britton, James. <u>Prospect and Retrospect: Selected Essays</u>. Ed. Gordon M.

    Pradl. London: Heinemann, 1982.

**8.** Book by a group or corporate author

Butterworths. <u>Education Statutes and Regulations of Ontario</u>. Toronto: Lexis-

    Nexis Group, 2001.

[When a corporation, organization, or group is listed as the author on the title page, cite it as you would a person.]

**9.** Work in a collection or anthology

Joe, Rita. "Wen net ki'l." <u>Native Poetry in Canada: A Contemporary Anthology</u>.

    Eds. Jeannette Armstrong and Lally Grauer. Peterborough: Broadview,

    2001.

**10.** Work reprinted in a collection or anthology

Sage, George H. "Sport in American Society: Its Pervasiveness and Its Study."

    <u>Sport and American Society</u>. 3rd ed. Reading: Addison-Wesley, 1980.

    4–15. Rpt. in <u>Physical Activity and the Social Sciences</u>. Ed. W. N. Wid-

    meyer. 5th ed. Ithaca: Movement, 1983. 42–52.

[First give complete data for the earlier publication; then add "Rpt. in" and give the reprinted source.]

11. Multivolume work

    Nichol, bp. <u>The Martyrology Books 7 &</u>. 7th bk. 9 vols. Toronto: Coach House,

        1998.

12. Reprinted (republished) book

    Richardson, John. <u>Wacousta</u>. 1832. Toronto: McClelland and Stewart, 1991.

    [When citing a republished book, give the original date of publication, fol-
    lowed by a period, then provide the publication information of the actual
    text you are citing.]

13. Later (second or subsequent) edition

    Gibaldi, Joseph. <u>MLA Handbook for Writers of Research Papers</u>. 6th ed. New

        York: MLA, 2003.

14. Book in translation

    Tougas, Gerard. <u>History of French-Canadian Literature</u>. 2nd ed. Trans. Alta Lind

        Cook. Toronto: Ryerson, 1966.

## Newspapers

15. Signed newspaper article

    Krebs, Emilie. "Sewer Backups Called No Problem." <u>Pantagraph</u> [Bloomington]

        20 Nov. 1985: A3.

    [If the city is not part of the name of a local newspaper, give the city in brack-
    ets, not underlined, after the newspaper's name.]

    Davidson, Diana. "William Blake Through Catherine's Eyes." <u>Edmonton Journal</u>

        8 Feb. 2004, sec. 4:11.

    [Note the difference between "A3" in the first example and "sec. 4.11" in the
    second. Both refer to section and page, but each newspaper indicates the sec-
    tion in a different way. Give the section designation and page number ex-
    actly as they appear in the publication.]

**16.** Unsigned newspaper article

"U.S. Says Vancouver Is Hub for People Smuggling." <u>Vancouver Sun</u> 26 Febru-

ary 2004, electronic ed., sec. 1, 1.

[If an edition is specified on the paper's masthead, name the edition (late ed., natl ed., final ed., electronic ed.) after the date and before the page reference. Different editions of the same issue of a newspaper contain different material.]

**17.** Letter to the editor

Banks, Sylvia. "Inner-City School Teachers Show Dedication and Humanity." Let-

ter. <u>The Vancouver Sun</u> 7 Apr. 2004: A15.

**18.** Editorial

"Separate but Not Equalized." Editorial. <u>The Daily News</u> [Halifax] 24 February

2004:14.

## Magazines and Journals

**19.** Article from a monthly or bimonthly magazine

Budak, Jasmine. "Born to Fly." <u>Up Here</u> 12 Mar. 2004: 15–18.

Lindsey, Fred. "Soul on Ice." <u>Black Issues Book Review</u> Nov/Dec 2000: 76.

**20.** Article from a weekly or biweekly magazine (signed and unsigned)

Coghlan, Andy. "Warring Parents Harm Children as Much as Divorce." <u>New Sci-

entist</u> 15 Jun. 1991: 24.

Mansbridge, Peter. "The Joys of Puck Fever." <u>Maclean's</u> 3 May 2004: 14.

**21.** Article from a journal with continuous pagination throughout the whole volume

Potvin, Raymond, and Che-Fu Lee. "Multistage Path Models of Adolescent Alco-

hol and Drug Use." <u>Journal of Studies on Alcohol</u> 41 (1980): 531–42.

22. Article from a journal that paginates each issue separately or that uses only issue numbers

    Holtug, Nils. "Altering Humans: The Case For and Against Human Gene Ther-

    apy." <u>Cambridge Quarterly of Healthcare Ethics</u> 6.2 (Spring 1997):

    157–60.

    [That is volume 6, issue 2.]

## Other Sources

23. Book review

    Mason, Ian Garrick. Rev. of <u>Cod: A Biography of the Fish That Changed the

    World</u> by Mark Kurlansky. <u>The Walrus</u> June 2004: 77–80.

24. Personal interview or letter

    Bowering, George. Personal interview. 9 Feb. 2004.

    Hjortsberg, William. Letter to the author. 16 May 2004.

    [Treat published interviews and letters like articles, with the person being interviewed as the author.]

25. Anonymous pamphlet

    <u>Parents Family Friends of Lesbians and Gays</u>. Parents Flag Organization, 2000.

26. Article from a reference work (signed and unsigned)

    "Psychopharmacology." <u>The Columbia Encyclopedia</u>. 5th ed. 1993.

    Johnson, J. K., and P. B. Waits. "Sir John Alexander Macdonald." <u>The Dictionary

    of Canadian Biography</u>. 2000 ed.

    [Treat a dictionary entry or an encyclopedia article like an entry from an anthology, but do not cite the editor of the reference work.]

27. Government publication

    Government of Canada. <u>Canada Gazette Part I</u>. 1.44. Ottawa: Queen's Printer,

    2003.

**28.** Film, videotape, or DVD

<u>Les Invasions Barbares (The Barbarian Invasions)</u>. Dir. Denys Arcand. Perf.

    Rémy Girard, Stéphane Rousseau, Dorothée Berryman. Astral/Pyramide,

    2003.

**29.** Lecture

Miller, Jonathan. "Shakespeare on the Stage." Stratford Festival Lecture Se-

    ries. Stratford, Ont. 15 Sept. 2002.

For any other sources (such as televised shows, performances, advertisements, recordings, works of art), include enough information to permit an interested reader to locate your original source. Be sure to arrange this information in a logical fashion, duplicating as far as possible the order and punctuation of the entries above. To be on safe ground, consult your instructor for suggestions about documenting unusual material.

## Electronic Sources

If you use material from a computer database or online source, you need to indicate that you read it in electronic form. In general, follow the style for citing print sources, modifying them as appropriate to the electronic source. Include both the date of electronic publication (if available) and the date you accessed the source. In addition, include the Uniform Resource Locator (URL) in angle brackets. If a URL must be divided between two lines, MLA style requires that you break it only after a slash and not introduce a hyphen at the break.

**30.** Article in an online reference book or encyclopedia

Daniel, Ralph Thomas. "The History of Western Music." <u>Britannica Online:</u>

    <u>Macropaedia</u>. 1995. Online Encyclopedia Britannica. 14 June 1995.

    ⟨http//www.eb.com:180/cgi-bin/g:DocF5macro/5004/45/0.html⟩.

**31.** Article in an online magazine

Yeoman, Barry. "Into the Closet: Can Therapy Make Gay People Straight?"

    <u>Salon.com</u> 22 May 2000. 23 May 2000.

    ⟨http://www.salon.com/health/feature/2000/05/22/exgay/html⟩.

**32.** Article from an online full-text database

To cite online material without a URL that you get from a service to which your library subscribes, complete the citation by giving the name of the database (underlined), the library, and the date of access.

Gomelsky, Victoria. "Canada's Diamond Business Boomed in 2003." <u>National</u>

<u>Jeweler</u> 16 Apr. 2004: 26. <u>ABI/INFORM</u>. U. of Western Ontario, Weldon

Lib. 21 May 2004.

**33.** Article from a commercial online service

Romano, Jay. "Terrorism Insurance, at a Price." <u>New York Times</u>. 9 Mar. 2003.

<u>Research Navigator</u>. U. of Western Ontario, Weldon Lib. 17 Mar. 2004.

[Research Navigator is both the database and the name of the online service.]

**34.** Material accessed on a CD-ROM

Shakespeare. <u>Editions and Adaptations of Shakespeare</u>. Interactive multi-

media. Cambridge, UK: Chadwick-Healey, 1995. CD-ROM. Alexandria:

Electronic Book Technologies, 1995.

"Silly." <u>The Oxford English Dictionary</u>. 2nd ed. CD-ROM. Oxford: Oxford UP,

1992.

**35.** Website

Noel, Wanda, and Gerald Breau. "Copyright Matters." <u>Education Network</u> 4 June

2004. <http://www.enoreo.on.ca/resources/copyright.htm>.

For more detailed information about citing electronic sources, consult The MLA Handbook for Writers of Research Papers, 6th ed. (2003), or the MLA's website (**www.mla.org**).

## The APA Documentation Style for the Social Sciences

The APA style puts more focus on the date of the source than the MLA style does; it is also called the author-date system. The year appears in the parenthetical documentation in the text, instead of only in the References list. It works this way:

**A.** Always mention your source and its date within the text of your paper in parentheses, like this:

The study reveals that children pass through identifiable cognitive stages

(Piaget, 1954).

**B.** Your readers can identify this source by consulting your References list at the end of your paper. The entry for the information above would appear like this:

Piaget, J. (1954). *The construction of reality in the child.* New York: Basic Books.

[Note the use of sentence capitalization for titles in the References section. Note, too, that APA style requires you to italicize the punctuation that follows underlined titles.]

**C.** If you are quoting directly or if you want to stress the authority of the source you are paraphrasing, you may mention the name of the source in your sentence. Then include just the date in parentheses, like this:

In *Woe Is I*, Patricia O'Conner (1996) underscores her preference for the use of

pronouns by advising us to "[s]tick to singular stand-ins for singular pronouns—

*he, she, it, his, hers,* or *its: Somebody forgot to pay his bill.* You may be tempted

to use *their* because you don't know whether the somebody is a he or a she.

Well, your non-sexist intentions are good, but your grammar isn't" (p. 16).

**D.** If the author's name is not given, then use a shortened title instead. Be sure to use at least the first word of the full title to send the reader to the proper alphabetized entry on your References page. The following is a reference to a press release entitled "Carmanah Wins National Environmental Award for Export Performance":

Canada's Environmental Leaders are celebrated at the 3rd Annual Globe

Awards for Environmental Excellence. Carmanah Technologies Corporation (TSX

Venture: CMH) is pleased to announce that it received the Industry Award for

Export Performance at the 2004 GLOBE Awards held in Vancouver, British Co-

lumbia on April 2, 2004 ("Carmanah," 2004).

**E.** If you are using a source written or edited by more than two people and fewer than six, cite all authors the first time you refer to the source. For all subsequent references use only the surname of the first person listed, followed by *et al.* (meaning "and others") in your lead-in:

Barnet et al. (2004) produced an anthology that was as good as any in its field.

When there are only two authors, join their names with the word *and* in the text:

Hale and Sponjer (1972) originated the Do-Look-Learn theory.

In parenthetical materials, tables, and reference lists, join the names with an ampersand (&):

The Do-Look-Learn theory (Hale & Sponjer, 1972) was taken seriously by educators across the country.

F.  If you are quoting more than *forty* words, begin the quotation on a new line and indent the entire quotation five spaces, but run each line to the usual right margin. Omit the quotation marks. Do not single-space the quotation.

In *Teenage Boys and High English* (2002), Bruce Pirie concludes that

> "English" can only be known by what English teachers do. We are double mirrors, reflecting the kinds of discourse that the subject allows, as well as reflecting back to the students their own possible roles within that discourse. For that reason, we must think carefully about the nature of the classroom contexts we are creating and the gender roles we are ourselves enacting. (p. 142)

G.  If there are two or more works by the same author in your References list, put the earliest one first. When more than one work has been published by the same author during the same year, list them alphabetically, according to the name of the book or article, and identify them with "a," "b," "c," following the date. (Include the "a," "b," "c," in your in-text citations, too.)

Graves, D. (1975). An examination of the writing processes of seven-year-old children. *Research in the Teaching of English, 9,* 227–241.

Graves, D. (1981a). *Writers: Teachers and children at work.* Exeter, NH: Heinemann Educational Books.

Graves, D. (1981b). Writing research for the eighties: What is needed. *Language Arts, 58,* 197–206.

## Sample Entries for a References List

The following models will help you write entries for most of the sources you will include in your References list. If you use a source not illustrated in these samples, consult the more extensive *Publications Manual of the American Psychological Association*, 5th ed. (Washington: APA, 2001), or ask your instructor.

Alphabetize your list by the author's last name. If there is no author given, alphabetize the entry by the title. Use hanging indention; use author's initials for given names; put the dates after the authors' names; and use sentence capitalization for article and book titles, but capitalize the first word in the subtitle after a colon.

## Books

1. Book by one author

   Bell, William (1986). *Crabbe.* Toronto: General Publishing.

2. Book by two or more authors

   Milner, J., & Milner, L. (2003). *Bridging English.* Upper Saddle River: Prentice

       Hall.

   Alvermann, D., Moon, J., & Hagood, M. (1999). *Popular culture in the class-*

       *room: Teaching and researching critical media literacy.* Newark: Interna-

       tional Reading Association.

   [Note: in the list of references, use the ampersand sign instead of writing the word *and*.]

3. Book by a group or corporate author

   National Library of Canada. (2004). *Read up on it.* Ottawa: Minister of Public

       Works and Government Services.

4. Book with an editor

   Gallegos, Bee (Ed.). (1994). *English: Our official language?* New York: Wilson.

5. Article in a collection or anthology

   Willinsky, J. (2000). A history not yet past: Where then is here? In B. Barrell &

       R. Hammett (Eds.), *Advocating change: Contemporary issues in subject*

       *English* (pp. 2–13). Toronto: Irwin.

6. Multivolume work

   Asimov, I. (1960). *The intelligent man's guide to science.* (Vols. 1–2). New York:

       Basic Books.

7. Later (second or subsequent) edition

Gibaldi, J. (2003). *MLA handbook for writers of research papers* (6th ed.). New
York: MLA.

## Periodicals

8. Article from a journal paginated by volume

Messner, M. (1990). When bodies are weapons: Masculinity and violence in
sport. *International Review for the Sociology of Sport, 25,* 203–220.

[Do not put quotation marks around article titles. Capitalize all important
words in journal or magazine titles.]

9. Article from a journal paginated by issue

Holtug, Nils. (1997). Altering humans: The case for and against human gene
therapy. *Cambridge Quarterly of Healthcare Ethics, 6*(2), 157–160.

10. Article from a magazine

Tenove, C. (2004, May/June). Bombs not bread. *Adbusters*, 65.

11. Article from a newspaper

Anthony, L. (2003, Mar. 11). Kids shown to reflect TV violence. *The London
Free Press*, C3.

## Other Sources

12. Personal or telephone interview

Not cited in References list, only within your paper.

13. Article from a specialized dictionary or encyclopedia

Treat as an article in a collection (item 5 above).

## Electronic Sources

14. Article retrieved from a database

Gomelsky, V. (2004, 16 Apr.) Canada's diamond business boomed in 2003.
*National Jeweler*, 26. Retrieved 21 May 2004 from *ABI/INFORM*.

**15.** Article from an online magazine

> Yeoman, B. (2000, May 22). Into the closet: Can therapy make gay people
>
> straight? *Salon.com*. Retrieved 23 May 2000 from
>
> http://www.salon.com/health/feature/2000/05/22/exgay/html

**16.** Article from an online newspaper

> Bradford, Keith. (2004, February 27). Terrifying Trip. *The Edmonton Sun*. Re-
>
> trieved February 27, 2004, from http://www.canoe.ca/NewsStand/
>
> EdmontonSun/News/2004/02/27/362497.html

**17.** Article from an online encyclopedia

> Pisani, E. (2001). Africa's struggle against AIDS. *Encyclopedia Britannica*
>
> *Online*. Retrieved November 17, 2001, from
>
> http://members.eb.com/bol/topic?tmap_id=4028008map_typ=by

Divide a URL only after a slash or before a period. There is no period after a URL at the end of a citation so that readers will not think the period is part of the URL. For more information, consult the APA website at **www.apastyle.org**.

## Other Styles of Documentation

As we noted earlier, different academic disciplines, and different instructors, may require the use of different style guides for citing and documenting your sources. While MLA and APA are most frequently used, it may be useful for you to be familiar with the following, which are also quite common. Your library or bookstore will have editions of these and, in many cases, relevant information can also be found online.

*The Chicago Manual of Style*. 15th ed. Chicago: University of Chicago Press, 2003.

*Citation Styles Online! A Reference Guide to Using Internet Sources.* (*www.bedfordstmartins.com/online/citex.html*)

*Scientific Style and Format: The CBE Manual for Authors, Editors, and Publishers*. New York: Press Syndicate of the University of Cambridge, 2002.

Turabian, Kate L. *A Manual for Writers of Term Papers, Theses, and Dissertations*, 6th ed. Chicago: University of Chicago Press, 1996.

Walker, Janice R., and Todd Taylor. *The Columbia Guide to Online Style*. New York: Columbia University Press, 1998. (*www.columbia.edu/cu/cup/cgos/idx_basic.html*)

Several established database sites are very useful, such as Research Navigator (**www.researchnavigator.com/index.html**), which contain summaries of all these major documentation guidelines. If your university library does not provide ready access to these databases, you may need an access code.

# Making Your Writing
# Clear and Correct

# Reviewing the Basics of Grammar

You do not need an extensive knowledge of grammar in order to write well. What you do need is a basic vocabulary, shared by you and your teachers and other writers, in which you can talk about sentences. Learning grammatical terms and concepts can help you identify and correct sentence fragments, comma splices, and run-on sentences; it can also help you decide where to put commas and semi-colons and how to untangle sentences that are marred by dangling modifiers or piled-up prepositional phrases.

## A Quick Look at the Parts of Speech

The sentence is the basic unit of communication in English. But sentences are, of course, made up of words, each of which can be classified as a *part of speech*. Learning these parts of speech and how they work will help you understand how sentences operate.

**NOUNS** are names. A noun may name a person, place, thing, or idea: *Maria, brother, Charlottetown, beach, shoe, cat, daffodil, iron, courage.*

Nouns have *number* (singular and/or plural); *case* (subject, object, or possessive); *gender* (feminine [*she, her*], masculine [*he, him*], neuter [*it*] or common [*all, some*]); and *person* (first [*I, we*], second [*you*], or third [*she, he, it, they*]).

| Classification | Definition | Examples (illustrating number) | |
|---|---|---|---|
| | | Singular | Plural |
| **Common** | • things | • *house* | *houses* |
| | | • *freedom* | *freedoms* |
| **Proper** | • persons, places | • *Jennifer* | *Jennifers* |
| | | • *Moncton* | *Monctons* |
| **Concrete** | • refers to specific things | • *house* | *houses* |
| | | • *medium* | *media* |
| **Abstract** | • refers to qualities or ideas | • *freedom* | *freedoms* |
| | | • *truth* | *truths* |
| **Collective** | • refers to a group or class | • *herd* | *herds* |
| | | • *committee* | *committees* |
| **Possessive** | • indicates ownership | • *Bob's* hat | *Bobs's* hats |
| | | • *committee's* decision | *committees'* decisions |

**FIGURE 11.1** *Grammar Details: Nouns*

## EXERCISE 11.1: NOUNS

Underline each of the nouns in the following sentences and identify its classification. Note that, in some cases, nouns have more than one classification; for instance, in the sentence "They sold their house," *house* is both common and concrete.

**1.** After the tornado, they put the pieces of their lives back together.

**2.** Equality is an ideal often expressed but rarely achieved.

**3.** Calgary was buried under a late spring blizzard.

**4.** "We hold these truths to be self-evident," was one plantation owner's vision of freedom.

**5.** The gaggle of geese saved the city from destruction.

## EXERCISE 11.2: PLURALS

Write the correct plural form of each of the following nouns:

| | |
|---|---|
| banjo | hippopotamus |
| dwarf | encylopedia |
| cargo | gymnasium |
| campus | 7 |
| thesaurus | antifreeze |

**PRONOUNS** replace or refer to nouns. The noun that a pronoun replaces or refers to is called the *antecedent* of that pronoun:

antecedent                              pronoun

Paula took three suitcases with <u>her</u> to Vancouver.

English has several different kinds of pronouns; the most frequently used are the *personal pronouns: I, me, you, she, her, him, it, we, us, they,* and *them*. Figure 11.2 lists other types of pronouns as well. (Note that, like nouns, pronouns have number, case, gender, and person.)

## EXERCISE 11.3: PRONOUNS

For each of the following sentences, underline the pronouns and identify their classification.

**1.** Samuel Richardson's *Clarissa* is not only a monument of the English canon, but was for Richardson himself a remarkable personal accomplishment.

**2.** Its heroine, who is kidnapped and raped, vindicates her honour when she wills herself to die.

**3.** By the twentieth century, it had become one of the greatest unread masterpieces.

**4.** While its epistolary style is no longer popular, many scholars acknowledge it to be the forerunner of the stream-of-consciousness technique.

**5.** Its interior monologues certainly enabled Richardson to convey remarkable psychological insight.

| Classification | Definition | Examples |
|---|---|---|
| **Personal** | • refers to specific persons, things | • *I, me, you, she, her, him, we, us, they, them* <br> • *it* (may be called "impersonal") |
| **Possessive** | • indicates ownership | • *mine, yours, hers, his, its, ours, theirs* |
| **Intensive** <br> (also "emphatic") | • emphasizes the noun or pronoun | • *myself, yourself, herself, himself, itself, ourselves, yourselves, themselves* <br> • The prime minister *herself* made that claim. |
| **Reflexive** | • indicates that the receiver of an action is identical to the doer | • *myself, yourself, herself* (same as above) <br> • The prime minister hurt *herself* playing golf. |
| **Relative** | • introduces a subordinate clause that provides additional information | • *who, whom, whose, which, that* <br> • The car *that* he drove was given to him by his uncle *who* was a mechanic in the factory. |
| **Demonstrative** | • indicates or identifies a noun, pronoun, adjective | • *this, that, these, those* <br> • *That* is her house. *This* is mine. |
| **Indefinite** | • refers to non-specific persons or things | • *all, another, everyone, each, anyone, both, either, several, none, some, few, nobody* |
| **Reciprocal** | • indicates a dual reception of the action of the verb | • *each other, one another* <br> • The two senators argued with *each other*. <br> • The four children tired *one another* out. |
| **Interrogative** | • asks questions | • *who, whom, whose, which, what* |

**FIGURE 11.2** *Grammar Details: Pronouns*

## EXERCISE 11.4: PRONOUN PROBLEMS

Correct the pronoun problems in the following sentences:

1. The farmer went to his neighbour and told him that his cattle were in his field.
2. Charles's duplicity was revealed to James by a letter to his wife.
3. Everybody admires their grandmother.
4. The student angrily left the building and drove away in their car.
5. If anybody wants to attend, they need to purchase a ticket in advance.

**ADJECTIVES AND ARTICLES** describe or limit the meaning of nouns (and sometimes pronouns).

Descriptive adjectives answer the question "what kind?":

*red* hair, *heavy* load, *expensive* car, *unbelievable* story

Descriptive adjectives have three degrees: positive, comparative, and superlative:

*heavy, heavier, heaviest; expensive, more expensive, most expensive*

A few adjectives are irregular in "degree formation" (*bad, worse, worst*) and adjectives with more than two syllables often use *more, most* (*colourful, more colourful, most colourful*). Check a dictionary if you are uncertain.

Limiting adjectives tell "which one" or "how many":

*this* problem, *any* car, *few* questions, *his* hair

Limiting adjectives do not have comparative or superlative forms.

Articles are essentially a specialized form of adjective, although some sources consider them a separate part of speech.

| Classification | Definition | Examples |
|---|---|---|
| **Qualitative** | • describes aspect of a noun | • *big, small, purple, thin, happy* |
| **Quantitative** | • describes number, amount | • *ten, several, few, many* |
| **Demonstrative** | • indicates specific noun | • *this, that, these, those*<br>• *These* apples are riper than *those*. |
| **Possessive** | • indicates ownership | • *your, her, his, my, our, their*<br>• *Your* car is better than *my* car. |
| **Interrogative** | • asks about specific noun | • *whose, which, what*<br>• *What* child is this? |

**FIGURE 11.3** *Grammar Details: Adjectives*

| Classification | Examples |
|---|---|
| **Definite** | • *the*<br>• *The* textbook in question is on *the* table in Room 21. |
| **Indefinite** | • *a, an*<br>• Please sit at *a* table where there is *an* examination booklet. |

**FIGURE 11.4** *Grammar Details: Articles*

## EXERCISE 11.5: ADJECTIVES

Write the adjective form for each of the following nouns. We have completed the first one for you.

beauty                     *beautiful*

bombast

fear

love

destruction

light

rock

blue

scandal

horror

recreation

## EXERCISE 11.6: ADJECTIVE ERRORS

Identify and correct the adjective errors in each of the following sentences:

1. He was the oldest of the two men.
2. Due to the inclement weather, the schools were closed.
3. Each of the assistants is giving up their lunch hour next Tuesday.
4. The apples taste nowheres near as sweetly as the pears.
5. That BMW is the most expensive car of any on the lot.
6. The bad dancers danced bad!
7. She missed her plane stopping for a smoke.
8. Her son likes that kind of a book.

**VERBS** say something about the subject of a sentence. They express actions, describe occurrences, or establish states of being.

**Action**:          The umpire <u>called</u> the runner out.

**Occurrence**:     A hush <u>settled</u> over the stadium.

**State of being**:   The umpire <u>was</u> wrong.

A complete sentence always has a main verb. Many verbs combine with *auxiliary* (or *helping*) verbs; the most common auxiliaries are forms of *be, have,* and *do:*

Silvio <u>is</u> <u>taking</u> a course in ballroom dancing. He <u>has</u> <u>taken</u> three lessons already. The instructor <u>did</u> <u>tell</u> him not to give up too soon.

A great deal of information, often in technical jargon, surrounds the grammatical understanding of verbs. Figure 11.5 and the following exercises provide a bird's-eye view of this grammatical territory. Irregular verbs are discussed in Chapter 13.

You create a *split infinitive* when you place a word between *to* and the verb in the infinitive form, as in the well-known phrase from *Star Trek*: "*to boldly go* where no one has gone before." While this practice is generally accepted, your writing style will usually be more effective if you avoid using split infinitives. The infinitive is a set grammatical structure in English and, for an ear tuned to the rhythm of the language, splitting the infinitive compromises the flow and power of your writing. Thus, the second sentence that follows is more effectively written than the first:

She began to slowly walk down the road and to gloriously sing.

She began to walk slowly down the road and to sing gloriously.

There are, of course, exceptions. Arguably, the following sentences seem best expressed through the splitting of the infinitive:

The school wanted to strongly encourage its students to stop smoking.

They wanted to really help the fundraising.

| Classification | Definition | Examples |
|---|---|---|
| **Transitive** | • expresses action done to a particular thing<br>• often followed by an object, a receiver of action (ask "what?" or "who?" after verb) | • She *purchased* two tickets. (She purchased [*what?*] two tickets. *Tickets* is the object of the transitive verb.)<br>• Two tickets *were purchased* by her. (Transitive passive verbs have no direct object.) |
| **Copula** | • expresses a state of being instead of an action<br>• followed by a subjective completion, a noun or noun substitute that completes or is an important link to the subject of the sentence | • *be (is, are, am, was), seem, appear, become, feel, taste, smell, grow, turn, prove, look*<br>• She *is* a doctor. (The copula verb *be* functions as an equal sign between *she* and *doctor*, with the subject *she* being "completed" by *doctor*.)<br>• The band *sounded* heavenly.<br>• The team *seems* unprepared. |
| **Intransitive** | • expresses action, but the action is not done to anything in particular (no answer to the question "what") | • Money *talks*.<br>• Sunflowers *grow* very tall.<br>• They *departed* late.<br>• *Sit* down! |

**FIGURE 11.5** *Grammar Details: Verbs*

## EXERCISE 11.7: VERB CLASSIFICATION

Indicate the classification of the underlined verb in each of the following; then rewrite the sentences by changing the verbs (where possible) from active to passive voice. We have done the first one for you.

1. They <u>purchased</u> two hockey sticks.

   *Transitive:* Two hockey sticks were purchased by them.

2. She <u>gave</u> the cat some milk.

3. The gymnast <u>won</u> a gold medal for Canada.

4. The agile squirrel <u>is</u> a skilful climber.

5. The young motorist <u>drove</u> carefully through the traffic.

6. The tiger <u>is</u> a ferocious beast and <u>burns</u> brightly on occasion.

## EXERCISE 11.8: VERB ERRORS

Identify and correct the verb errors in each of the following sentences:

1. The programmers and the president walks to the restaurant each afternoon.

2. Although Ed died on that Juno beach, Jon, his pal, rushes on, intending to bravely charge to victory in his friend's memory.

3. Neither Tom nor Jane are running for re-election and not one of all of their ministers are interested.

4. A large crowd of screaming fans were present; it tried to fiercely get in the East Gate.

5. Yesterday she had run in the marathon.

## EXERCISE 11.9: SUBJECT–PREDICATE AGREEMENT

Choose the correct verb to agree with the bare subject of each of the following:

1. The teacher and her students (visit, visits) the museum.

2. Bread and jam (taste, tastes) good with tea.

3. The Queen (has, have) a limousine for state events.

4. The students said they (saw, seen) them at the mall.

**ADVERBS** usually modify verbs, describing *how, when, where,* and *how much* the action of the verb is performed:

Garfield <u>ran</u> *upstairs quickly.* Robert <u>will</u> <u>arrive</u> *soon.*

Some adverbs can modify an adjective or another adverb:

Ian <u>is</u> a *very* cautious driver. He <u>drives</u> *quite* carefully.

Although many adverbs in English are formed by adding *-ly* to an adjective (*happily, expensively*), many others are not: *already, always, seldom, never, now, often, here, there, up, down, inside,* and so forth. Like adjectives, many adverbs change form from the positive to indicate the comparative and superlative degree: *carefully, more carefully, most carefully.*

| Classification | Definition | Examples |
|---|---|---|
| **Interrogative** | • indicates a question about the modified word | • *why? how? where? when? what?*<br>• *Why* did he do it?<br>• *Where* were the police at the time? |
| **Manner** | • indicates a quality about modified words | • *swiftly, quickly, kindly, discreetly*<br>• The truck *slowly* turned the corner.<br>• Children grow up too *quickly*. |
| **Degree** | • indicates a quantity with regard to modified words | • *far, near, much, more, probably, certainly, too*<br>• She was *far* better today than yesterday.<br>• Children grow up *too* quickly. |
| **Time** | • answers the question "when" about modified words | • *late, today, now, then, often, ever*<br>• The parade was *late* because of the accident.<br>• They lived happily *ever* after. |
| **Place** | • answers the question "where" about modified words | • *there, here, everywhere*<br>• *There* is our mayor.<br>• *Here* is the heartland of the country. |
| **Negation** | • indicates nullification of words modified | • *not, never, no*<br>• We shall *not* go to the party.<br>• The outcome was *never* in question. |

**FIGURE 11.6** *Grammar Details: Adverbs*

## EXERCISE 11.10: ADVERB ERRORS

Identify and correct the adverb errors in the following sentences:

1. Please lock the door careful and nail the shutters tight to winterize the cottage.
2. Lilacs are blooming there now abundantly.
3. The felon answered often rudely.
4. He was sure happy that the holidays had arrived.
5. Eddie has nowhere near enough money to buy that CD player.
6. The Niagara River roared loud over the Falls.
7. After the final bell of June, most all of the students raced quiet from the school.
8. The firefighter escaped nearly breaking his neck when the floor collapsed suddenly.
9. We watched the tornado awfully silent as it ripped through the trailer park.
10. Some claim that rock music continues to be a real bad influence on youth.

## EXERCISE 11.11: ADVERBIAL PUNS

Try creating some clever adverbial puns, generally known as *Tom Swifties*. (These puns mimic the often zestful use made of the adverb in the hundred or so *Tom Swift* novels written since 1910 by several writers, including Edward Stratemeyer, Howard Garis, and James Lawrence.) Here is an example:

"I cut myself with the razor," Tom said *sharply*.

**1.** "My pencil is dull," Tom said _____.

**2.** "Please pass the sugar," Tom said _____.

**3.** Tom sat in the Emergency Room, _____.

**4.** "I work repairing photocopiers," Tom said _____.

**5.** "This impressive piano costs $1000," Tom said _____.

**6.** "I couldn't find the bananas or peaches," Tom said _____.

**7.** "This arrangement is missing a flower," Tom said _____.

**8.** "I want to take a picture now," Tom said _____.

**9.** "Now, I'll NEVER dance," Tom said _____.

**10.** "Let's get married," said Tom _____.

**PREPOSITIONS** are connecting words. Each of the following prepositions shows a different relation between the noun *stump* and the actions expressed by the verbs:

> The rabbit jumped *over* the stump, ran *around* the stump, sat *on* the stump, hid *behind* the stump, crouched *near* the stump.

The group of words beginning with a preposition and ending with a noun or pronoun (its *object*) is called a *prepositional phrase*. For a list of common prepositions, see Figure 11.7.

| | | | |
|---|---|---|---|
| about | below | in | since |
| above | between | into | through |
| across | by | like | till |
| after | down | of | to |
| against | during | off | until |
| at | except | on | up |
| before | for | outside | upon |
| behind | from | over | with |

Prepositions made up of more than one word are called *compound prepositions*:

| | | |
|---|---|---|
| according to | in addition to | in spite of |
| because of | in back of | instead of |
| contrary to | in case of | on account of |
| except for | in front of | out of |

**FIGURE 11.7** *Common Prepositions*

| Definition | Examples |
|---|---|
| • a *structure word* (meaning that it never changes its form) that links a noun or pronoun to another word in the sentence and that indicates their relationship | • The family drove *to* the mall. (The preposition *to* connects *mall* and *family*, indicating where the family drove.) <br> • They parked their car *in front of* the video store. |

**FIGURE 11.8 *Grammar Details: Prepositions***

Try to avoid ending a sentence with a preposition. While it is not considered a grammatical error, this practice can often make your sentences stylistically awkward. The second sentence that follows is more effective than the first:

He did not know which novel to begin his study with.

He did not know with which novel to begin his study.

### EXERCISE 11.12: PREPOSITION ERRORS

Identify and correct the preposition errors in the following sentences:

1. She was happy that the winter was over with.
2. I just don't know where the time went to.
3. Due to lateness, Michael was not selected when the interviews were held.
4. He plans on borrowing some money off of Tom.
5. Which vehicle were you riding in?

### EXERCISE 11.13: PREPOSITIONS

Replace the prepositions omitted in the following passage from Mary Shelley's *Frankenstein*.

_____ a few minutes, I heard the creaking _____ my door, as if some one endeavoured to open it softly. I trembled _____ head _____ foot; I felt a presentiment _____ who it was, and wished to rouse one _____ the peasants who dwelt _____ a cottage not far _____ mine; but I was overcome _____ the sensation _____ helplessness, so often felt _____ frightening dreams, when you _____ vain endeavour to fly _____ an impending danger, and was rooted _____ the spot.

**CONJUNCTIONS** join words or groups of words.

A *coordinating conjunction* (*and, but, or, nor, for, yet, so*) joins words or word groups of the same kind and same importance:

Clovis forgot the extra nails *and* sealing tape. He also stepped on the drywall *and* ruined it. We wanted to fire him, *but* his dad owns the business.

A *subordinating conjunction* (*if, because, although, when,* etc.) joins a dependent (subordinate) group of words to an independent sentence:

*If you love me*, you will buy me a new car.

I love you *because you are so generous.*

*Conjunctive adverbs* are adverbs used as conjunctions or transitional words. The most common are *however, thus, therefore, consequently, indeed, furthermore,* and *nevertheless.*

He used the wrong nails to put up the drywall; *thus,* they popped right out when spring came. His daughter told him to use special nails; *however,* he neglected to follow her advice.

| Classification | Definition | Examples |
|---|---|---|
| **Coordinate** | • joins two, or more, equal items (nouns, verbs, clauses, etc.) | • *and, but, or, nor* (sometimes *for, so, yet*)<br>• Punch *and* Judy were famous puppets.<br>• They ran *and* jumped in the field.<br>• Neither the corn *nor* the beans were ready to harvest. |
| **Subordinate** | • joins two or more items, one of which is of more significance than the other or others | • *that, which, who, since, because, if*<br>• Carla, *who* was an expert, taught the seminar. (The fact that Carla taught the seminar is given greater significance here than the fact that she is an expert; this latter idea is of lesser importance, or subordinate.)<br>• Schools were closed *because* of the blizzard. (Again, the most important idea is that the schools were closed.) |
| **Correlative** | • pairs of conjunctions that join words or groups of words of equal value | • *both . . . and; either . . . or; neither . . . nor; not only . . . but also*<br>• *Both* Edith *and* Archie were memorable characters.<br>• The black Lab was *not only* wet *but also* muddy. |
| **Conjunctive Adverbs** (sometimes called "adverbial connectives," or "sentence adverbs") | • join two sentences or principal clauses, and modify the second | • *however, therefore, nevertheless, so, thus, still, consequently, accordingly, finally, indeed*<br>• The tea was cold; *however,* the scones were hot.<br>• She enjoys Baroque music, *so* she has a large collection of CDs of that period. |

**FIGURE 11.9** *Grammar Details: Conjunctions*

## EXERCISE 11.14: CONJUNCTIONS

Complete the following sentences by adding a suitable conjunction (or two).

1. _____ you cannot make it, we will reschedule the party.
2. We must hurry, _____ the last ferry is at 1:00 a.m.
3. Either Kelly _____ I will help you move the sofa.
4. Please wait _____ the intersection is cleared.
5. Ali _____ Rachel were the best of friends.
6. Do not begin the examination _____ you are given complete instructions.
7. _____ Sir John A. Macdonald _____ George Brown were Fathers of Confederation.
8. _____ you visit Victoria, you must have tea at the Empress Hotel.
9. My brother wanted to go to the University of Saskatchewan _____ Queen's.
10. Margaret Avison _____ P. K. Page, _____ all is said and done, are two of our best poets.

## EXERCISE 11.15: COORDINATION

Use coordinating conjunctions (*and, but, or, nor, for, so, yet*) to make the following sets of sentences into one sentence:

1. He has a bat. He has a glove.
2. Spring is the most dangerous time for avalanches. Avalanches can happen almost any time of the year.
3. The London turnpike was busy. It was snowing. He still needed to get to Hyde Park quickly.
4. *Who Has Seen the Wind* is written by W. O. Mitchell. *Jake and the Kid* is written by W. O. Mitchell. Both novels are set on the prairies. Both novels are coming-of-age stories.
5. The heron was standing still. The heron was perched high on the pole. The heron readied itself to dive into the water.

**INTERJECTIONS** are words used to designate expressions that individuals might utter—*wow, oh, eh, huh*, and the like.

| Definition | Examples |
|---|---|
| • an expression of surprise, anger, etc. | • *"O brave new world, that has such people in't!"*<br>• *Alas!* poor Yorick, I knew him, Horatio . . ." |

**FIGURE 11.10** *Grammar Details: Interjections*

**EXPLETIVES** are words or phrases that have no grammatical meaning. For instance, when we write "It is raining," the expletive "It" has no antecedent, and hence no specific meaning; it is simply used to fill out the sentence.

Expletives are also swear words used as an exclamation. When we hit our thumbs with hammers while pounding nails, we may utter a certain imprecation connoting that we would like to make love with that hammer, but of course that is not what we literally mean. The frequent inclusion of the words "expletive deleted" in the transcripts of Richard Nixon's infamous Watergate tapes provides another example of the meaning of the term in this context.

| Definition | Examples |
|---|---|
| • an introductory word that forces the subject to appear later in the sentence, often adding emphasis to the subject<br>• has no grammatical correlation | • *It* is frightening to think that going out at night could be dangerous. (*It* has no antecedent; the actual subject of this sentence is *going out at night could be dangerous.*)<br>• *There* are eleven players on a team.<br>• *It* is the only one I value. |

**FIGURE 11.11** *Grammar Details: Expletives*

# Putting the Words Together

Knowing a word's part of speech tells only part of the story. You must understand how the word operates in the pattern or structure of a particular sentence to get the full message.

## Basic Sentence Patterns

There are five basic patterns for sentences in English. Each pattern contains a subject and a predicate. Depending on the nature of the verb, the pattern may also contain *objects* or *complements* that complete the meaning of the verb.

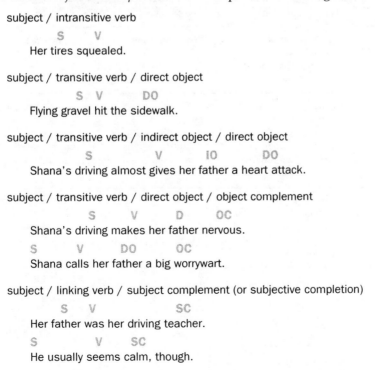

subject / intransitive verb

    S    V
Her tires squealed.

subject / transitive verb / direct object

    S  V    DO
Flying gravel hit the sidewalk.

subject / transitive verb / indirect object / direct object

    S    V  IO    DO
Shana's driving almost gives her father a heart attack.

subject / transitive verb / direct object / object complement

    S  V    D    OC
Shana's driving makes her father nervous.

S    V    DO    OC
Shana calls her father a big worrywart.

subject / linking verb / subject complement (or subjective completion)

    S  V    SC
Her father was her driving teacher.

S    V  SC
He usually seems calm, though.

## Phrases

A phrase is a string of related words that does *not* include a subject and verb combination. The common types of phrases are shown in Figure 11.12.

| Phrases | Definition | Examples |
|---|---|---|
| **Noun Phrase** | • a phrase composed of a noun and its modifier<br>• functions as subject, object, or complement of a sentence | • *The delicious six-foot submarine sandwich* was too big for three people.<br>• "The delicious six-foot submarine sandwich" is a noun phrase that acts as subject of the sentence. |
| **Prepositional Phrase** | • a phrase introduced by a preposition<br>• functions as adjective or adverb | • The boys *from the academy* went *to the store.*<br>• "from the academy" is a prepositional adjective phrase that modifies the bare subject "boys."<br>• "to the store" is a prepositional adverb phrase that modifies the bare predicate "went." |
| **Participial Phrase** | • a phrase introduced by a participle<br>• functions as an adjective | • *Tacking into the wind*, the sailboat slowly crossed the lake.<br>• "tacking" is a participle introducing the phrase "tacking into the wind," which modifies the bare subject "sailboat." |
| **Gerund Phrase** | • a phrase introduced by a gerund<br>• functions as a noun or noun equivalent | • *Telling a lie* is rarely wise.<br>• "telling" is a gerund introducing the phrase "telling a lie," which functions as subject of the sentence. |
| **Infinitive Phrase** | • a phrase introduced by an infinitive<br>• functions as noun, adjective, or adverb | • The walrus began *to talk of many things.*<br>• "to talk" is an infinitive that introduces the phrase "to talk of many things," which modifies the bare predicate "began." |
| **Appositive Phrase** | • phrase names identical thing as noun or pronoun<br>• follows noun or pronoun in subjective or objective case | • Swift's politicians, *amazing rope dancers*, rarely miss a step.<br>• "amazing rope dancers" is in apposition to "politicians"; that is, it means the same thing (one could be exchanged for the other). |
| **Absolute Phrase** | • phrase is grammatically separate from the rest of the sentence<br>• modifies whole sentence or clause | • *The wind howling outside*, the fire began to feel warmer.<br>• "the wind howling outside" is separate ("absolute") from the sentence. |

**FIGURE 11.12** *Grammar Details: Phrases*

## Clauses

Clauses contain both subjects and predicates plus all their related modifiers and complements. The two kinds of clauses are *independent* (sometimes called *main*) and *dependent* (sometimes called *subordinate*).

**INDEPENDENT CLAUSES.** An independent clause is a complete sentence. It contains a subject and a verb plus any objects, complements, and modifiers of that verb. We have already described the typical patterns for independent clauses: see the Basic Sentence Patterns, pages 181–82.

**DEPENDENT CLAUSES.** A dependent clause does not sound like a complete sentence when it is spoken or written by itself. It *depends* on an independent clause to complete its meaning. The word that makes all the difference is the subordinating conjunction or relative pronoun that introduces the clause. For instance, suppose a stranger walked up to you and said, "I eat blue bananas." You would understand those words as a complete, though odd, utterance. In contrast, suppose the stranger said, "Since I eat blue bananas" or "That I eat blue bananas" or "After I eat blue bananas." You would think this even more unusual: you would want the stranger to finish the sentence. The words *since, that,* and *after* make the clauses dependent.

Dependent clauses can be used as nouns, adjectives, and adverbs, as shown in Figure 11.13.

| Dependent Clauses | Definition | Examples |
|---|---|---|
| **Noun Clause** | • functions as a noun<br>• subject or object | • I know *who ate the banana.*<br>• "who ate the banana" is a noun clause that is the direct object of the bare predicate "know."<br>• *Why he ate it* does not concern me.<br>• "Why he ate it" is a noun clause that is the subject of the sentence. |
| **Adjective Clause** | • found in complex sentences<br>• modifies nouns or pronouns | • The lawyer *whose doughnut you ate* is famous.<br>• "whose doughnut you ate" is an adjective clause that modifies the bare subject "lawyer." |
| **Adverb Clause** | • found in complex sentences<br>• modifies verb, adjective, or adverb | • The fans arrived earlier *than did the band.*<br>• "than did the band" is an adverb clause and modifies the adverb "earlier." |

**FIGURE 11.13** *Grammar Details: Dependent Clauses*

## ▓ EXERCISE 11.16: CLAUSES AND PHRASES

In the following sentences, label the independent and dependent clauses and the phrases.

1. Many cures for insomnia exist.

2. Drinking warm milk is a common home remedy for sleeplessness.

3. Milk contains calcium, which is a natural tranquilizer.

4. When you heat the milk, you make the calcium easier for your body to absorb.

5. The warm milk cure does not work for everyone.

6. Some people believe in counting sheep.

7. This boring activity quickly makes them drowsy.

8. Others claim that long nineteenth-century novels will produce sleep efficiently.

9. Alarmed at such barbarism, nineteenth-century fiction scholars are frantically trying to find alternative sedatives.

10. Their most recent work, which is now in experimental stages, involves Wordsworth's *Prelude*.

When we speak, we nod, gesture, change facial expression, and raise and lower the tone and volume of our voices to help communicate the meanings of our words. When we write, the only aids we have are word choice, word order, and punctuation. The conventions for punctuating our written sentences are not numerous, but they are complicated and flexible enough to give some writers more trouble than help.

## Separating and Connecting

Punctuation marks have one main function: to signal the separation between ideas. For example, if you want to show that two ideas are completely separate, you put a period or question mark after one and start a new sentence. On the other hand, if you want to show that two parts of a sentence (like the subject and verb) are closely connected, you do not put in any punctuation at all. The following list of punctuation marks describes the amount of separation (from most to least) that you can signal within and between sentences:

- period, question mark, exclamation mark: maximum separation
- semicolon: medium separation
- colon: medium separation (anticipatory)
- dash: medium separation (emphatic)
- comma: minimum separation
- no mark: no separation

As the list suggests, the colon and the dash signal more than just the amount of separation. Their precise uses will be explained later.

Another way of understanding the differences among these punctuation marks is to look at the grammatical units they separate. These units can be divided into two kinds: independent clauses and non-independent elements. You will remember that an independent clause is a group of words that contains a subject and a predicate and can stand alone as a sentence. Non-independent elements include words, phrases, and dependent clauses that do not stand alone as sentences. Figure 12.1 presents the list of punctuation marks arranged according to the grammatical units they separate.

With these differences in mind, we can now look at the specific conventions for using punctuation marks both within and between independent clauses. And we will begin with the most frequently used mark of punctuation, the comma.

| | |
|---|---|
| *To separate independent clauses* | Use **periods, question marks, or semicolons** |

Canadian poet Al Purdy was born in Wooler, Ontario, in 1918. When he was in his teens he rode the rails and then spent six years serving in the RCAF.

Have you read any of Purdy's poems? Many of them deal with his experiences travelling across Canada.

Eventually Purdy settled in Ameliasburgh; he built an A-frame cottage on Roblin's Lake.

| | |
|---|---|
| *To separate independent clauses or to separate non-independent elements from independent clauses* | Use **dashes or colons** |

It was in settling in Ameliasburgh that Purdy discovered his unique voice—as he poetically claimed, he found "a place to stand."

The great subjects of Purdy's art began to appear in his poems: a sense of history, a vision of Canada, and the significance of everyday occurrences in being human.

| | |
|---|---|
| *To separate non-independent elements from independent clauses* | Use **commas** |

Leaving behind the stilted and derivative style of writing used in his early chapbooks, Purdy's engaging conversational voice saturated his writings of the 1960s and beyond.

Several of his early books, such as *The Caribou Horses* and *North of Summer,* include lyrics that examine specific Canadian landscapes through direct and personal observation.

*In Search of Owen Roblin,* however, is a book-length poem, uncovering the mythic in the local through an imaginative exploration of the life of an entrepreneurial Ameliasburgh pioneer.

Through the course of his career, which included more than thirty books of poetry and numerous editorials, critical articles, a novel, and other writings, Al Purdy became an architectural force in Canadian literature.

Purdy, who died of cancer at the age of eighty-two, is buried in Ameliasburgh in a cemetery not far from the place where Owen Roblin's mill once stood.

**FIGURE 12.1** *Using Punctuation to Separate Sentence Elements*

## Punctuation Within Sentences: Using Commas

*Commas* are used to set off non-independent elements within sentences. Learn to look at a basic English sentence—with a subject, verb, and completer—as a single structure (an independent clause):

| subject | verb | completer |
|---------|------|-----------|
| Dilip | loves | cleaning the house. |

You do not want to separate the three parts of an independent clause with commas. But when you attach non-independent elements (words, phrases, dependent clauses) to this structure, you need to put in commas.

You can add non-independent attachments in three places: before the independent clause, after the independent clause, and in the middle of the independent clause.

(**before**)  Though it seems odd to most of us, Dilip loves cleaning the
house.

(**after**)  Dilip loves cleaning the house, a preference we find hard to
believe.

(**middle**)  Dilip, who hates to do laundry, loves cleaning the house.

These non-independent additions are usually separated from the independent clause by commas. If you leave the commas out, the reader may be confused or disconcerted, because your punctuation has not marked off where the main (independent) clause begins and ends.

## Using Commas to Set Off Beginning Elements

Put a comma after an introductory word or phrase, a dependent clause, or a long phrase that precedes an independent clause. Dependent clauses, you will remember, contain a subject and a verb but do not make complete sense by themselves. (See page 183 for more information about dependent clauses.)

After a heavy downpour with lightning and high winds, the yard was littered with branches.

Surprisingly, the roof was still intact.

Before going outside, my roommate checked the basement.

Indeed, he found four centimetres of water down there.

Because the electricity had gone out, the sump pump quit working.

Sighing heavily, we got out the wet-vac and went to work.

## Using Commas to Set Off Ending Elements

Put a comma before a word, phrase, or dependent clause tacked on the end of an independent clause.

The counsellor intended to help you, obviously.

Her advice wasn't all that bad, considering the hopelessness of the situation.

Do not be angry with her, whatever you decide to do.

She was completely honest, which suggests she had your best interests at heart.

Dependent clauses that begin with *after, as soon as, before, because, if, since, unless, until,* and *when* are not set off with a comma when they follow an independent clause:

You will feel better after you get a good night's sleep.

But dependent clauses that begin with *although, even though, though,* and *whereas* convey a contrast and are usually set off when they come after an independent clause:

The play seemed to go on for hours, although my watch said it lasted only forty minutes.

## Using Commas to Set Off Elements in the Middle

Put commas before and after a word, phrase, or dependent clause that interrupts the flow of thought in an independent clause.

Honesty, in my opinion, should always be tempered with kindness.

Being totally honest is, after all, sometimes an excuse for being cruel.

Winifred, my friend from school, has taught me a lot about etiquette.

A noncommittal remark may be, it seems, the proper response to questions about personal appearance.

George, taking into account my frame of mind, told me that my swimsuit had beautiful colours.

My swimsuit, which is bright red and flaming orange, does fit a bit tightly.

**TIP!**
**You can use this dropout rule to decide whether to enclose an interrupter in commas.**

In those last two sentences, the interrupters (the parts between commas) could be dropped out of the sentence without changing the overall meaning, like this:

George told me that my swimsuit had beautiful colours.

My swimsuit does fit a bit tightly.

## Using Dashes and Parentheses to Set Off Elements

You can also use dashes or parentheses instead of commas to set off non-independent elements.

A *dash* is a comma with clout. Dashes are used for emphasis or variety—to highlight whatever they set off.

In the twentieth century it has become almost impossible to moralize about epidemics—except those which are transmitted sexually.

—Susan Sontag

The real interest rate—the difference between the nominal rate and the rate of inflation—has averaged about 3 to 4 percent over long periods.

—Milton Friedman

If the interrupting material contains commas, dashes will help make the sentence easier to read:

But when TV is forced upon us, all the things that give it power—intimacy, insularity, intensity—are deadened.

—Jennifer Cowan

*Parentheses* function just the opposite of dashes. (Parentheses downplay whatever they enclose.) Use parentheses to separate material that is indirectly related or less crucial to the main idea in a sentence.

> John Stuart Mill (1806–1873) promoted the idea of women's equality.

> Although Jean-Luc has lapses of memory (often forgetting what he went to the store to buy), he is the best auditor in the company.

## Using Commas to Separate Items in a Series

Put commas between elements in a series—words, phrases, or short parallel clauses. The comma before the final item (usually before the *and*) is now optional, but in certain circumstances, for emphasis or clarity perhaps, you may need to use it.

> The restaurant in the elegant shopping mall specialized in fresh fish, lobster, shrimp, clams and crabs.

> We strolled through the mall, looked at expensive clothes, and admired the fountains.

> Jeanne lusted for a diamond pin, she panted for a crystal vase, she pined for a chiffon gown, but she bought a pair of pre-torn blue jeans.

When writing descriptive modifiers in series, put in a comma only if you could insert the word *and* between the modifiers:

> Jeanne loves fresh, creamy lobster thermidor.

You could easily say "fresh *and* creamy." You could not sensibly say "creamy *and* lobster," though. Nor would you say "lobster *and* thermidor." Consider this one:

> Jeanne bought pre-torn, stonewashed blue jeans.

You could say "pre-torn *and* stonewashed," so the comma is all right. But you cannot reasonably say "stonewashed *and* blue jeans," nor would you say "blue *and* jeans."

## Using Semicolons with Items in a Series

If one or more of the items in a series already includes commas or if the individual items are lengthy, *semicolons* will increase the amount of separation and help the reader sort out the boundaries between items:

> Rich asked me to bring wine, preferably a chablis; baby Swiss cheese; and freshly baked whole wheat rolls.

**T I P !**

**Remember the difference between a hyphen and a dash: hyphens connect, dashes separate.**

On your keyboard, strike two hyphens to make a dash.

**T I P !**

**For variety you can sometimes omit the *and*:**

Some values never go out of style: love, compassion, honesty, caring.

**For emphasis, you can replace the commas with *ands*:**

We could all be more loving and compassionate and honest and caring.

## Using Commas with Dates, Addresses, and Titles

In dates, the year is set off from the rest of the sentence with a pair of commas:

On May 5, 1993, I moved to Alberta.

If you give only the month and year, you do not need to separate them with a comma:

July 2003 was an extremely hot month.

The elements in an address or place name are separated by commas, although a postal code is not preceded by a comma:

My new address will be 3742 Dundas Street, London, Ontario N6G 5K3.

Our aunt in Prince Albert, Saskatchewan, sent us some gold-plated candlesticks.

If a title follows a name, separate it from the rest of the sentence with a pair of commas:

The committee chose Delores Sanchez, lawyer, to represent them.

**TIP!**
Do not write an unclear sentence and depend on a comma to make it intelligible. If in doubt, rewrite the sentence.

## Using Commas to Prevent Confusion

Occasionally you may need to put in a comma simply to make the sentence easier to read:

The main thing to remember is, do not light a match.

Everything that we thought could happen, happened.

Before kicking, a player may want to visualize her target.

### EXERCISE 12.1: COMMAS

Try your hand at putting commas in the following sentences to separate non-independent elements from the independent clause and to separate elements in series.

1. My father who leads a sheltered life took a dim view of my being arrested.
2. My mother however saw the injustice involved.
3. All students who cannot swim must wear life jackets on the canoeing trip.
4. Natasha's cousin who cannot swim has decided to stay home.
5. Date rape after all occurs in a culture that still expects men to be assertive and women to be resistant.
6. Before you complete your plans for vacationing at Lake Louise you should make plane reservations.
7. Reservations which may be submitted either by mail or by phone will be promptly acknowledged.

8. Reservations that are not secured by credit card or cheque will be returned.

9. If you go out please get me some cheese crackers pickles and a case of cola.

10. Anyone who wants the most from a university or college education must study hard.

11. Maureen who was born November 15 1950 in Whistler British Columbia moved to Flin Flon Manitoba before she was old enough to ski.

12. Before getting all excited we should find out if the money is real.

13. Irving cannot seem to pass math although he studies for hours and hours.

14. My cousin Clarice is the tall willowy red-haired girl with the short bow-legged long-haired dog.

15. Robert Frost tells of a minister who turned his daughter his poetry-writing daughter out on the street to earn a living saying there should be no more books written.

# When Not to Use Commas

Remember that commas separate or set off non-independent elements from the rest of the sentence. If you toss in commas whenever you feel the need, you may confuse or mislead your readers. Here are some situations that seem particularly tempting to comma abusers.

1. *When main sentence parts are long*

   Some writers mistakenly separate the subject from the predicate or the predicate from the complement. These are required parts of the independent clause and should not be separated from each other.

   | | |
   |---|---|
   | **(misleading)** | A lively lecture followed by a good discussion, is entertaining, and instructive. |
   | **(clear)** | A lively lecture followed by a good discussion is entertaining and instructive. |
   | **(misleading)** | I was told by several people, that this speaker would be boring. |
   | **(clear)** | I was told by several people that this speaker would be boring. |

   In that second example, the dependent clause serves as the completer of the verb *told* and thus should not be set off with a comma.

2. *When a restrictive clause occurs in the sentence*

   The term *restrictive* means that the modifier is necessary to the meaning of the sentence or is needed to identify the word it modifies.

   | | |
   |---|---|
   | **(restrictive)** | People who compose on word processors can use spell checkers to catch their misspellings. |

In this example, the modifier "who compose on word processors" identifies the subject of the sentence, "people"; it tells us which people are being talked about.

**(nonrestrictive)**   Enrico, who composes on a word processor, is too lazy to use the spell checker.

In this example with the subject identified as *Enrico*, the modifier adds some information but does so without changing the basic meaning of the sentence. Since you could drop the modifier out, you set it off with commas—one before and one after.

3. *When the word* and *appears in the sentence*

Some people always put a comma before the word *and*, and they are probably right more than half the time. It is correct to put a comma before *and* when it joins the last item in a series or when it joins independent clauses. But when *and* does not do either of these things, a comma before it is usually inappropriate.

**(nonstandard)**   His problems with spelling, and his reluctance to proofread make Ned's writing seem illiterate.

**(standard)**   His problems with spelling and his reluctance to proofread make Ned's writing seem illiterate.

4. *When two or more independent clauses should be separate sentences*

Some writers have the habit of linking separate sentences that express independent ideas with commas instead of using periods to create stand-alone sentences. Generally, this creates a run-on sentence known as a comma-splice error.

**(nonstandard)**   Upon his return, Odysseus found his house filled with suitors, every one of the suitors wanted the hand of Penelope and the land of the absent king, he devised a deadly plan.

**(standard)**   Upon his return, Odysseus found his house filled with suitors. Every one of the suitors wanted the hand of Penelope and the land of the absent king. He devised a deadly plan.

**(standard)**   Upon his return, finding his house filled with suitors, every one of whom wanted the hand of Penelope and the land of the absent king, Odysseus devised a deadly plan.

## Punctuation Between Sentences

Most of your writing will consist of multiple independent clauses. To guide your readers through your sentences and paragraphs, you need to mark the places where the independent clauses begin and end. If you do not, your writing will be confusing and difficult to follow.

There are two devices for marking the boundaries of independent clauses: conjunctions and punctuation marks. The rules for using these devices effectively are not complicated, but they offer you several choices that require thought and understanding.

## Using Periods and Other End Marks

A period, question mark, or exclamation mark provides the greatest amount of separation between independent clauses. Each of these marks tells the reader to come to a full stop.

Use a *period* to end sentences that make statements or give mild commands:

Professional tennis players keep their eye on the ball until the point of impact with the raquet.

Keep your head down, and swing through the ball.

Also use a period to close an indirect question, one which reports a question instead of asking it directly:

The players wondered whether the tournament will start on time.

Many parents ask if their children need individual tutoring.

Use a *question mark* to end a direct question. Direct questions often begin with an interrogative word (such as *who, when, what, how, why,* and so forth) and usually have an inverted word order, with the verb in front of the subject.

When will the tournament start?

Does my child need individual tutoring?

Use *exclamation points* to end sentences that express very strong feelings or deserve special emphasis.

There are a lot of bleeding hearts around who just don't like to see people with helmets and guns. All I can say is go and bleed!
—Pierre Elliott Trudeau, October 13, 1970

I'm mad as hell, and I'm not going to take it anymore!
—Paddy Chayefsky, *Network*

But do not use an exclamation point just to punch up an ordinary sentence; instead, write a good emphatic sentence.

**(ineffective)** LeRoy was in a terrible accident!
**(improved)** LeRoy, whose motorcycle collided with a semi on Confederation Bridge, lies near death from head injuries.

**T I P !**

If the independent clauses are short and parallel in structure, separate with commas for stylistic effect.

We shall fight on the beaches, we shall fight on the landing grounds, we shall fight in the fields and in the streets, we shall fight in the hills; we shall never surrender.

—Winston Churchill

## Using Coordinating Conjunctions and Commas

To mark the boundary between two independent clauses, you can use a coordinating conjunction (*and, but, or, nor, for, yet,* and *so*) with a comma before it.

Children's reactions to grief vary, *yet* educators have found a well-defined set of common responses.

Children intuitively know something is wrong, *and* they fill in the gaps with their fantasy thinking.

Educators must pay attention to the warning signs, *for* the key to successful grief counselling is early intervention.

Children at this age are interested in tangible things and want to know the facts about death, *but* they are also interested in causality and want to know why someone has died.

Notice that there are three coordinating conjunctions in that last example, but a comma precedes only one of them. The *ands* connect compound verb phrases ("are interested in *and* want to know"), not independent clauses the way the *but* does. Thus, a comma before a coordinating conjunction signals your readers that another complete sentence is coming up.

If the independent clauses are short and parallel, you can use the coordinating conjunction without the comma:

Adults seek emotional help but children do not.

## Using Semicolons

A *semicolon* functions very much like a period but does not provide as much separation. Thus, you can use a semicolon between two independent clauses that are closely related in thought.

Sebastian Lareau must rethink his strategy; he is losing more games than he's winning.

Perhaps he needs better equipment; a wider racquet and some lightweight tennis shoes might help him.

You should also use a semicolon to separate two independent clauses, even though they appear to be connected with a conjunctive adverb (*therefore, nevertheless, consequently, then, thus, however, indeed, furthermore, besides, otherwise, moreover, hence, meanwhile, instead*).

Practising more might help Sebastian; however, he already practises four hours a day.

He should skip the next tournament; then he and his coach can decide how to improve his game.

For more on conjunctive adverbs, see page 179.

Notice that when independent clauses are connected with a coordinating conjunction *(and, but, or, for, nor, yet, so)*, you do not need a semicolon. A comma is enough.

> Practising more might help Sebastian, but he already practises four hours a day.

> He should skip the next tournament, and he and his coach can then decide how to improve his game.

Both clauses connected by a semicolon should be independent clauses.

> (**nonstandard**)   I thought surely Lareau would win the tournament; although I didn't bet any money on him.
>
> (**standard**)   I thought surely Lareau would win the tournament, although I didn't bet any money on him.
>
> (**standard**)   I thought surely Lareau would win the tournament; I didn't bet any money on him, though.

**T I P !**
Memorize the seven coordinating conjunctions—*and, but, or, for, nor, yet, so*—so that you will not be fooled into mistaking a conjunctive adverb for a coordinating conjunction.

## Using Colons

You can use a *colon* to separate independent clauses, but the colon marks more than a separation. It also signals that an explanation or summary is coming. So use a colon between independent clauses only when the second clause summarizes or explains the first, as these examples demonstrate:

> John Merrick, the Elephant Man, was not a pretty sight: his forehead and the right side of his face were so hideously deformed that he always wore a large bag over his head.

> The students had an inspired idea: they would publish a course guide for next year's class.

If the second clause poses a question, begin with a capital letter:

> Our policy makers should ask themselves this question: Are we doing everything we can to reduce poverty?

You can also use a colon after a single independent clause to call attention to a list or a quotation.

> You will need the following supplies for this course: three camel's hair brushes, one watercolour pad, and ten tubes of paints.

> Oscar Wilde's epigrams are often thought-provoking: "I am not young enough to know everything."

## Marking Sentence Boundaries Clearly

If you run independent clauses together without any punctuation or with only a comma, you may confuse some readers and annoy others. Sentences that are run together with no conjunction or no punctuation are called *fused* or *run-on sentences.* Here is an example:

> **(run-on)** Oubykh is a highly complex language it has eighty-two consonants but only three vowels.

As we noted earlier, sentences that are separated by just a comma are called *comma splices.* A comma alone is not enough to divide independent clauses.

> **(comma splice)** Almost all languages change in one way or another, the written form of Icelandic is a rare exception.

## Using Conjunctive Adverbs and Semicolons

Only coordinating conjunctions—*and, but, or, nor, for, yet, so*—can link two independent clauses with just a comma. If you use another connective word with a comma, you will write a comma splice:

> **(comma splice)** We read our papers aloud first, then we discussed them.

Other connective words—also known as *conjunctive adverbs*—may seem like coordinating conjunctions, but they are not. Figure 12.2 provides a list of the most commonly used conjunctive adverbs.

| | | | |
|---|---|---|---|
| also | however | nevertheless | still |
| besides | indeed | next | then |
| consequently | instead | nonetheless | therefore |
| finally | likewise | otherwise | thus |
| furthermore | meanwhile | similarly | hence |

**FIGURE 12.2** *Commonly Used Conjunctive Adverbs*

One way to tell a conjunctive adverb from a coordinating conjunction is to see if you can reasonably move the word around in the sentence. If you can move it, it is a conjunctive adverb:

> We read the poem first; *then* we analyzed it.

> We read the poem first; we *then* analyzed it.

> We read the poem first; we analyzed it *then.*

If you use a conjunctive adverb between independent clauses, you must put a semicolon in front of it:

> Learning a language is a challenging experience; therefore, a learner must be persistent and hardworking.

Children pick up languages easily; however, the older we get, the harder it becomes to learn a new language.

Many common transitional expressions also act like conjunctive adverbs:

| | | |
|---|---|---|
| as a result | in addition | of course |
| for example | in fact | on the other hand |

You should put a semicolon in front of these expressions when you use them between two independent clauses:

Language acquisition is natural; in fact, every normal human child learns to speak at least one native language.

## Revising Run-Ons and Comma Splices

You can revise these two sentence boundary problems—*run-ons* and *comma splices*—in a number of ways. You have to decide which method fits your writing situation.

1. *Use a semicolon.*

   Oubykh is a highly complex language; it has eighty-two consonants but only three vowels.

2. *Use a period and a capital.*

   Almost all languages change in one way or another. The written form of Icelandic is a rare exception.

3. *Use a comma plus a coordinating conjunction.*

   Oubykh is a highly complex language, for it has eighty-two consonants but only three vowels.

4. *Use a semicolon plus a conjunctive adverb.*

   Almost all languages change in one way or another; however, the written form of Icelandic is a rare exception.

5. *Use subordination to eliminate one independent clause.*

   Although almost all languages change in one way or another, the written form of Icelandic is a rare exception.

### ▨ EXERCISE 12.2: REVISING

Revise any run-ons or comma splices in the following sentences. You may be able to revise them in more than one way.

1. Many people are left-handed, some of them belong to an organization called Left-handers International.

2. Lefthanders International fights discrimination against the left-handed, it informs the public about the special problems of left-handed people.

3. More men than women are left-handed hand preference does not become established until about the age of six.

4. The right side of the brain controls the sense of space, in addition it governs the left side of the body.

5. Left-handed people can drive or sew or paint as well as any right-hander, still it is not easy for them to use many ordinary tools and mechanical gadgets.

6. Stores now sell objects designed especially for left-handed people these include watches, scissors, cameras, and pencil sharpeners.

7. Creativity is not the same thing as intellect, in fact there is no relation between intelligence and originality.

8. Intelligence tests measure knowledge and skill, however they do not accommodate inventiveness.

9. Creative people ask questions intelligent people want to know the answers.

10. Creative scientists have a lot in common with creative artists, they both prefer things to be complex instead of simple.

## EXERCISE 12.3: REVISING

Rewrite the following paragraph; revise the six run-on sentences and comma splices by using the methods described in this chapter.

### WATER SUPPLY

Years ago river water and rain water provided all the water people needed. The farmer working in the fields used river water, the people in the towns used rain water. There was no shortage in the water supply, however, population growth and town development have changed the situation. Nowadays geologists are looking for new underground reserves, engineers are trying to find cheap ways to get drinking water from the salty sea. Newspaper advertisements ask people to save water towns have passed ordinances against watering lawns in the summer, farmers who have no irrigation system fear a dry winter. Townsfolk once disliked the winter rains, they now wait for the clouds that will bring the needed water.

## Recognizing and Revising Sentence Fragments

A *sentence fragment*, as the term suggests, is only part of a sentence but punctuated as if it were a complete sentence. Many accomplished writers use fragments for emphasis, or simply for convenience, as in the portions we have italicized in the following examples:

Man is the only animal that blushes. *Or needs to.*

—Mark Twain

As a rule, more thought goes into the purchase of a stereo than a tattoo. *With predictable results.*

—John Gray

If there is to be a new etiquette, it ought to be based on honesty, mutual respect and responsiveness to each other's real needs. *Regardless of sex.*

—Lois Gould

Although professional writers sometimes use grammatically incomplete sentences for emphasis and variety, the writing you do in college or university and in business should be in complete sentences. To make sure you are not writing sentence fragments, you first need to be able to recognize a complete sentence. Then, you need to know how to revise the fragments.

## Recognizing a Complete Sentence

A group of words must meet three grammatical tests to be a complete sentence:

1. It must contain a subject.

2. It must contain a predicate.

3. It must contain at least one clause that does not begin with a subordinating word.

Groups of words that do not pass all three tests are fragments and need to be revised.

There is one exception: the subject of a sentence can be implied, as often happens in sentences that are commands. For example, you might say to your dog, "Sit." This is a complete sentence, in that the bare predicate is "sit" and the subject, although it is not actually written down, is the implied "you."

**SUBJECTS AND PREDICATES** Look at the following examples, and notice the difference between the ones that contain a subject and a predicate (the sentences) and the ones that do not (the fragments). Subjects are underlined once and bare predicates are double underlined.

(sentence)  My <u>uncle</u> in Quebec <u>has</u> <u>worked</u> in a nickel-copper mine most of his life.

(fragment)  My uncle in Quebec.

(sentence)  This <u>mine</u> in Quebec <u>produces</u> some of the highest grade nickel-copper concentrate in the world.

(fragment)  Produces some of the highest grade nickel-copper concentrate in the world.

**DEPENDENT CLAUSES** Some groups of words may contain a subject and a predicate but do not pass the third test for grammatical

**T I P !**

A clause is a group of words that has a subject and a predicate. Subordinating words—such as *if, when, although, who, which, that*—turn independent clauses into dependent fragments.

completeness: they need at least one clause that does not begin with a subordinating word. Look at the following examples to see the difference:

**(fragment)** When I was twelve years old.
**(sentence)** I started mining when I was twelve years old.

**(fragment)** Who worked here forty years ago or more.
**(sentence)** On the walls I can read the names of miners who worked here forty years ago or more.

**(fragment)** Although mining may not be the easiest job in the world.
**(sentence)** Although mining may not be the easiest job in the world, I do not think it is dangerous.

**(fragment)** Because the mine is never too hot or too cold.
**(sentence)** I like working underground because the mine is never too hot or too cold.

Word groups that begin with a subordinating word are fragments because they *depend* on another statement to complete the thought. *When I was twelve years old* leaves the reader hanging, expecting to find out what happened when the writer was twelve years old. These word groups are called *dependent clauses*. Unlike independent clauses, which can stand alone as sentences, dependent clauses do not make complete sense by themselves. Figure 12.3 gives you a list of words that begin dependent clauses. Whenever you begin a sentence with one of these words, be sure to attach it to another clause so that the whole thought sounds complete.

| | | |
|---|---|---|
| after | in order that | when, whenever |
| although | once | where, wherever |
| as | since | whereas |
| as if | so that | whether |
| because | than | which |
| before | that | while |
| even though | though | who, whom, whose |
| ever since | unless | whoever |
| how | until | why |
| if, even if | what, whatever | |

**FIGURE 12.3 *Subordinating Words***

**VERBAL PHRASE FRAGMENTS** Some groups of words that appear to be grammatically complete may be verbal phrases. These fragments usually begin with a word that looks and sounds like a verb but is not. Some words ending in *-ing* (*working, repairing, using*) or with *to* in front of them (*to love, to produce*) name actions but are not complete verbs. Notice the differences in the following examples (subjects are underlined once and bare predicates are double underlined):

**(verbal phrase)**  Working underground for eighteen months.
  **(sentence)**  <u>Daniel Flores</u> from Argentina <u>has</u> <u>been</u> working underground for eighteen months.

**(verbal phrase)**  To love his job in the mine.
  **(sentence)**  <u>He</u> <u>seems</u> to love his job in the mine.

**(verbal phrase)**  Repairing machinery in the mine.
  **(sentence)**  <u>Richard Vreeland</u> <u>has</u> <u>worked</u> for five years repairing machinery in the mine.

**(verbal phrase)**  Using modern machinery.
**(verbal phrase)**  To produce the richest zinc ore in the world.
  **(sentence)**  The <u>miners</u> <u>work</u> nearly 2000 feet under the ground, using modern machinery to produce the highest-grade concentrate in the world.

## Revising Sentence Fragments

In general, you can revise a fragment by combining it with an independent clause or by turning it into an independent clause. The following examples will show you how to eliminate sentence fragments from your writing:

1. A group of words that lacks a subject or verb can often be joined to the independent clause that comes before or after it, like this:

   **(fragment)**  A steeplejack paints and fixes church roofs, clocks, and steeples. *The highest parts of tall church buildings.*
   **(revised)**  A steeplejack paints and fixes church roofs, clocks, and steeples—the highest parts of tall church buildings.

   **(fragment)**  *The entire O'Neil family, Jerry O'Neil, his wife Beverly and their two sons and the sons' wives.* They all work as steeplejacks.
   **(revised)**  The entire O'Neil family, Jerry O'Neil and his wife Beverly and their two sons and the sons' wives, all work as steeplejacks.

2. Dependent clauses can be attached to a nearby independent clause or rewritten as complete sentences:

   **(fragment)**  *Because many old church buildings became damaged by wind and water.* Their roofs began to leak, the paint peeled, and the decorations wore off.
   **(revised)**  Because many old church buildings became damaged by wind and water, their roofs began to leak, the paint peeled, and the decorations wore off.

**(fragment)**    The church members then decided to hire someone to make repairs. *Which can be very expensive.*

**(revised)**    The church members then decided to hire someone to make repairs, which can be very expensive.

**(revised)**    The church members then decided to hire someone to make repairs. Such work can be very expensive.

3.  Verbal phrases can be combined with an independent clause or turned into separate sentences:

**(fragment)**    The O'Neils enjoy working together. *Travelling around the country. Finding jobs as they go.*

**(revised)**    The O'Neils enjoy working together, travelling around the country and finding jobs as they go.

**(revised)**    The O'Neils enjoy working together. They travel around the country, finding jobs as they go.

### EXERCISE 12.4: REVISING

Rewrite the following paragraphs, correcting any fragments that you find. The first one has three fragments in it.

> **T I P !**
>
> **It is acceptable to use fragments in asking and answering questions, even in formal writing.**
>
> When should the reform begin? At once.
>
> How? By removing self-serving politicians from office.

**1.**    Next year I am going to cooking school. I got the idea from a friend of my brother's. A business manager for a cruise line. He said that cruise ships build their reputations on the meals they serve. Which must be superbly prepared and elegantly presented. Consequently, cruise lines are always looking for chefs. Trying to find people who are well trained as expert cooks.

**2.**    There are many ways to exercise and have fun at the same time. Such as, swimming, hiking, or playing tennis. But some people are exercise puritans. Insisting that exercise must be serious and painful. My next door neighbour, for example, makes fun of me because I prefer walking to jogging. But I walk several kilometres every day. While he jogs only once or twice a week. I figure that exercise is not going to help if a person does not do it regularly. So why not find something enjoyable to do?

**3.**    To do their work, steeplejacks have to sit on seats that hang down from ropes. Attached to the very tops of the church steeples. If you watch them at work, you can see them. Swinging gently in midair. While they repair a roof. Or replace the old numbers on a church clock. With newly painted ones. Would you have the nerve to do that kind of work? Probably not. Most people would not.

# Coping with Apostrophes

*Apostrophes* probably cause more problems than any other mark of punctuation. Even experienced writers sometimes feel uncertain about their use. If you study carefully the various uses of the apostrophe, you should be able to straighten them out.

**1.** *Use an apostrophe plus* s *with singular nouns to show possession.*

| | |
|---|---|
| the length of the rope | the rope's length |
| the star of the show | the show's star |
| a lease of one year | a year's lease |

As you can see from the above examples, the *'s* ending is a substitute for a phrase beginning with *of* that shows possession.

**2.** *Do not use an apostrophe to form the plural of a noun.*

You may have problems with the apostrophe plus *s* ending because the letter *s* gets pressed into service in a number of ways. Its most common use is to show that a noun is plural (more than one of whatever the noun names). No apostrophe is needed:

three professors
two encyclopedias
two athletes

**3.** *Use an apostrophe with plurals that are possessive.*

three professors' letters of recommendation
two encyclopedias' different interpretations
two athletes' difficulties with drugs

You do not need another *s* after the apostrophe in the above examples because it cannot be pronounced aloud.

In deciding where to place an apostrophe to show possession with plural nouns, first write down the plural form. Then add just an apostrophe to those plurals ending in *s*.

| Singular | Plural | Plural Possessive |
|---|---|---|
| lady | ladies | ladies' lunch |
| society | societies | societies' problems |
| bartender | bartenders | bartenders' tips |

But if the plural does *not* end in *s,* then you have to add an apostrophe plus *s:*

| | | |
|---|---|---|
| child | children | children's clothes |
| man | men | men's fashions |

4. *Use an apostrophe plus* s *with singular nouns ending in* s.

| | |
|---|---|
| the boss's daughter | Janis's singing |
| Keats's poetry | the albatross's curse |

If pronouncing the added 's would be awkward, some writers use only the apostrophe. Either use is acceptable.

| | |
|---|---|
| Jesus' teachings | Jesus's teachings |
| Socrates' death | Socrates's death |

5. *Do not use an apostrophe with any of the possessive pronouns.*

You will not even be tempted to use an apostrophe with most of the possessive pronouns—*his, hers, theirs, ours, yours.* But one of these pronouns—*its*—causes considerable grief because it gets confused with the contraction *it's,* which, of course, means *it is.* Notice the difference:

That dog just bit *its* kindly owner.
*It's* an ungrateful beast.

6. *Use an apostrophe to show omissions in contractions and numbers.*

The apostrophe goes where the letters are left out, not where the two words are joined.

does not = doesn't (not *does'nt*)
will not = won't (not *wo'nt*)
would not = wouldn't (not *would'nt*)
class of 1975 = class of '75

7. *If you wish, use an apostrophe in forming the plural of numerals, letters, words used as words, and abbreviations.*

Your 5's look like 8's to me.
This paragraph has three *very*'s in it.
Her last name contains three m's.
The 1960's were years of great social change.
He claims to have three Ph.D.'s.

You may also correctly add the *s* with no apostrophe.

> Your 5s look like 8s to me.
> The 1960s were years of great social change.

## ▮ EXERCISE 12.5: APOSTROPHES

Copy the following sentences, inserting an apostrophe or an apostrophe plus s as needed.

1. Many adults distrust of computers stems from a lack of understanding the way that the machines function.
2. Childrens love of computers may indicate that they are not concerned with the machines internal workings.
3. Grade school teachers are often surprised by their students achievements on computers.
4. One students accomplishments were the main topic of talk in the teachers lounge.
5. Students attendance improves when they are allowed to do assignments in class on computers.
6. When he was given a computer, James attitude changed completely, greatly to his mothers surprise.
7. "For goodness sake," his mother exclaimed. "I used to question James intelligence."
8. Many of societys problems have been eased by computer use.
9. But the computers usefulness is offset by problems caused by programmers mistakes.
10. A computers mistake can ruin a persons credit, for instance.

## ▮ EXERCISE 12.6: *ITS* OR *IT'S*

Using *its* or *it's*, fill in the blanks in the following sentences with the correct form.

1. The army forces _____ recruits to do aerobic exercise.
2. Undoubtedly _____ a good idea to keep the soldiers fit.
3. The military needs _____ forces in fighting shape.
4. To gain _____ full benefits, exercise must be performed strenuously.
5. In order to exercise regularly, _____ helpful to have a "drill sergeant" force you.

# Punctuating Quotations

If you want to report the actual words that someone has spoken or written, you need to enclose those words in *quotation marks*. It is customary to use a *reporting tag* to identify the person being quoted: "she said" or "he replied" or "Darwin observed" or some such phrase. For variety, these reporting tags can appear at the beginning, in the middle, or at the end of the quoted material.

## Identifying Quotations at the Beginning

Put a comma after the reporting tag and before the opening quotation marks:

> Samuel Johnson observed, "Marriage has many pains, but celibacy has no pleasures."

If you quote a full sentence, capitalize the first word in that sentence, unless it blends into the sentence that introduces it:

> In his essay on punctuation Lewis Thomas writes, "The commas are the most useful and usable of all the stops."

> It is Thomas's opinion that "exclamation points are the most irritating of all."

## Punctuating the Ends of Quotations

If the quotation ends the sentence, put a period, a question mark, an exclamation mark, or a dash before the final quotation marks:

> The mayor announced, "Our landfills are completely full."
> The city manager asked, "What are we going to do?"
> A concerned citizen shouted, "We *must* begin recycling!"

> One board member smugly observed, "I'm recycling already, but you folks—"

The dash in this last example indicates that the speaker stopped in mid-sentence—or was interrupted.

If a question mark or an exclamation mark belongs to the whole sentence, not just to the quoted material, put this mark after the closing quotation marks:

> Did the mayor actually say, "Let's postpone this issue"?

> I could not believe that the mayor said to the council, "Let's table this recycling business tonight"!

If you are not reporting the exact words that were spoken, you do not need quotation marks:

> Did the mayor actually want to postpone recycling?

> He told the city council he wanted to table the recycling proposal.

## Identifying Quotations in the Middle

If your reporting tag interrupts a sentence, set it off with commas:

> "I hope," sniffed the mayor, "that we can remain civil about this matter."

If a complete sentence comes before the reporting tag, put a period after the reporting tag and capitalize the first word of the rest of the quoted material:

> "You cretin!" shouted the concerned citizen. "Can't you see that this is a pressing issue?"

> "What do you mean?" asked the mayor. "I don't feel any great need for haste."

If the reporting tag is placed between two independent clauses that are separated by a semicolon, the semicolon follows the tag:

> "Everyone needs to calm down," pleaded the city manager; "we must try to discuss this issue rationally."

## Identifying Quotations at the End

If the quoted sentence would ordinarily end in a period, put a comma before the quotation marks:

> "We must come to some decision tonight," said the city manager.

But use a question mark or an exclamation mark when it is appropriate:

> "Why do we have to decide tonight?" the mayor asked.

> "Because time is running out!" yelled the manager.

In these cases, do not add a comma as well.

## Punctuating Dialogue

When you are writing dialogue or reporting a conversation, you should start a new paragraph when there is a change in speaker, no matter how brief the quoted remarks may be:

> "I saw you listening to those two little creeps," she hissed. "Were they talking about me?"
> "I don't know," I said.
> "You don't know! Why not?"
> "They were speaking Spanish."

## Quoting Within Quotations

When you need to put quotation marks around material that is *already* inside quotation marks, use single quotation marks around the material inside.

> Jim whispered, "I think I heard one of them say, 'We launch the attack as soon as it gets dark.'"

Notice that both single and double quotation marks go outside the period.

## Using Quotation Marks to Punctuate Titles

Put quotation marks around the titles of short works—such as the titles of short stories and poems that are usually part of a longer work like a book or magazine:

"A Cap for Steve"—a short story by Morley Callaghan

"We Real Cool"—a poem by Gwendolyn Brooks

"Not Poor, Just Broke"—an essay by Dick Gregory

"Your Reflex Systems"—a chapter in a book by Jonathan Miller

### EXERCISE 12.7: QUOTATION MARKS

Copy the following paragraphs, inserting quotation marks in the appropriate places.

Motherhood is not for every woman, moaned Michelle, as she wiped up the milk. Why doesn't anyone ever tell you that having children can be hazardous to your health?

Do you mean your mental health? inquired her friend Laverne, who was holding the dripping Billy at arm's length.

That too! snapped Michelle, stripping off the milk-soaked T-shirt. This makes the third time today I've changed Billy's clothes. And it's not even afternoon yet!

But he's so cute, observed Maureen, glancing at the grinning Billy who was already planning more mischief. Isn't he your pride and joy?

Maybe, if I live through his childhood, sighed Billy's mother, I may be able to see some profit in this venture. But right now I agree with Roseanne: When my husband comes home at night, if those kids are still alive—I've done my job.

# Using Italics (Underlining)

Italic type slants upward to the right. We use *italics* to set off words and phrases for emphasis or special consideration. In handwritten or typed papers, you underline material that would be italicized if set in type.

## Italicizing Titles and Names

We generally italicize (or underline) the titles of long or complete works. Figure 12.4 gives you a list of examples of titles to italicize.

The titles of sacred books, such as the Bible or the Koran, and of public documents, like the Charter of Rights and Freedoms or the Constitution, are not italicized or underlined. The titles of shorter works—such as poems, short stories, songs, essays, and the titles of specific television episodes—are enclosed in quotation marks: "In Flanders Fields," "Girls and Boys," "The Wreck of the *Edmund Fitzgerald*," "St. Urbain Street Then and Now." The same is true for sections of works, such as chapter titles ("The Rise of the Middle Class") or titles of magazine articles ("An Interview with Adrienne Clarkson").

| **Books** | **Long Poems** |
|---|---|
| *The Dance of the Happy Shades* | *The Odyssey* |
| *The Internet for Dummies* | *In Memoriam* |
| **Plays** | **Films** |
| *Letter from Wingfield Farm* | *The Sweet Hereafter* |
| *A Midsummer Night's Dream* | *Citizen Kane* |
| **Long Musical Works** | **Paintings and Sculptures** |
| Gershwin's *Rhapsody in Blue* | Rodin's *The Thinker* |
| The Beatles' *Abbey Road* | the *Mona Lisa* |
| **Television and Radio Programs** | **Magazines and Newspapers** |
| *Da Vinci's Inquest* | the *St. John's Telegram* |
| *As It Happens* | *Saturday Night* |

**FIGURE 12.4** *Titles to Italicize*

## Italicizing Words and Phrases

We italicize (underline) foreign words and phrases that have not yet been adopted into English:

> Standing *en pointe* is useful only if the candy bars are on the top shelf.

Words and phrases used so frequently that they have become part of the English language—for example, "pasta," "bon voyage," "habeas corpus," and "karate"—do not need to be italicized or underlined. Most dictionaries will tell you whether the words you want to use should be marked for italics or underlined.

We also italicize (or underline) words, letters, or numbers referred to as words:

> In current usage, the pronouns *he*, *him*, and *his* outnumber *she*, *her*, and *hers* by a ratio of almost 4 to 1.

> Some people have trouble pronouncing the letter *r*, especially when it follows an *i* or an *a*.

## Using Italics for Emphasis

Italics (or underlining) can add emphasis to written language:

> We want our freedom *today*, not tomorrow.

But this means of adding emphasis is obvious and easy to overdo. It is usually more effective to create emphasis through sentence structure and word choice.

## Using Hyphens

1. Use a *hyphen* to connect two or more words that go together to modify a noun.

   | | |
   |---|---|
   | hard-hearted lover | up-to-date sources |
   | lighter-than-air balloon | world-renowned pianist |

   Do not hyphenate the modifiers when they come after the noun.

   | | |
   |---|---|
   | lover with a hard heart | sources that are up to date |
   | balloon lighter than air | pianist who is world renowned |

   Do not use a hyphen between an *-ly* adverb and the word it modifies:

   | | |
   |---|---|
   | a hopelessly dull person | a happily divorced couple |

2. Use a hyphen to connect *all-*, *self-*, *ex-*, and *-elect* to other words.

   | | | | |
   |---|---|---|---|
   | self-esteem | ex-wife | all-important | mayor-elect |

   Never use a hyphen with the following words:

   | | | |
   |---|---|---|
   | yourself | himself | itself |
   | themselves | herself | oneself |
   | ourselves | myself | selfless |

3. Use a hyphen when spelling out fractions and compound numbers from twenty-one to ninety-nine.

   People over fifty-five make up almost two-fifths of the population.

4. Use a hyphen to avoid ambiguous or awkward combinations of letters. For instance, *re-creation* means "create anew"; the hyphen distinguishes it from *recreation*, which means "a refreshing or diverting activity." Words like *anti-inflammatory*, *cross-stitch*, and *bell-like* are easier to read with the hyphens.

5. Consult a dictionary about compound words: some are two words, some are hyphenated, some are written as a single word. Usage changes rapidly and is unpredictable. Even compounds that begin with the same word are treated differently: *blue cheese, blue-collar, blueprint.*

6. Use a hyphen to divide a word at the end of a line of type. Words can be divided only between syllables. Consult your dictionary when in doubt. The tendency today is to *avoid* dividing words if at all possible.

## ■ EXERCISE 12.8: PUNCTUATION

Punctuate each of the following passages. First punctuate for meaning; then, if necessary, refer to the rules.

**1.** Matthew was not looking at her and would not have seen what she was really like if he had been but an ordinary observer would have seen this a child of about eleven garbed in a very short very tight very ugly dress of yellowish gray wincey she wore a faded brown sailor hat and beneath the hat extending down her back were two braids of very thick decidedly red hair her face was small white and thin also much freckled her mouth was large and so were her eyes that looked green in some lights and moods and gray in others

—L. M. Montgomery, *Anne of Green Gables*

**2.** robert jordan was climbing down into the framework of the bridge the girders were cold and wet with dew under his hands and he climbed carefully feeling the sun on his back bracing himself in a bridge truss hearing the noise of the tumbling water below him hearing firing too much firing up the road at the upper post.

—Ernest Hemingway, *For Whom the Bell Tolls*

**3.** above all things a hun must be loyal disagreement is not necessarily disloyalty a hun who in the best interest of the tribe disagrees should be listened to on the other hand a hun who actively participates in or encourages actions that are counter to the good of the tribe is disloyal these huns whether warrior or chieftain must be expeditiously removed their ability to influence and discourage loyal huns is a contagious disease in cases where disloyal actions and attitudes cannot be changed harsh action must be taken to rid ourselves of those among us who see no value in and subvert our cause

—Attila the Hun, *Leadership Secrets of Attila the Hun* (Wess Roberts)

**4.** i told some of you last Thursday of the principle of the time machine and showed you the actual thing itself incomplete in the workshop there it is now a little travel worn truly and one of the ivory bars is cracked and a brass rail bent but the rest of its sound enough i expected to finish it on Friday but on Friday when the putting together was nearly done i found that one of the nickel bars was exactly one inch too short and this i had to get remade so that the thing was not complete until this morning it was at ten o'clock to-day that the first of all time machines began its career i gave it a last tap tried all the screws again put one more drop of oil on the quartz rod and sat myself in the saddle i suppose a suicide who holds a pistol to his skull feels much the same wonder at what will come next as i felt then i took the starting lever in one hand and the stopping one in the other pressed the first and almost immediately the second i seemed to reel i felt a nightmare sensation of falling and looking round i saw the laboratory exactly as before had anything happened for a moment i suspected that my intellect had tricked me then i noted the clock a moment before as it seemed it had stood at a minute or so past ten now it was nearly half-past three

—H. G. Wells, *The Time Machine*

**5.** where are you john asked his sister it is very dark in here

**6.** i interviewed him before the fatal accident the reporter said and he joked i am very careful driving on city streets is more dangerous than racing i cannot believe that he is gone.

# Working with Verbs

You probably remember from somewhere back in high school that subjects have to agree with their verbs, or bare predicates, in *number*, meaning a singular subject takes a singular verb and a plural subject takes a plural verb. You also need to watch out for irregular verbs. Most of the time getting your verbs right is easy, but complications can occur.

## Getting Subjects and Predicates to Agree

When the Bible declares that "The wages of sin is death," believers are not supposed to question—either grammatically or theologically. But if you write "The wages at McDonald's is lousy," you will likely get corrected by someone saying your subject–verb agreement is off. There is no point in protesting the inequity of this double standard. Just grant poetic licence to the Bible and concentrate on making your own subjects and verbs agree.

### Singular Verb Forms

In English the only singular verb form occurs in the present tense. We add an *-s* or *-es* ending to a present-tense verb when its subject is a singular noun or the pronoun *he, she,* or *it.*

> Our biology <u>instructor</u> <u>wants</u> us to write three lab reports a week. <u>She</u> <u>expects</u> them to be handed in on Friday.

> My <u>roommate</u> <u>washes</u> his hair twice a day. <u>He</u> <u>flosses</u> his teeth after every meal.

> That <u>colour</u> <u>looks</u> good on you; <u>it</u> <u>matches</u> your eyes.

Two verbs—*have* and *be*—are exceptions to this rule. *Have* changes to *has,* and *be* changes to *is.*

> My <u>uncle</u> <u>has</u> false teeth.

> <u>He</u> <u>is</u> only thirty-five years old.

*Be* is the only verb that has a singular form in the past tense. Use *was* with *I,* with singular nouns, or with *he, she,* or *it.*

> <u>I</u> <u>was</u> late for class yesterday.

> My <u>teacher</u> <u>was</u> not happy with me.

Otherwise, use *were.*

> The other <u>students</u> <u>were</u> all on time.

Most of the time subject–predicate agreement poses no problem. With a plural subject *(wages)*, supply a plural verb *(are)*, and everybody's happy:

The <u>wages</u> at McDonald's <u>are</u> lousy.

Only it is not always that simple because we do not always use the normal *subject-followed-by-verb* sentence pattern. In this chapter, we will explain a few of the less-than-simple situations. For variety, we shuffle the order around so that sometimes the bare predicate gets ahead of the subject—or sometimes modifiers crop up between the subject and the predicate, causing confusion. Another construction you need to watch out for involves *expletives,* words that often pose alluringly like subjects, even though they are not. (See Chapter 11 for more on expletives.) You also have to be alert for collective nouns and indefinite pronouns, which can sometimes lead to agreement problems.

## Subject–Predicate Reversals in Questions

You naturally expect one of the first words in a sentence to be the *subject*—what the sentence is about. Usually the *bare predicate* follows, telling what is going on with the subject or what the situation is, like this:

These <u>papayas</u> <u>taste</u> delicious.

But questions often reverse this normal order:

Where <u>are</u> the <u>papayas</u>?

As you can see, the reversal will not necessarily make sense. But the real subject becomes clear—*papayas* (plural)—so the bare predicate should be *are* (plural). No problem.

The going sometimes gets tricky when the questions get longer, like this:

> **(wrong)** Which version of the ending has the show's producers decided to use?

If you turn that into a statement, you can see that the agreement is off:

> **(wrong)** The show's producers has decided to use which version of the ending.

Since the subject—*producers*—clearly is plural, you need a plural bare predicate:

> The show's producers <u>have</u> decided to use which version of the ending.
>
> **(right)** Which version of the ending <u>have</u> the show's producers decided to use?

If you have difficulty with agreement in questions, get into the habit of quickly changing them into statements as part of your editing process. Once you get the subject and verb in the normal order, you are not likely to go wrong.

**T I P !**

**To find the subject, turn the question into a statement.**

If you can make a statement out of a question, you will usually end up with the subject at the beginning of the sentence:

The <u>papayas</u> <u>are</u> where.

## Subject–Bare Predicate Reversals for Style

Sometimes you may deliberately put a predicate ahead of its subject as a stylistic device. If not overdone, this technique can be effective. The variation from the expected sentence pattern automatically produces emphasis:

> **(wrong)**  In poverty, injustice, and discrimination lie the cause of many social problems.

But just glance at that sentence again. What is the subject? Not *poverty, injustice, and discrimination*: those words are the object of the preposition *in*. Since a noun cannot serve as the subject *and* as an object in the same sentence, you need to look elsewhere. The subject actually is *cause*—and *the cause lie* does not sound right. It should be *the cause lies* or *the causes lie.* You could change either word, but both words have to be singular or both plural to make subjects and predicates agree.

> **(right)**  In poverty, injustice, and discrimination lies the cause of many social problems.

> **(right)**  In poverty, injustice, and discrimination lie the causes of many social problems.

Of course, we know that most people probably would not be much bothered by the lack of agreement in that sentence. But see if you pick up the problem in this less complex construction:

**(wrong)**     Here comes the defending champions.

Of course it should be

**(right)**     Here <u>come</u> the defending <u>champions</u>.

**(right)**     There <u>are</u> a few <u>flaws</u> in your plan.

**(right)**     Here <u>is</u> a small <u>case</u> of larceny.

> **T I P !**
>
> ***Here* and *there* can never be subjects.**
>
> If a sentence begins with either of those words, turn it around, find the true subject, and make the bare predicate agree.

## Agreement with Intervening Modifiers

Sometimes even when the subject–bare predicate order is normal, a modifier gets sandwiched between them and confuses things, like this:

> **(wrong)** The seriousness of these injustices have been revealed to the public.

*Injustices have been revealed* sounds fine, but the subject of that sentence happens to be *seriousness*, with *injustices* serving as the object of the preposition *of* (which means that it cannot also be the subject). So, how does *The seriousness have been revealed* sound? Not good, since *seriousness* is clearly singular. The sentence should read

> **(right)** The <u>seriousness</u> of these injustices <u>has</u> <u>been</u> <u>revealed</u> to the public.

Because this problem will not be revealed by simply turning the sentence around, let us look at a few more examples. You have to recognize the intervening modifiers and take them out in order to get the subject and bare predicate next to each other. Try this sentence:

> (**wrong**) The boredom of dusting furniture, folding laundry, cleaning floors, cooking meals, and washing dishes have driven many women to drink.

The sentence does not sound bad, does it? But actually all those plural-sounding tasks are objects of the preposition *of.* The true subject is quite singular—*boredom.* The sentence should read

> (**right**) The <u>boredom</u> of dusting furniture, folding laundry, cleaning floors, cooking meals, and washing dishes <u>has</u> <u>driven</u> many women to drink.

Here is one more:

> (**wrong**) Ling's reasons for developing his gymnastics style was essentially the same as Jahn's—to promote nationalism.

*Style was* sounds fine. But *style* is not the subject. It is the object of the gerund *developing*; the subject is *reasons.* So, *reasons was* cannot be right. The verb needs to be plural:

> (**right**) Ling's <u>reasons</u> for developing his gymnastics style <u>were</u> essentially the same as Jahn's—to promote nationalism.

## Agreement with Compound Subjects

Sentences having *compound subjects* (meaning more than one subject) usually cause no bother. With singular compound subjects connected by *and*, you can apply simple arithmetic:

> The <u>pitcher</u> and the <u>catcher</u> <u>are</u> both fine players.

*Pitcher + catcher* = two people = plural subject requiring plural verb. But matters can get more complicated:

1. *When you have more than one singular subject connected with* but, or, *or* nor

   These subjects take singular verbs, even though the idea expressed may be quite plural:

   > Not only the pitcher <u>but</u> the catcher also <u>is</u> tired.

   Both are tired, but the verb arbitrarily should be singular. If you use *nor*, the agreement is at least a bit more logical:

   > Neither the pitcher <u>nor</u> the catcher <u>is</u> <u>playing</u> well.

   Both are still tired but neither one is playing well.

2. *When you have one singular and one plural subject*

The verb agrees with the one that is closest:

Champagne or sad <u>movies</u> <u>remind</u> me of you. Sad movies or <u>champagne</u> <u>reminds</u> me of you.

3. *When you have subjects that sound plural but really are not*

Singular subjects followed by any of these terms remain singular:

| | | |
|---|---|---|
| with | like | along with |
| besides | including | together with |
| as well as | namely | no less than |

The meaning of the sentence may be distinctly plural but the subject is still grammatically singular:

The owner of the Flames, as well as the general manager, is responsible for that trade.

Obviously, two people are responsible, but the verb remains faithful to the singular subject. This next example is more logical:

Seymour, together with his St. Bernard, his pet alligator, and his seventeen goldfish, is planning to move in with us.

Although the group moving in is incontestably plural, only Seymour is doing the planning. As you can see, commas often set off these constructions, giving you a good clue that the subject remains separate.

4. *When you have a compound subject that names one person, thing, or idea*

Some ideas that are joined to form compounds as a whole refer to one thing; for example, *bread and butter, strawberries and cream, gin and tonic.* Each of these is actually a single food or drink. With such compounds, use a singular verb:

Bread and water is the traditional diet of the prisoner.

The secretary and treasurer of the lodge is a two-year appointment.

## The Expletive *There*

Although an indispensable little word, the expletive *there* causes more than its share of bother. As we noted in Chapter 11, an *expletive* is a filler word that often stands at the beginning of a sentence, looking for all the world like the subject, when actually it is nothing of the kind. It is just taking up space until the real subject comes along. The word *there* is either an expletive or an adverb. You need to find out what the subject really is before sliding in a verb.

**(wrong)** There is among all the weeds in my garden several exquisite begonias.

The actual subject is *begonias*:

    **(right)**  There <u>are</u> among all the weeds in my garden several exquisite <u>begonias</u>.

**EXPLETIVES IN QUESTIONS.** Do not forget that *there* can complicate questions as well as statements (and *there* will not necessarily be the very first word, either):

    **(wrong)**  Is there in this line of work many opportunities for advancement?

Ask yourself, *what* is? Answer: *opportunities is.* But *opportunities* always *are,* so the verb needs changing. Or you can make those *opportunities* singular and write the sentence that way.

    **(right)**   <u>Are</u> there in this line of work many <u>opportunities</u> for advancement?

    **(right)**   <u>Is</u> there in this line of work any <u>opportunity</u> for advancement?

## Collective Nouns and Indefinite Pronouns

*Collective nouns,* which name a group or a collection of people, usually are considered singular:

Theodore's <u>family</u> <u>is</u> quite small.

Our school <u>orchestra</u> <u>plays</u> extremely well.

The <u>audience</u> <u>was</u> <u>clapping</u> wildly.

Sometimes, if the members of the group are acting as individuals, a plural verb is used to indicate that the group is not considered a single unit:

The curriculum <u>committee</u> <u>disagree</u> on every issue.

Our old <u>gang</u> <u>have</u> <u>gone</u> their separate ways.

Even when a plural verb is used correctly with a collective noun, it may not sound correct. Some writers add a clearly plural noun, like *members,* to underscore the notion of individuality that the sentence is supposed to convey.

Some <u>members</u> of the curriculum committee <u>disagree</u> on every issue.

All the <u>members</u> of our old gang <u>have</u> <u>gone</u> their separate ways.

Several collective nouns (like *rest, remainder,* and *number*) and some *indefinite pronouns* (*some, all, enough, neither,* and *none*) can be either singular or plural, depending on how they are used:

    **(singular)**  The <u>rest</u> of the movie <u>is</u> sloppy and sentimental.
      **(plural)**  The <u>rest</u> of us <u>are</u> leaving.

    **(singular)**  <u>Some</u> of the pizza <u>has</u> anchovies on it.
      **(plural)**  <u>Some</u> of players <u>are</u> already on the bus.

    **(singular)**  <u>All</u> of the pizza <u>is</u> stone cold by now.
      **(plural)**  <u>All</u> of the seats <u>are</u> taken.

**T I P !**

**When referring to *a number,* use a plural verb; when referring to *the number,* use a singular verb.**

A <u>number</u> of students <u>are</u> ill; <u>the number</u> <u>is</u> getting larger every day.

**T I P !**

Be warned that some writers and educators insist that *none* should always be singular.

When the indefinite pronoun *none* is used alone, it takes a singular verb:

(singular)   None <u>is</u> immune to this disease.

But when followed by phrases with a plural meaning, usage varies:

(plural)   None of us <u>are</u> ever going to eat there again.

(singular)   None of us <u>is</u> sick today, at least.

The rest of the indefinite pronouns are singular and cause little trouble with verbs: *anyone, something, any, anybody, each, either, neither, everybody, everyone, everything, nobody, no one, somebody, someone.*

<u>Anyone</u> <u>is</u> <u>allowed</u> to attend.

<u>Everything</u> <u>seems</u> in order.

<u>Somebody</u> <u>is</u> <u>pounding</u> on the door.

### EXERCISE 13.1: AGREEMENT

Revise any of these sentences whose subjects and bare predicates do not agree. Some may be correct.

1. A child's personality and behaviour is influenced to a great extent by environment.
2. In this new stage of our relationship comes new adjustments.
3. There has never been any concerted attempts to solve the mystery.
4. Financial support, like volunteer workers and effective speakers, are hard to get.
5. Movies packed with violence is still a favourite with the public.
6. There by the bank of that stream is a mass of lovely flowers.
7. Melba Starstruck, along with her agent, her latest husband, and her Bengal tiger, are staying at the Plaza.
8. In the centre of the superstore lies various departments ranging from electronics to kitchenware.
9. Where has my toothbrush and the toothpaste gone?
10. The prime audience for advertising, mainly young people, are an easy target.

### EXERCISE 13.2: AGREEMENT

If you still feel shaky about subject–bare predicate agreement, see how you do choosing the correct word in the following sentences.

1. There (is/are) Yolanda and Chris, talking furiously.
2. Bananas and peanut butter (make/makes) a tasty snack.
3. Peanut butter and bananas (make/makes) a tasty snack.
4. The major impact of these statistics (has/have) not yet been analyzed.

**5.** Ingesting tar, as well as nicotine, (cause/causes) cigarette smoking to be hazardous to your health.

# Watching Out for Irregular Verbs

Although sometimes the language seems irritatingly irregular, English is actually a well-patterned language. Only because we are accustomed to its regularity do we get thrown off track by its quirks—like irregular verbs.

Old English (circa 400–1100) was a highly inflected language, meaning its grammar system relied on changing the forms of the words rather than their order (similar to Latin or present-day languages such as French or German). After the Norman conquest of 1066, which made French the dominant language in England for nearly 300 years, a considerable amount of inflection disappeared in English, and most words became regularized.

Thus, most verbs in English form their past tense and their past participle by adding -*d* or -*ed* or -*t*. The past participle is the form used with the helping verbs *has, have,* or *had* and with forms of *be* in passive verbs *(are used, was seen, will be changed)*.

| Today, I . . . | Yesterday, I . . . | In the past, I have . . . |
|---|---|---|
| hope | hoped | hoped |
| laugh | laughed | laughed |
| spend | spent | spent |

As you can see, the past tense and the past participle are the same for regular verbs.

But with the irregular verbs, the principal parts change. You just have to memorize them or, if you are unsure, check a dictionary. Here are the most common irregular verbs:

| Today, I . . . | Yesterday, I . . . | In the past, I have . . . |
|---|---|---|
| **(present)** | **(past)** | **(past participle)** |
| am | was | been |
| bring | brought | brought |
| begin | began | begun |
| break | broke | broken |
| burst | burst | burst |
| choose | chose | chosen |
| come | came | come |
| do | did | done |
| drag | dragged | dragged *(not* drug*)* |
| drink | drank | drunk |
| forget | forgot | forgotten *(or* forgot*)* |
| get | got | gotten *(or* got*)* |

| go | went | gone |
|---|---|---|
| know | knew | known |
| lay | laid | laid *(meaning* placed*)* |
| lead | led | led |
| lie | lay | lain *(meaning* reclined*)* |
| ride | rode | ridden |
| rise | rose | risen |
| run | ran | run |
| see | saw | seen |
| swim | swam | swum |
| take | took | taken |
| wake | waked *(or* woke*)* | waked *(or* woke*)* |

When you are looking up the principal parts of verbs in your dictionary and do not find any listed, that means the verb is regular—add -*d*, -*ed*, or -*t*.

### ■ EXERCISE 13.3: IRREGULAR VERBS

Complete the following chart by filling in the correct principal parts of these irregular verbs. If you are unsure, check a dictionary. What alternative forms are presented? Did any of these surprise you? If so, why?

| Today, I . . . | Yesterday, I . . . | In the past, I have . . . |
|---|---|---|
| slay | | |
| creep | | |
| flee | | |
| ring | | |
| swing | | |
| wring | | |
| say | | |
| beat | | |
| freeze | | |
| dive | | |
| awake | | |
| eat | | |
| think | | |

### ■ EXERCISE 13.4: IRREGULAR VERBS

In the following sentences insert the form of the verb given in parentheses beforehand. Check the verbs against the list above. The first one is done for you as an example.

1. (*break*: past participle) You have <u>broken</u> your promise.
2. (*lay*: past) Yesterday I _____ my watch on the sink.
3. (*lie*: past) She was so tired that she _____ down.
4. (*set*: past) I _____ my watch ten minutes fast.
5. (*lie*: past participle) We had just _____ down when the telephone rang.
6. (*lay*: past participle) The goalie _____ down his face mask and throat protector.
7. (*drown*: past) His son almost _____ in the pool.
8. (*cost*: past participle) It has _____ me a lot to move.
9. (*go*: past participle) She has _____ to Montreal.
10. (*begin*: past participle) I have just _____ to fight.
11. (*see*: past) The director _____ to it that I knew my part.
12. (*bring*: past participle) What have you _____ to the picnic?
13. (*be*: past participle) They had _____ soundly defeated.
14. (*do*: past participle) You have _____ it again.
15. (*swim*: past) We _____ to the other side of the lake.

## Staying in the Same Tense

Sometimes your prose gets rolling along and you shift into the wrong gear while moving, which causes an unpleasant grinding noise in your readers' heads. You should choose either present or past tense and stay with it. As a general preference, write in the present tense. Here is an example of present tense:

> Savio <u>is</u> <u>swimming</u> in his running shorts.

Past tense would be

> Savio <u>was</u> <u>swimming</u> yesterday, too.

or

> Savio <u>has</u> <u>been</u> <u>swimming</u> every day this week.

There is a good bit of variety within the tenses. These variations are summarized for you in Figure 13.1. The main point to remember is to choose one tense and stay in it—unless you have some reason to change, like this:

> Savio <u>is</u> <u>swimming</u> today, but yesterday he <u>played</u> tennis.

Here is an example of a faulty tense shift, the kind that happens by accident and needs to be changed when you revise:

(**inconsistent**)  Savio <u>was</u> <u>swimming</u> across the pool, when suddenly he <u>sinks</u> under the water and <u>failed</u> to come up. I <u>yell</u> and <u>jumped</u> in to rescue him, when he <u>shoots</u> to the surface and <u>laughed</u> at me.

**T I P !**

**Remember to be consistent: choose present tense or past tense and stick with it.**

The passage sounds much better this way:

(**consistent**)  Savio <u>was</u> <u>swimming</u> across the pool, when suddenly he <u>sank</u> under the water and <u>failed</u> to come up. I <u>yelled</u> and <u>jumped</u> in to rescue him, when he <u>shot</u> to the surface and <u>laughed</u> at me.

---

English has three simple tenses and three perfect tenses. There is a progressive form of each of these six tenses:

|  | **Basic Form** | **Progressive Form** |
|---|---|---|
| SIMPLE PRESENT | walk(s) | is (are) walking |
| SIMPLE PAST | walked | was (were) walking |
| SIMPLE FUTURE | will walk | will be walking |
| PRESENT PERFECT | has (have) walked | has (have) been walking |
| PAST PERFECT | had walked | had been walking |
| FUTURE PERFECT | will have walked | will have been walking |

Simple present describes habitual actions (*Jamal walks to work*) and events that are happening now (*I see a blue heron by the dock*). Simple past describes actions completed entirely in the past (*Yesterday Jamal walked to work*). Simple future describes actions that have not yet happened (*Jamal will walk to work tomorrow*).

Present perfect describes actions that began in the past and might still be going on (*Jamal has walked to work for years*) or actions that occurred at some unspecified time in the past (*The leaves have turned yellow already*). Past perfect describes a past action that ended before another past action began (*Jamal hailed a cab after he had walked several blocks in the rain*). Future perfect tense describes actions that will be completed before or by a certain future time (*Jamal will have left by the time you get there*).

Progressive forms describe actions in progress: *Jamal is walking to work this morning. He was working on our tax accounts last night; he has been working on them for three days and will be working on them again this weekend.*

---

**FIGURE 13.1 *Survey of Tenses***

## Using the Literary Present Tense

If you are writing about literature, you will probably want to use the present tense even though you may be referring to works written decades ago, authors long dead, and characters never alive. The use of the present tense makes sense if you consider that the works, the authors, and the characters still live in our imaginations.

*Anne of Green Gables* by L. M. Montgomery <u>is</u> one of our most beloved Canadian novels.

Although she created many other characters, Anne <u>remains</u> the one that everybody associates with Montgomery's literary career.

Anne <u>gets</u> herself into scrape after scrape but her honesty and sincerity always <u>win</u> the day.

## ▨ EXERCISE 13.5: WRITING

Think about some person, some friend or relative, whom you have known for years. How has this person changed? How does he or she act toward you now that you are older? Write a paragraph that describes how your friend or relative has changed. Use present tense verbs to describe how the person is now and past tense verbs to describe how the person used to be.

## ▨ EXERCISE 13.6: REVISING

The following paragraph contains uncalled-for tense shifts. First, revise it to make all the verbs present tense; then go through it again and make all the verbs past tense.

(1) Bowser, the huge sheepdog who lives next door, had a shaggy coat and a loud, resounding bark. (2) He was friendly and loves to be petted, but his size frightened children. (3) He got so excited when kids came around that he knocks them down like bowling pins. (4) So, he spent his time barking at squirrels, or else he gallops along the fence and terrorized our tiny fox terrier. (5) Bowser really needed to live on a farm and have animals his own size to play with.

## ▨ EXERCISE 13.7: REVIEW

Correct whatever errors you find in each of the following sentences:

1. It is you, not your friends, who have to take responsibility for the accident.
2. Some of the teams are coming to the celebration.
3. Cell phones and email, to a great extent, has changed the way people communicate.
4. In the dean's office was a student and his parents.
5. There's many students who have not had the pleasure of life in a residence.
6. He should not have drank with his friends the night before the exam.
7. "The Whiteoaks of Jalna," based on the novels of Mazo de la Roche and largely scripted by Timothy Findley, were a very successful television series on CBC.
8. The manager and the assistants, working together, refuses to use those tactics.
9. Neither the winners nor the losers were happy.
10. The interior of the newest lecture theatres were not very attractive.

Pronouns, for the most part, do not cause any more bother than do nouns, the words they replace. But remember that pronouns must agree with their antecedents in number (singular or plural), person (first, second, third), and gender (male or female). Gender never causes agreement problems, but agreement in number and person can sometimes be troublesome.

And modifiers usually know their place, but an occasional one will stray off and nudge up next to the wrong word, leaving your readers either puzzled or amused. But more on that later. We will consider pronoun agreement first.

## Sorting Out Agreement with Indefinite Pronouns

The indefinite pronouns that have been decreed singular (such as *everyone, everybody, anyone, anybody, everything*) can cause confusion with pronouns referring to them. Consider these grammatically correct sentences:

*Everyone* applauded, and I was glad *he* did.

After *everybody* finished writing, the instructor passed among *him* and collected the papers.

The lack of logic in such constructions has always made the rule difficult to follow. In general, standard usage is changing to allow these once singular indefinites to be followed by plural pronouns:

*Everyone* should wear *their* seat belts.

*None* of those arrested would admit *they* were involved.

## Strategies for Avoiding Sexist Pronouns

If your indefinite pronoun is singular in meaning, standard English once required you to write,

*Each* student must show *his* permit to register.

Writers now take care to avoid sexist language that makes all people appear to be male. You can totally eliminate the difficulty by writing in the plural:

*Students* must show *their* permits to register.

Or you can do it this way:

*Each* student must show *a* permit to register.

**T I P !**

**Be warned: some people do not like this usage.**

Some may declare you in error if you write *everyone* followed by *their*. To avoid ruffling such readers, you can use both singular pronouns this way:

*Everyone* should wear *his or her* seat belt.

*None* of those arrested would admit *he or she* was involved.

Or rewrite to avoid the issue:

Everyone should wear *a* seat belt.

None of those arrested would admit being involved.

Occasionally, you may need to write a sentence in which you emphasize the singular:

> *Each* individual must speak *his* own mind. *or* Each individual must speak her own mind. *or* Each individual must speak her or his own mind.

But the sentence will be just as emphatic this way:

> *Each one of us* must speak *our* own mind.

> **T I P !**
>
> **If you write in the plural, the problem disappears.**

### EXERCISE 14.1: PRONOUNS

In the following sentences, select one or more pronouns to fill in the blanks. If you cannot think of suitable words, rewrite the sentences in the plural.

1. Anyone living outside town should leave _____ job early to avoid getting _____ car stuck in a snow drift.

2. A good student does _____ own homework.

3. Someone has left _____ car lights on.

4. Anyone wishing to improve _____ tennis game should work on _____ backhand.

5. Each must cast _____ own vote.

## Confusion with the Pronouns *This* and *Which*

Most of the time when you use the pronoun *this,* your meaning is clear. You say, "This is my new hockey stick," and because you are standing there holding it, your meaning is quite clear. But at other times, when you use *this* to refer to ideas or events, your meaning becomes hazy, especially if the pronoun gets too far away from its antecedent (the noun that names the idea or event you are talking about).

> **T I P !**
>
> **Whenever you use the word *this*, try to follow it with a noun telling what *this* refers to.**

If you are going to write,

> The importance of this becomes clear when we understand the alternatives.

at least give your readers a clue: this *plan,* this *principle,* this *problem,* this *stipulation,* this *qualification,* this *dichotomy,* this *stalemate,* this whatever. And if you have trouble supplying a noun to follow *this,* that is nature's way of telling you that the whole idea is vague, and you need to go back and clarify what *this* means in your own mind before you totally befuddle your readers.

The word *which* causes similar problems. Often this handy pronoun refers to an entire clause preceding it. Sometimes the meaning is clear, sometimes not. Suppose you write,

> **(unclear)** Germaine has received only one job offer, which depresses her.

That sentence can be interpreted two ways:

Germaine is depressed about receiving only one job offer, even though it is a fairly good one.

or

Germaine has received only one job offer—a depressing one at that.

Whenever you use the word *which,* make sure that your readers will be able to tell exactly what it means.

### EXERCISE 14.2: REVISING

Revise the following sentences to eliminate any unclear pronoun reference.

1. Al asked if Jose allowed a speck of egg yolk or a particle of grease to get into the egg whites. This might keep the whites from fluffing up the way they should.
2. Meg ate Chinese food and went out jogging, which caused her to feel unwell.
3. Eating a simple meal in an outdoor setting, which I prefer, relaxes me after a hard day.
4. This makes all my symptoms of stress disappear.
5. I was late and skipped dinner, which got me in trouble.

## Choosing Pronoun Case—*I* or *Me? He* or *Him?*

Nouns do not change form when they move from being subjects to objects in a sentence. For instance, you can write,

Kesha resembles my sister.

My sister resembles Kesha.

But, as a holdover from Old English, pronouns still show *case* (subjective, objective, or possessive). So, with pronouns, we write,

*She* resembles my sister.

My sister resembles *her.*

The case forms are easy.

| Subject | Object | Possessive |
| --- | --- | --- |
| I | me | my, mine |
| he | him | his |
| she | her | her, hers |
| you | you | your, yours |
| it | it | its |
| we | us | our, ours |
| they | them | their, theirs |
| who | whom | whose |

Except for the confusion of *its* with the contraction *it's* and *whose* with *who's*, the possessives cause no concern. But you must make choices among the other forms in constructions like these:

1. *When you have more than one subject or object*

    (wrong)   Adrian and *me* went to a lecture.

    (right)   Adrian and *I* went to a lecture.

    (wrong)   LaWanda sat with Seymour and *I*.

    (right)   LaWanda sat with Seymour and *me*.

Drop the word before (or after) the "and" to see how the pronoun sounds alone.

    *Me* went to a lecture or *I* went to a lecture?

    LaWanda sat with *I* or LaWanda sat with *me*?

Your choice is now a no-brainer.

2. *When pronouns are used as appositives*

You remember what appositives are. They go like this:

| | |
|---|---|
| we football fans | us football fans |
| we pizza lovers | us pizza lovers |
| we students | us students |
| we teachers | us teachers |

Whether you choose *we* or *us* depends on whether the construction is the subject or the object.

    (wrong)   *Us* fitness freaks are slaves to exercise.

    (right)   *We* fitness freaks are slaves to exercise.

    (wrong)   Weather can be bad news for *we* joggers.

    (right)   Weather can be bad news for *us* joggers.

3. *When pronouns are used in comparisons*

    (wrong)   My sister is smarter than *me*.

    (right)   My sister is smarter than *I*.

Just finish the incomplete comparison in your mind. Would you say, "My sister is smarter than *me* am"? If so, you are right about your sister but wrong about the pronoun. Most of us would say, "smarter than *I* am."

**T I P !**

Although prepositions are usually short words (*in, on, at, by, for,* and the like), a few are deceptively long— *through, beside, among, underneath, between.* Long or short, prepositions always take object pronouns:

    between Clyde and *me*

    among Clyde, Clarence, and *him*

    beside Clyde and *me*

**T I P !**

If you are in doubt, just drop the appositive. Would you say "*Us* are slaves" or "*We* are slaves"? Your ear should tell you that *we* is the correct choice. And would it be "bad weather for *we*" or "bad weather for *us*"? Of course, it is "bad weather for *us*."

**4.** *When choosing between "who" and "whom"*

In writing, you must determine when to use *who* and when to use *whom*.

Kate Chopin was a superb writer (who/whom) literary critics have neglected until recently.

Substitute the subject *he* (or *she*) or the object *him* (or *her*). Then ask yourself, "Critics have neglected *she*"? or "Critics have neglected *her*"? We would all choose *her,* of course. Because *her* is an object, the sentence needs the object *whom*:

Kate Chopin was a superb writer *whom* literary critics have neglected until recently.

> **T I P !**
>
> **You can sometimes avoid the choice by using *that*:**
>
> Kate Chopin was a superb writer *that* literary critics have neglected until recently.

**5.** *Do not substitute* which *for* who *or* whom

Standard usage still does not allow *which* to refer to people.

(**unacceptable**)   the candidate *which* I admire

(**acceptable**)   the candidate *whom* I admire

(**acceptable**)   the candidate *that* I admire

### EXERCISE 14.3: PRONOUNS

Choose the correct pronoun in each sentence.

**1.** You can't win if you run against Malcolm and (she/her).

**2.** At the prom next Saturday Ashley and (I/me) are going to wear blue jeans.

**3.** For too long (we/us) taxpayers have been at the mercy of Parliament.

**4.** (Who/Whom) is going to deliver the keynote address?

**5.** Stanley went to visit his mother (who/whom) he called "Muma."

**6.** Renato and (I/me) are planning to become vegetarians as soon as we finish our Big Macs.

**7.** Did both (she/her) and Cecil promise to come early to help?

**8.** The member of Parliament is the person on (who/whom) I base all hope for the future.

**9.** We should be spared commercials (who/whom/that/which) are an insult to our intelligence.

**10.** We arranged to study for the big exam with Selina and (she/her).

## Revising Dangling and Misplaced Modifiers

The word *modify* means to change. Thus a modifier in a sentence changes in some way the meaning of whatever it modifies. Here is a sentence with no modifiers:

Maria graduated.

We will add a couple of modifiers in italics:

*Yesterday* Maria graduated *with honours.*

Positioning modifiers is usually easy, but sometimes they get stranded with nothing to modify—or else they stray off and modify the wrong thing, as in the following examples.

The cookbook tells how to make a chocolate cake clearly.

A woman was running down the sidewalk with long grey hair.

A mountain lion suspected of killing at least two suburban dogs was shot to death after a warden spotted it taking a report near the scene of the latest attack.

## Repairing Dangling Modifiers

Modifiers that dangle are not always funny. They can be annoying because they indicate that the writer is not paying attention, like this:

Driving through the lush, pine-scented forest, the air was suddenly fouled by the sulphurous belchings of a paper mill.

Clearly the *air* is not driving though the forest. The opening modifier dangles with nothing in the sentence to modify. You can revise in a couple of ways:

As we drove through the lush, pine-scented forest, the air was suddenly fouled. . . .

Driving through the forest, we gasped as the air was suddenly fouled. . . .

To catch wayward modifiers, read your last draft carefully, paying attention to each sentence individually.

Modifiers often dangle in passive constructions, so take special care with the passive voice. The passive voice allows you to omit the person or entity doing the acting, thus positively inviting dangling modifiers:

**(faulty)** Knowing that the airliner was off course, only two conclusions can be drawn.

Clearly, it was not the "conclusions" that knew the plane was off course. Whoever did the knowing got left out of the sentence entirely. When you revise in active voice, you will need to supply a subject for the modifier:

**(revised)** Knowing that the airliner was off course, *the investigators* could draw only two conclusions.

## Moving Misplaced Modifiers

Misplaced modifiers may not be quite as annoying as dangling ones, but they can still mess up the meaning of your sentence, like this:

> **(faulty)**  Once married, the Church considers that a couple has signed a lifelong contract.

It is not the Church that is getting married, so you need to move the modifier:

> **(revised)**  The Church considers that a couple, once married, has signed a lifelong contract.

Sometimes a misplaced modifier can badly skew the meaning of a sentence, as in this example taken from a university newspaper:

> **(faulty)**  DARE is sponsoring a series of presentations on drugs for university students.

That sentence wrongly gives the impression that DARE is in the business of acquainting university students with drugs to use. The meaning is less ambiguous this way:

> **(revised)**  DARE is sponsoring a series of presentations for local university students on the dangers of drug use.

As you revise, check your sentences for lapses in logic caused by misplaced modifiers.

## EXERCISE 14.4: REVISING

Revise the following sentences to eliminate all misplaced or dangling modifiers. You may need to add information to help some of these make sense.

1. After deciding which section will be sewn first, the material must then be cut.
2. I had been driving for forty years when I fell asleep and had an accident.
3. Otis was robbed at gunpoint in the elevator where he lives.
4. At university I hope to start singing with a scholarship.
5. A crutch is a device used to take weight off an injured leg by sticking it under the arm and leaning on it.
6. I do not see my Aunt Frieda much in Montreal.
7. With this total lack of responsibility, more and more items were purchased.
8. Consider this letter to the editor of an urban newspaper a few years ago.
9. The poem exemplifies the patriarchal success of the socialization of women.
10. After reading the essays, papers were written discussing the ideas.

## EXERCISE 14.5: REWRITING

Explain how the following sentences might be misread. Then rewrite them to make the meaning clear and unambiguous.

1. The company packages natural meals for children that can be shipped anywhere.
2. North Dakota citizens' groups are sending volunteers to help flood relief workers in Manitoba.

3. The House of Commons plans to resume consideration of legislation to restrict campaign contributions next week.

4. Bob Gainey signed a contract to manage the Montreal Canadiens yesterday.

5. A municipal task force announced its plan to increase parking at a city hall press conference.

6. The plan will increase parking in congested areas.

7. The superintendent called for a meeting to talk about increasing teenage drug use with members of the school board.

8. The passengers wanted their ordeal to end desperately.

9. The Grishams decided their daughter would be a lawyer before she was ten years old.

10. The restaurant had many autographs of celebrities on the walls that had eaten there.

**CHAPTER**

*Usage* means the way the language is used. But different people use the language in different ways. And even the same people use the language differently on different occasions. You probably speak one way in the classroom or on the job and another way at a party or a hockey game. Good usage, then, is a matter of using language *appropriate* to the occasion.

In this chapter we describe the current usage of terms that are often confused and misunderstood; we also point out when words and expressions are unacceptable or questionable for formal or even informal writing. (To refresh your memory about the characteristics of the various levels of language, see pages 16–19.) In making decisions on usage, we have been guided by *Fowler's Modern English Usage*, 3rd ed.; *The Oxford Guide to Canadian English Usage*; the *Nelson Canadian Dictionary of the English Language*; the *Canadian Oxford Dictionary*, with supplement; and several popular composition handbooks.

If you are still in doubt about some terms or have questions about words that do not appear in this chapter, consult your trusty dictionary. But be sure it is a recent one: even the best dictionaries will be out of date on usage within ten years. You may also need to consult Chapter 11 to check pertinent grammatical terms and concepts.

## Hazardous Usage

*Standard usage* means the language used by educated people, *nonstandard usage* means any language that fails to conform to this accepted standard. Dialectical expressions are considered nonstandard. Some dictionaries label such usage as *illiterate*, which seems harsh, but you should be advised that many people are unalterably opposed to nonstandard English in business and academic writing. The following words are considered nonstandard *or* are often confused by writers who employ them in nonstandard ways. Use them with extreme care; in some cases, avoid using them at all.

**ain't** People have been using this word in speech for at least 200 years, but it is still considered nonstandard. Do not use it unless you are writing dialogue or trying to get a laugh. Use *am not, are not,* or *is not.*

**a lot** It is still two words: *a + lot* (a noun meaning a large extent or amount).

> Your complaints have caused *a lot* of trouble.

> We are feeling *a lot* better.

**analyzation** The standard term is analysis; tacking on extra syllables does not make it any grander—only incorrect.

**anyways/anywheres**    These are a nonstandard formations: use *anyway* and *anywhere*.

> They decided to go to the dance *anyway*.

> They could not find the missing ring *anywhere*.

**could of/should of/would of**    These phrases are nonstandard for *could have, should have, would have*.

**due**    *Due* is an adjective and must modify a noun or noun equivalent, as in "What is the due date of the essay?" *Due* can also be used after a copula verb that links it to a noun, as in "The essay is due next Tuesday." Avoid the incorrect use of *due* as a preposition, as in the following example.

> The essay is *due* today, but classes are cancelled because of (not *due to*) the storm.

**enthused**    Many people prefer that you use *enthusiastic*.

> **(familiar)**  The critics were *enthused* about our performance.
> **(preferred)**  The critics were *enthusiastic* about our performance.

**etc.**    This abbreviation means "and the rest" (from the Latin *et cetera*). Do not use it just to avoid thinking of good examples, and avoid ending a list with *etc.* unless the other examples are obvious (like large cities: Paris, Rome, London, etc.). Even then, it is usually more effective to end with an example or to use the more graceful phrase *and so on*. Never write *and etc.*; it is redundant.

**hardly**    This adverb carries a negative meaning, so do not combine it with a negative verb.

> **(nonstandard)**  She *can't hardly* see without her glasses.
> **(standard)**  She *can hardly* see without her glasses.

> She *can't* see without her glasses.

**hisself**    This word is nonstandard. Use *himself*.

**irregardless**    Use *regardless*, never *irregardless*, which is not accepted as standard English.

> She continued her pursuit, *regardless* of the forces against her.

**is when/is where/is because**    Avoid these usages—the copula verb *to be* requires a subjective completion. Add a subjective completion or replace the verb with *occurs* or *happens*.

> **(nonstandard)**  The climax is when the hero dies.
> **(standard)**  The climax is the moment when the hero dies.
> **(standard)**  The climax occurs when the hero dies.

**myself** This word is a reflexive or intensive pronoun; use it only when an antecedent appears in the same sentence: *I cut myself shaving* (reflexive); *I will fix the faucet myself* (intensive). Do not use *myself* in place of *I* (a subject pronoun) or *me* (an object pronoun).

> They gave awards to Harry and me (not *myself*).
>
> Khari and I (not *myself*) won last year.
>
> I myself will fix the car. I taught myself all I need to know.

**quote** *Quote* is a verb:

> Leroy quotes Shakespeare in his sleep.

In writing avoid using *quote* or *quotes* as a shortened form of *quotation* or *quotation marks*.

**suppose to/use to** These are nonstandard; the correct forms are *supposed to* and *used to*. Be careful to add the *-d* in writing, even though you do not hear it in speech. In negative constructions of *used to,* the *-d* can be omitted ("I did not use to know").

**theirself/theirselves/themself** These are all nonstandard forms of *themselves*.

## Double Trouble: Words That Are Easily Confused

The English language is filled with words that look alike or sound alike or are alike in meaning, and they cause problems for many writers. The only way to handle these similar terms is to stay alert for them and double-check their every use when you proofread. It is not just a matter of learning how to spell the words correctly; you also have to match the spelling with the meaning. Keeping a list of the ones that give you trouble will increase your awareness and save you time when you edit. And remember: the spell checker on your computer will not help you with these words that sound and look alike.

**a/an** Use *a* before words that begin with consonant sounds; use *an* before words that begin with vowel sounds (*a, e, i, o, u*).

| | |
|---|---|
| a martini | an Irish coffee |
| a tree toad | an armed |
| a hopeful sign (the *h* is sounded) | an honest decision (the *h* is silent) |
| a hostile crowd (sounded *h*) | an hour-long exam (silent *h*) |
| a one-car accident (*o* sounds like *w*) | an only child |
| a university (*u* sounds like *y*) | an unusual request |

*An* was once used before unaccented syllables beginning with *h*: *an historian, an hotel*. But that usage has changed; it is now acceptable to write *a historian* or *a hotel*.

**accept/except** *Accept*, a verb, means "to receive or to agree with."

We *accept* your gracious apology.

*Except*, a preposition, means "other than" or "leaving out."

He did not utter a word *except* to complain.

Everyone will attend the banquet, *except* Alain.

*Except* can also be a verb meaning "to exclude."

Senior citizens are *excepted* from paying full price.

**advice/advise**   *Advice* is a noun; *advise* is a verb. When you *advise* someone, you are giving *advice*.

vb.

We *advise* you to stop smoking.

n.

Sun-Lee refuses to follow our good *advice*.

**affect/effect**   In general usage the verb *affect* means "to influence," and the noun *effect* means "the result of some influence."

n.                    vb.

The *effect* on my lungs from smoking should *affect* my decision to quit.

vb.

Smoking adversely *affects* our health.

n.

Carleton smokes expensive cigars for *effect*.

To complicate matters further, *effect* can also be a verb meaning "to bring about some event or change" and *affect* can be a verb meaning "to put on or simulate."

vb.

We need to *effect* [bring about] some changes in the system.

vb.

He *affects* [puts on] the petulance of a rock star.

Occasionally, in the context of psychology, *affect* can be used as a noun meaning "emotional response."

n.

Psychologists say that inappropriate *affect* [emotional response] is a feature of schizophrenia.

These last three meanings are seldom confused with the more widely used words above. Concentrate on getting those first common meanings straight.

**all right/alright**    Although *alright* is gaining acceptance in the world of advertising, you should stick with *all right* to be safe. *Alright* is definitely not *all right* with everybody yet.

**allude/elude**    *Allude* means "to make an indirect reference to"; *elude* means "to escape."

She *alluded* to the events of her childhood several times during her talk.

The escaped felon did not manage to *elude* the RCMP for very long.

**allusion/illusion**    *Allusion* is a reference; *illusion* is an erroneous or misleading conception.

James Joyce's great modern novel contains many *allusions* to classic mythology, including those ghostly *illusions* once encountered by Odysseus in Hades.

**almost/most**    See *most/almost.*

**already/all ready**    *Already* means "before, previously, or so soon."

Gabrielle has *already* eaten two cheeseburgers.

*All ready* means "prepared."

Pedro is *all ready* to deliver his anti–junk food lecture.

**altogether/all together**    *Altogether* means "entirely, thoroughly."

Emil's analysis is *altogether* absurd.

*All together* means "as a group."

Let us sing the last chorus *all together.*

**ambiguous/ambivalent**    *Ambiguous* implies "more than one meaning"; *ambivalent* means "indecisiveness or mixed feelings."

For Melville, the colour white had many shades of meaning; the great whale was similarly *ambiguous.*

Having read the book, she felt *ambivalent* about its themes.

**among/between**    Use *among* when referring to more than two items. Use *between* when referring to only two.

Ashley found it difficult to choose from *among* so many delectable desserts.

She could not decide *between* the raspberry torte and the butterscotch mousse.

**amount of/number of**    *Amount of* refers to a general, unspecified quantity; *number of* refers to a quantity that can be counted.

The *amount of* time wasted trying to find the perfect font was remarkable.

A *number of* actors have appeared on the series.

**anymore/any more**   Use *any more* if you mean "any additional." Use *anymore* with negative verbs if you mean "any longer."

> Ashley won't be eating *any more* desserts.

> She doesn't eat desserts *anymore*.

Do not use *anymore* with positive verbs; use *now* or *nowadays*.

> **(familiar)**  All she eats *anymore* is salad and fruit.

> **(preferred)**  All she eats *nowadays* is salad and fruit.

(Note, however, that some Canadian sources consider *anymore* an American form.)

**apprise/appraise**   To *apprise* means to "inform or serve notice." To *appraise* means to "evaluate or judge."

> The judge *apprised* the defendant of her right to counsel.

> The fugitive *appraised* the situation and caught the next flight to South America.

**assure/ensure/insure**   *Assure* means "to state positively"; *ensure* means "to make certain or sure"; *insure* means to cover with insurance.

> Let me *assure* you that his company is reliable and would be able to *ensure* your safety.

> Those who rent should always *insure* the contents of their dwellings.

**bad/badly**   *Bad* is an adjective; use it after linking verbs (*be, feel, seem, appear, look, become, smell, sound, taste*). *Badly* is an adverb; use it to modify verbs.

> We feel *bad* about missing your birthday.

> I feel *bad* because I'm coming down with a cold.

> The car is vibrating *badly*.

> The car was *badly* damaged.

If you just cannot remember these distinctions, choose another word.

> We feel sorry about missing your birthday.

> I feel awful because I'm coming down with a cold.

> The car is vibrating alarmingly.

> The car was seriously damaged.

**between/among**   See *among/between*.

**can/may**   *Can* indicates an ability to do something; *may* indicates a request.

> She *can* compete at the master's level; whether or not she *may* participate is a decision to be made by the commission.

**censure/censor/censer**  *Censure,* as noun or verb, concerns "an extreme expression of criticism, of disapproval"; *censor,* as noun, is "one who determines what is objectionable" and, as verb, is "the act of expurgation." A *censer* is a container for burning incense.

The government's film *censors* forwarded a letter of *censure* to the importers.

**choose/chose**  *Choose* (rhymes with *ooze*) means a decision is being made now. *Chose* (rhymes with *toes*) means a choice has already been made.

Please *choose* a new lab partner for me.

The one you *chose* for me last semester was incompetent.

**cite/site/sight**  *Cite,* a verb, means "to quote as an authority or example." *Site,* a noun, means "a particular place."

In his speech Paul Martin *cited* three passages from the Charter of Rights and Freedoms.

We found a perfect *site* to hold our rally.

As a verb, *sight* means "to observe or notice."

Astronomers recently *sighted* a new comet.

As a noun, *sight* means something that is seen or foreseeable or worth seeing.

There is no end in *sight* to this heat wave.

One of Quebec's most famous *sights* is the Citadel fortress.

**compare/contrast**  These words overlap in meaning. While *compare* generally means to focus on similarities and *contrast* means to focus on differences, you are comparing when you make a contrast.

**complement/compliment**  *Complement* is a verb meaning "to go together with or complete" and a noun meaning "something that completes."

Aimée's lilac scarf *complements* her lavender sweater.

The scarf is also a good *complement* to her whole outfit.

*Compliment* is a verb meaning "to praise or flatter" and a noun meaning "an expression of praise or flattery."

Many people *complimented* Aimée on her clothes.

She received many *compliments* on her sense of style.

**conscious/conscience**  *Conscious* refers to one's awareness of one's environment and self; *conscience* is one's internal sense of ethics or morality.

Macbeth is *conscious* of the actions he takes and, as such, is often described as a killer with a *conscience.*

**continual/continuous**   There is a slight difference between these two words, although many people treat them the same. *Continual* describes an action that is repeated at intervals; its synonyms are *recurrent* or *intermittent*. *Continuous* means something that is extended or prolonged without interruption; its synonyms are *uninterrupted* or *incessant*.

> The *continual* banging of the shutters kept me awake.

> They kept a *continuous* watch for approaching storms.

**council/counsel**   *Council* is a noun and refers to a group of people; *counsel* is a verb and means "to give advice."

> The executive *council* met every other Tuesday to receive *counsel* from its committee chairs.

**desert/dessert**   People who get their just *deserts* are getting what they deserve. People who get *desserts* are eating something like cheesecake or pie with ice cream at the end of a meal. Neither is to be confused with an arid, desolate landscape.

**device/devise**   *Device* is a noun and refers to "a thing or object"; *devise* is a verb and means "to plan or design."

> The *device* was *devised* to work at lower speeds.

**disinterested/uninterested**   Although the distinction between these words is important, many people confuse them. *Disinterested* means "impartial or objective." *Uninterested* means "not interested."

> You need a totally *disinterested* counsellor to help you with your marriage problems.

> Andre is totally *uninterested* in environmental causes.

**dominant/dominate**   *Dominant* is an adjective. *Dominate* is a verb.

> Luis has a *dominant* personality.

> Brown eyes are genetically *dominant*.

> Cecil's brothers *dominate* him.

**effect/affect**   See *affect/effect*.

**everyday/every day**   Use *everyday* as an adjective to modify a noun. Use *every day* to mean "daily."

> Jacques is wearing his *everyday* clothes.

> It rains in Juneau almost *every day*.

**farther/further**   *Farther* (or *farthest*) refers to "physical distance"; *further* refers to "advancement along a non-physical dimension (degree, time, space)."

Sheila could walk no *farther*. It was *further* proof that a life of coffee and cigarettes had taken its toll.

**fewer/less** *Fewer* refers to things that can be counted; *less* refers to uncountable amounts.

The *fewer* the campers, the *less* destruction happens to the environment.

**forceful/forcible/forced** *Forceful* is someone or something that is "filled with force or strength"; *forcible* refers to actions "accomplished by the use of physical force"; and *forced* is "used to describe an act or condition brought about by control or an outside influence."

The winds of the thunderstorm were extremely *forceful*.

There was evidence of *forcible* entry at the rear of the store.

The airplane successfully completed a *forced* landing.

**hung/hanged** These are the past and past participle forms of the verb "to hang." If you are talking about hanging inanimate objects, then *hung* is the correct form but if you are referring to executing people by suspending them by the neck, then *hanged* is the one you want.

The people at the art museum *hung* the pictures upside down.

They *hanged* the prisoner at dawn.

**illicit/elicit** *Illicit* means "illegal or outside of law or custom"; *elicit* means "to bring out or arrive at something."

The *illicit* drug trade is a societal problem that never seems to go away.

The instructor attempted to *elicit* a better response from the class.

**imply/infer** *Imply* means to state indirectly or throw out a suggestion. *Infer* means to draw a conclusion or take in a suggestion.

Theo *implied* that he was a computer expert.

The boss *inferred* that Theo had exaggerated his credentials.

**in/into** *In* is a preposition that is primarily used to indicate a location; *into* is a preposition that is usually used with verbs indicating motion.

The laundry was *in* the hamper.

The old television was moved *into* the basement.

**its/it's** Do not confuse these two terms. Memorize the two definitions if you have trouble with them, and when you proofread, check to be sure you have not confused them accidentally. *Its* is a possessive pronoun. *It's* is a contraction of "it is" or "it has."

That dog wags *its* tail whenever *its* owner walks into the room.

*It's* a great day for taking the dog for a walk.

*It's* been a long time since you walked the dog.

**T I P !**

**If you never can keep the two straight, quit using the contraction. Write *it* is or it has.**

**lay/lie**   *To lay* means to put or place; *to lie* means to recline. Be sure you know the principal forms of each verb; then decide which verb you need:

> **(to place)**   lay, laid, laid, laying

> **(to recline)**   lie, lay, lain, lying

Remember that *lay* requires a direct object: you always *lay* something. But you never *lie* anything: you just *lie down,* or *lie quietly,* or *lie under a tree,* or *lie on a couch.*

> **(no direct object)**   Duncan *lies* in the hammock.

> **(direct object)**   Duncan usually *lays* the mail on the hall table.

If you absolutely cannot keep these verbs straight in your mind, choose another word.

> Duncan *lounges* in the hammock.

> Duncan usually *puts* the mail on the hall table.

**lead/led**   Pronunciation causes the confusion here.

*Lead* (rhymes with *bed*), a noun, means "a heavy, greyish metal."

> Our airy hopes sank like *lead.*

*Lead* (rhymes with *seed*) is the present tense of the verb meaning "to guide."

> He *leads* me beside the still waters.

*Led* (rhymes with *bed*) is the past tense of the verb *lead.*

> Marcelo *led* the march last year, but he vows he will not *lead* it again.

**lessen/lesson**   To *lessen* is a verb meaning "to reduce or decrease"; *lesson* is usually a noun meaning "something to be learned."

> Strategies to *lessen* one's daily level of stress was the *lesson* of the lecture.

**lose/loose**   This is another problem in pronunciation and spelling.

*Lose* (rhymes with *ooze*) is a verb meaning "to fail to keep something."

> If we *lose* our right to protest, we will ultimately *lose* our freedom.

*Loose* (rhymes with *goose*) is an adjective meaning "not tight."

The noose is too *loose* on your lasso.

**most/almost**   *Most* is colloquial when used to mean "almost."

(familiar)  *Most* everyone in the office took Friday off.

(preferred)  *Almost* everyone in the office took Friday off.

**passed/past**   *Passed* is a verb; *past* is an adjective or noun.

In the *past* year, she *passed* all of her courses.

**practice/practise**   *Practice* is a noun; *practise* is a verb.

After the basketball *practice*, she stayed to *practise* her free throws.

**precede/proceed**   *Precede* means "to come before"; *proceed* means "to go ahead or continue."

A brief social gathering will *precede* the meeting; then the committee will *proceed* with business.

**prejudice/prejudiced**   *Prejudice* (without the *-d*) is a noun. *Prejudiced* (with the *-d*) is the past participle of the verb *to prejudice*; it means "affected by prejudice." Do not leave off the *-d* when using this word as an adjective.

*Prejudice* remains engrained in our society.

adj.                                                              n.

A *prejudiced* person is someone who harbours *prejudice*.

pred. adj.

Our society remains *prejudiced* against minorities.

**principal/principle**   *Principle* means a rule or fundamental truth: a person of high moral *principle,* a primary *principle* of physics, the *principle* of equal justice. You can remember the *-le* spelling by association with the *-le* ending of *rule.* All other uses end with *-al*: a high school *principal,* the *principal* of a loan, a *principal* cause or effect, the *principal* (main character) in a film or play.

**probable/probably**   Both of these words mean "likely." *Probable* (sounds at the end like *capable*) is an adjective, and *probably* (ends with a long *e* sound, like *capably*) is an adverb.

adj.                                      adv.

The *probable* involvement of CSIS *probably* reduced the security threat.

**quite/quiet**   *Quite* means "entirely" or "truly"; use it to qualify adjectives and adverbs: *quite* suddenly, *quite* often, *quite* right. *Quiet* means the opposite of "loud."

Carlos was *quite* ready to yell, "Be *quiet*, please!"

**raise/rise**   You never *rise* anything, but you always *raise* something. Prices *rise,* spirits *rise,* curtains *rise,* temperatures *rise,* and the sun *rises;* but you *raise* children, *raise* corn, *raise* prices, *raise* a ruckus, or *raise* the window.

> Taxes are *rising* because the government has *raised* the health-care budget again.

If you cannot keep these verbs straight, avoid them.

> Taxes are going up because the government has increased the health-care budget again.

**real/really**   Do not use *real* as an adverb or qualifier in writing.

> **(familiar)** Maya saw a *real* interesting movie.

> **(standard)** Maya saw a *really* interesting movie.

**rise/raise**   See *raise/rise.*

**sensuous/sensual/sensory**   *Sensuous* refers to any type of pleasure (intellectual, spiritual, and so on) experienced through our senses; *sensual* generally is used in reference to gratification or indulgence of our more carnal natures; *sensory* tends to be neutral, referring to the senses in a purely physical way.

> The music of Sarah McLachlan conveys a *sensuous* ambience.

> Their *sensual* dance captured the rapt attention of all who were present.

> The brain receives *sensory* input of many different kinds.

**sit/set**   You seldom *sit* anything. You *sit* down or *sit* for a while or *sit* in a chair. One notable exception: *sit* can mean "to cause to be seated." Thus, it is quite correct to write "The parole officer should *sit* Buffy down and give her a lecture."

But you always *set* something. You *set* a glass down or *set* a time or *set* the table. Exceptions: in some common phrases *set* does not have an object—the sun *sets,* Jell-O and concrete *set,* and hens *set*—but these uses seldom cause trouble.

**stationary/stationery**   *Stationary* is an adjective meaning "in a fixed position"; *stationery* is a noun referring to "the paper on which one writes."

> The author's hand was *stationary*, her pen hovering above the *stationery*.

**than/then**   See *then/than.*

**that/which**   As a relative pronoun, *that* is used to introduce a clause that is essential; *which* is used to introduce incidental information that could be omitted.

> The only goal *that* she wants to achieve by the end of the year is to compete in a marathon. The Ottawa Marathon, *which* occurs in October, is a reasonable possibility.

**their/there/they're**   These words are easy to confuse because they sound exactly alike. But their meanings and uses are quite different.

*Their* is a possessive modifier or pronoun.

> *Their* dog is friendly. That dog is *theirs*.

*There* is an adverb or an expletive (a filler word that delays the subject).

> **(adverb)**  Sylvia is over *there*.
> **(expletive)**  *There* is no one with her.

*They're* is a contraction of *they are*.

> *They're* gone now.

**then/than**   These words have quite different meanings. *Then* means "at that time in the past" or "next in time, space, or order." *Than* is used in comparisons.

> We were all much younger *then*.

> We watched the late movie and *then* went to bed.

> No one talks more *than* Michael does.

> Claudia would rather talk *than* eat.

**to/too/two**   *To* is usually a preposition and sometimes an adverb; it also introduces an infinitive.

> *to* the depths, push open the door *to*, *to* swing

*Too* is a qualifier or an adverb meaning "also."

> Don't make *too* much noise. (qualifier of "much")

> Clement is going, *too*. (means "also")

*Two* is the number.

> *two* paycheques, *two* kilometres

**unique**   *Unique* is an absolute, suggesting the only one of its kind. Avoid using any adjectives, such as *more unique* or *very unique*. Other absolute words that follow the same rule include *equal, fatal, infinite, omnipotent, parallel, perfect, unanimous.*

**weather/whether**   *Weather* is what goes on outside; *whether* introduces an alternative. Using the wrong one causes serious misunderstandings.

> We cannot decide *whether* the *weather* will be suitable for a picnic.

**who/which/that**   Use *who* to refer to people (or to animals you are personifying).

> The person *who* lost the car keys. . . .

> Lenin, *who* is Susie's cat, . . .

Use *which* to refer to animals and nonliving things.

The earth, *which* blossoms in the spring, . . .

The cat, *which* is sitting in the window, . . .

Use *that* to refer to either people or things.

The person *that* lost the car keys . . . (*who* is preferred in formal usage)

The earth *that* blossoms in spring . . .

The cat *that* is sitting in the window. . . .

**who/whom**   *Who* is used in the subjective case; *whom* is used in the objective case (see Chapter 14).

*Who* is responsible? To *whom* did you lend the book?

**who's, whose**   *Who's* means "who is"; *whose* is a possessive pronoun.

*Who's* going to the movie and *whose* car are we taking?

**your/you're**   *Your* is a possessive modifier or pronoun. *You're* is a contraction of *you are.*

Here is *your* book; this book is *yours.*

Let me know when *you're* leaving.

**allegory** a narrative in which the events and characters represent historical, mythic, or abstract concepts (for example, Spenser's *The Faerie Queene*)

**alliteration** the repetition of initial consonants in two or more nearby words (for example, "seven slimy snakes")

**allusion** a reference to another person, place, literary work, or passage

**analyze** to examine parts and make connections/conclusions about the whole

**antecedent** the noun or substantive to which a pronoun refers

**anthropomorphism** the attribution of a human appearance or form to a non-human entity (for example, the mountain named "the finger" in Earle Birney's *David*)

**archetype** an original pattern, prototype, or character type that occurs repeatedly in literature, folklore, myth, religion. Northrop Frye defines archetype as "a symbol, usually an image, which recurs often enough in literature to be recognizable as an element of one's literary experience as a whole."

**aside** in drama, a speech or comment not heard by others on stage

**atmosphere** the emotion or feeling conveyed to the reader or audience by a literary work

**bathos** a "lapse into the ridiculous" that results when a work of literature overshoots its sincere intention and achieves instead a ludicrous effect

**blank verse** in verse, lines of iambic pentameter that are unrhymed (for example, Milton's *Paradise Lost*)

**Boolean logic** the logical relationship among online search terms; the main operators are AND, OR, and NOT

**catharsis** the purification of the emotions; one of the traditional functions of tragedy for an audience

**citation** a restatement of another's idea or a direct quotation

**comic relief** the use of humour to contrast the tension in serious fiction or drama (for example, the Porter's scene in *Macbeth*)

**conflict** the struggle that occurs between opposing forces, usually expressed as person versus self, person versus person, or person versus nature

**connotation** the meaning that is associated with or implied by a word, as distinct from or in addition to its literal meaning (or *denotation*); for example, the denotation of *home* is "a place where one lives"; its connotations may include safety, retreat, love

**couplet** in verse, two successive lines that usually rhyme and that have a similar metre ("If this be error and upon me proved, / I never writ, nor no man ever loved," William Shakespeare, "Sonnet 116")

**database** an organized collection of information for computer access

**discuss** to analyze, compare, or evaluate information; *discuss* typically tends to mean many different things to different people

**documentation** the acknowledgment of one's sources of research

**dramatic irony** the effect produced when the reader or audience knows something that characters do not (for example, as Romeo commits suicide in grief over the body of Juliet, the audience knows she is still alive)

**dramatic monologue** a poem in which a single character speaks his or her mind while another listens silently (for example, Robert Browning's "My Last Duchess")

**essay** a composition, traditionally in prose, that attempts to express a point of view or persuade the reader to accept a thesis on some subject

**fallacies** *pathetic fallacy* is the attribution of human qualities to nature; *intentional fallacy* is the error of analyzing a work with reference to the intention of its author; *affective fallacy* involves evaluating a work based exclusively on its emotional effects

**foil** a character whose qualities or actions emphasize those of the protagonist or another character by means of contrast (for example, Laertes functions as Hamlet's foil)

**foreshadowing** suggestions or hints about what will happen later in a literary work

**free verse** a form of poetry that is generally written in irregular line lengths and that lacks rhyme and a regular stress pattern (for example, Ezra Pound's "In a Station of the Metro"); the French term is *vers libre*

**Freytag's Pyramid** a diagrammatic metaphor invented by Gustav Freytag in 1863 to illustrate the structure of a five-act tragedy; generally characterized by an inciting moment, rising action, a climax, falling action, and denouement

**genre** types or categories into which works can be grouped (tragedy, comedy, satire, romance, pastoral, epic, short story, novel/novella, poetry, essay, drama, film, sitcom, reality TV, and so on)

**hamartia** originally used by Aristotle, refers to a frailty, error, or mistake in judgment that principally causes the downfall of a hero in a tragedy (Macbeth is often said to be too ambitious; Romeo, too impetuous)

**hubris** great pride or overwhelming self-confidence that leads the protagonist to her or his downfall; *nemesis* (named after Nemesis, the Greek goddess of vengeance) is the term applied to the just punishment the protagonist receives (in the classical myth of Icarus, for example, he is overconfident in his new ability to fly with his wings made of wax, gets too close to the sun, and is destroyed)

**hyperbole** extravagant exaggeration; see *understatement*

**hypothesis** an idea or guess used as a starting point for additional exploration

**image/imagery** combinations of words used to create sensory or word pictures (cold day, long day, cucumber day); *imagery* refers to the collection of images used

**irony** a phrasing or statement that implies/contains more than one meaning

**metaphor** an indirect comparison of two generally dissimilar objects. According to I. A. Richards, metaphors have two elements: the *tenor* is the idea or subject of the comparison and the *vehicle* is the image by which the comparison is expressed. In "My love is a rose," for example, *love* is the tenor and *rose* is the vehicle.

**metonymy** the substitution of the name of an object associated with a word for the word itself (for example, *crown* for monarch: "That decision will be left up to the crown.")

**mood** see *atmosphere*

**motif** from *leitmotif*, refers to the recurrence of an event, pattern, phrase, or image in a literary work (for example, stones are a motif in Robertson Davies's *Fifth Business*)

**narrative point of view** the perspective(s) from which a story is told. While many nuances are possible, stories are typically told from one of four points of view: main character; secondary character; omniscient; or shifting points of view, in which more than one character tells the tale (Faulkner's *The Sound and the Fury* is a good example of this.)

**nemesis** see *hubris*

**ode** a long lyric poem with a serious subject, elaborate form, and elevated style (for example, Keats's "Ode on a Grecian Urn")

**onomatopoeia** a word whose sound echoes its sense (for example, *hiss, buzz*)

**pathos** a moment in literature or drama that evokes feelings of sympathy in the reader or audience

**peripeteia** the turning or reversal of fortune for a protagonist

**persona** a mask; the "second self" that an author creates as the speaker of a poem or story

**personification** the attribution of human characteristics to inanimate objects, animals, or the like

**plagiarize** to use someone else's words or ideas as one's own without giving credit

**primary/secondary research** *primary research* involves original work, such as making personal observations, conducting surveys, reading original materials, undertaking lab experiments; *secondary research* involves the examination of articles, books, and research completed by other researchers and writers

**protagonist** the main character in a work

**pun** a play on words (for example, the mortally wounded Mercutio in *Romeo and Juliet* says, "Ask for me tomorrow, and you shall find me a *grave* man")

**repetition** the reiteration of a particular word or phrase, often used to particular effect in speeches and in song

**rhyme/rhyme scheme** the similarity of sound between words; many different types of rhyme are used for different purposes in verse. The *rhyme scheme* is the pattern in which rhyme sounds occur and is usually analyzed by ascribing an alphabetic value to each rhyming word; for example, *abab cdcd efef gg.*

**scheme** the structure or arrangement of words or ideas in a work

**setting** the time and place in which a work is located

**simile** a direct comparison of two dissimilar objects using *like* or *as* (for example, Robert Burns's "My love is like a red, red rose")

**soliloquy** in drama, the convention in which, alone on stage, a character speaks to himself or herself (for example, Hamlet's "To be or not to be" speech)

**sonnet** traditionally, a lyric poem consisting of fourteen lines with an intricate rhyming scheme. The *Italian* or *Petrarchan* sonnet is typically divided into two parts: an *octave* of eight lines that poses a problem and a *sestet* of six lines that offers a solution or resolution to the problem. The *English* or *Shakespearean* sonnet consists of three quatrains, each of which states and/or restates the problem, and a rhyming couplet that provides a solution or resolution.

**sound** sound is created and used in literature in many ways and for many purposes. *Assonance* is the repetition of similar vowel sounds in nearby words that end with different consonant sounds (qu*ie*t, ch*i*ld); *consonance* is the repetition of a sequence of consonants with a different intervening vowel sound (hea*rer*, ho*rror*). *Cacophony* is language that is rough or harsh to the ear; *euphony* is language that sounds pleasant and smooth.

**stichomythia** in drama, a rapid exchange of one liners (for example, the encounter between Richard and Lady Anne in *Richard III*, Act 1.2)

**suspense** anxiety or uncertainty created in a work about the outcome of events

**symbol/symbolism** an object that represents an idea; *symbolism* is the extended development or use of symbols (for example, Piggy's spectacles in *Lord of the Flies*; the sled named Rosebud in *Citizen Kane*)

**synecdoche** the use of a part to represent the whole, or the whole to represent a part (for example, "all hands on deck")

**theme** the central message or main idea of a work; most literary works have many themes

**thesis** a topic stated with an argument; the central contention of an essay

**tone** in literature, the attitude that the author conveys toward the subject of the work and/or the audience

**trope** a figure of speech that conveys a meaning beyond the literal meaning of the words

**understatement** the deliberate minimizing of an idea or fact in order to produce an ironic effect

**vers libre** see *free verse*

**voice** the distinctive features of a work, including its tone and style, that are conveyed by the speaker or author

# Answer Key

This section provides acceptable answers for most of the exercises included in this book; in several cases, alternative answers are possible.

## EXERCISE 2.1: REVISING

2. The management liked the writer's report.
3. Some companies will fire employees who live unacceptable lifestyles.
4. Pioneers depended on wood for fuel.
5. His friends enthusiastically beat up the other gang.
6. The committee feels that workplace relations need improvement.

## EXERCISE 2.2: TONE

2. People who want to lose weight and gain energy should adopt an exercise program.
3. Desdemona is a passive victim who just lies down and dies.
4. When running for office, a candidate must always try to look superior to the opponent.
5. The very people who most annoy are often those who most want to please.
6. We must suppose, then, that the figures cited are acceptable.
7. You cannot help expressing yourself, unless you reside in a vacuum.
8. If you want to hold the attention of your reader, you should cultivate a captivating style.
9. Scientists have recommended that one strategy for alleviating the threat of global warming is to reduce automobile emissions.

10. The premier explained his reform proposal at length, but the audience was clearly inattentive and did not understand.

## EXERCISE 2.5: GENDERED LANGUAGE

2. Anyone with a brain can see the dangers of using atomic reactors.
3. A homeowner can pay taxes by mail, at the municipal offices, or at the bank.
4. The gregarious dog is a human's best friend, but the aloof cat keeps its distance.
5. Women outnumber men on campus by almost two to one.
6. Deepa's mother repairs computers for the university.
7. The surgeon who performed Adrian's bypass operation has a medical degree from the University of Toronto.
8. The hippopotamus is happiest when half-submerged in mud.
9. Canadian pioneers loaded up their wagons and moved their families westward.
10. "As long as humans are on earth, they are likely to cause problems. But the employees at General Electric will keep trying to find answers."

## EXERCISE 2.6: EUPHEMISMS

1. the firing of workers
2. used car
3. drug addiction
4. pornography
5. spying

6. prison
7. old people's residence
8. failing students
9. librarians
10. taxation
11. unsafe buildings
12. rerun

## EXERCISE 4.2: DESCRIPTION (SAMPLE ANSWER)

The old, red barn sat in the wind-swept field. It had not been used for many long years. The ancient rail fences that had once enclosed its bustling paddocks were twisted and lost among the jungle of weeds and shrubs that flourished there. Its once sturdy loft, which had often held an entire winter's sustenance for the livestock below, had finally given in to the will of time and gravity. As each inevitable winter came and went, the barn sank more into desolation and decay. And it was not alone—it merely served as a symbol, a touchstone, of what had happened to all the small farms that had once thrived along this country road.

## EXERCISE 4.5: TRANSITIONS

Billy Bishop, a Canadian from Owen Sound, Ontario, was one of the most famous and successful of all Allied aces in World War I, actually being credited with over seventy "confirmed victories," as they were termed, by the end of the war. As a matter of fact, his escapades even included an encounter with the infamous Red Baron, from which, incidentally, both pilots flew away relatively unscathed. Eventually, Bishop rose to the rank of Marshal in the RCAF and, ultimately, was awarded the Croix de Guerre with Palm and the Victoria Cross. Nevertheless, Bishop's feats became a subject of controversy. Much of it revolved around certain uncorroborated combat reports that he submitted; namely, on June 2, 1917, he reported having engaged in a dogfight with four enemy aircraft over a heavily armed aerodrome, destroying all four. Although his deeds were acknowledged after nine weeks of investigation by the command authority, it was reported that many of his colleagues felt that his account was pure fiction. The "Bishop Controversy," furthermore, has been refuelled in recent years with the publication of Brereton Greenhous's *The Making of Billy Bishop* and the National Film Board documentary *The Kid Who Couldn't Miss,* both of which challenge the authenticity of Bishop's descriptions of his exploits. Conversely, other accounts, such as Dan McCaffery's *Billy Bishop: Canadian Hero* and David Bashow's chapter on Bishop in *Knights of the Air*, present different sides of the controversy. Therefore, just as he emerged from the battle-ravaged skies of World War I, so Billy Bishop remains today—larger than life in word and deed, a tantalizingly complex figure of wonder and mystery.

## EXERCISE 5.1: SENTENCE COMBINING

2. Uncle Zou, who lives in Edmonton and drives a bus there, is coming on the early train to stay with us for a week.

3. My garden, which is in the backyard, had lettuce, which the rabbits ate, tomatoes, which the worms got, and cucumbers, which somebody trampled.

4. After getting off work at 4:30, I pick up the kids from daycare, fix dinner, wash the dishes, and then fall asleep in front of the TV.

5. All the characters in this bestseller are stereotypes, including the Idealistic Young Man, the Disillusioned Older Man, the Scheming Siren, and the Neglected Wife.

## EXERCISE 5.2: SENTENCE COMBINING

1. Flowers serve an important role in Cather's "Paul's Case," and are therefore worthy of closer examination.

2. The boy's illusion is conveyed even more clearly when Joyce describes the girl as turning a silver bracelet on her wrist.

3. Learning to swim was such a big achievement for Edna that she shouted for joy.

4. The numerous similarities between Dr. Sloper and Morris Townsend can be seen throughout the book.

5. Dr. Sloper, who sees so many of his own weak points in his daughter's suitor, warns her about the dangers of marrying Morris.

## EXERCISE 5.3: SENTENCE COMBINING

1. "Boys and Girls," by Alice Munro, is a good example of a type of story in which theme predominates.

2. Unlike a character or action story in which the main character is faced with a critical decision, Munro's story places its protagonist in a situation that is beyond her control but illuminating.

3. If the main character does not act the way she does, she will be caught and destroyed, as Flora is.

4. The main character, who begins to be aware of many new things about herself, the world in which she lives, and the difference between herself and her family, comes to understand the unfairness of the roles society casts for girls and for boys.

## EXERCISE 5.5: ON CONCISENESS

2. Call me Ishmael.

3. You need to think about the complexity of this problem before you reach a conclusion.

4. The ineffective parents regularly accepted the behaviour of their obnoxious child as normal.

5. Based on what I had read, I came to feel that the food we buy at supermarkets is often bad for us.

## EXERCISE 5.6: REVISING

2. The referee blew the whistle.

3. The police believed the child was kidnapped.

4. Cosmo never forgot the day he discovered sex.

5. The officers violated some basic human rights.

6. The city engineer frequently accepted bribes.

## EXERCISE 5.10: REVISING

2. The final step involves making a ninety-degree kick-turn and starting the pattern over from the beginning.

3. European trains are frequent and punctual, have easy connections, and travel at high speeds.

4. In the movies college men are portrayed as being single, driving a nice car, being well-off financially, having good looks, and wearing cool clothes.

5. Progressive education aims to teach children to be open-minded, to use logic in their thinking, to make wise choices, and to practise self-discipline and self-control.

6. This proposal would alert society to the fact that, although sexual assault is a prevalent crime, only a few convictions are made each year.

## EXERCISE 5.12: REVISING

1. The Rites of Spring Festival has been postponed because too many students are sick with the flu.

2. Illegally parked vehicles are towed away at the owners' expense.

3. Times of crisis must be handled with cool judgment.

4. My second qualification for an ideal roommate is an easygoing nature.

5. Choosing whether or not to go to college has both problems and rewards.

6. Miss Brill tries to convince herself that she makes a significant contribution to society.

7. By no means does the novel glorify war.

8. Being loved or not no longer mattered to her.

9. Mrs. Pontellier carried herself in such a way that people thought she would be the mother only of strong, gallant sons.

10. Remaining married is important in Edna's society.

11. Mosquitoes bred in containers may be carriers of disease.

12. The controversial changes in school busing were intended to correct inequalities in educational opportunities.

## EXERCISE 5.13: CONSTRUCTING SENTENCES (SAMPLE ANSWERS)

1. Smelling smoke, Carol ran into the kitchen and rushed to the stove.

   Having smelled smoke, Carol ran into the kitchen and rushed to the stove.

   Carol smelled smoke, ran into the kitchen, and rushed to the stove.

   Having smelled smoke and run into the kitchen, Carol rushed to the stove.

2. Kelly reached the blueline, saw her right-winger breaking into the clear, and fired the puck across the ice.

   Kelly fired the puck across the ice when she reached the blueline and saw her right-winger breaking into the clear.

   Reaching the blueline, Kelly saw her right-winger breaking into the clear and fired the puck across the ice.

## EXERCISE 5.14: CORRECTING SENTENCES

1. He drove into town, purchased the supplies he needed, and drove home.

2. The students' council made a grand profit of—twenty-two cents.

3. If the employees like a company's orders, they will obey them.

4. The woman, who was clever, wrote editorials.

5. Last Sunday our aunt from Edmonton visited and we went to the mall.

6. The weather was very cold while our dog was recovering from surgery. To make matters worse, our car had a flat tire and the Open House was cancelled.

7. Last night's tornado ripped through the trailer park.

8. For their March vacation they would like to golf in South Carolina or ski in Banff.

9. Although Sally did not want to serve on the committee, she did not wish to have her opinion ignored.

10. The team could go neither by plane nor train.

## EXERCISE 6.1: REVISION

1. Tell me the name and birthplace of the author.

2. He knew neither the meaning nor spelling of the word.

3. Many adults believe that wealth equals success.

4. The blackflies stung my father and my sister and me as well.

5. The success of a television program depends on its promotion, its actors, and its recognition as a distinct genre.

6. I knew both boys when they were young and their father owned the grocery store at the corner of our street.

7. Hamburgers smothered in onions were served to all the guests.

8. Since Duddy felt that success in life depended on his owning property, he tried to purchase land using whatever means necessary.

9. Ophelia was reported to have said to the Queen, "These are the flowers I gather."

10. It has been said that there are only two indigenous Canadian art forms: Native pictographs and Inuit carvings.

## EXERCISE 6.2: REVISION

1. The main character in the story, a farmer, was just barely making a living and his family was nearly starving. After a short illness, his only mule died and, to make matters worse, the owner of the land demanded his rent in advance. The man stared at the sunset, not knowing what to do.

2. He had seen men blinded and smashed to pieces in the war and he had seen prisoners tortured and killed. He had held the hand of his closest friend and watched him die by inches. He could not understand how the citizens of his country could remain unchanged, doing the same things, thinking the same thoughts, watching the same television programs, complaining about their same little problems—truly, he thought, he would never be able to go home again.

3. Men and women blessed with political freedom, willing to work and able to find work, rich enough to maintain their families and educate their children, contented with their lot in life and friendly with their neighbours, will defend themselves to the utmost but will never consent to take up arms for an unjust war of conquest.

4. Let me give you an example of rationalization. I have said to myself that I made a good grade on an examination which, deep in my heart, I knew I did not do that well on, at least not as well as I could have. Finally, though, in spite of my true feelings, I convinced myself that I did make a good grade—now that is rationalization.

5. Most enterprises look for ways to manufacture their wares at a lower cost so that they can sell them at a slightly lower price than their competitors, a practice that often leads to inferior products.

## EXERCISE 6.3: SPELLING

In February the quiet nurse surprised everybody and gave up her profession. She had finally decided to try a different business. What could she do? The answer, she thought, was to study grammar and become an editor. That would surely be more interesting than medicine.

She separated herself from her friends and spent her time at the library, among books. She spent hours every day with usually only ten minutes for a light lunch. It was definitely hard work. She worked until her head was filled with opinions.

At last she was ready. She drove across the country looking for an excellent editing opportunity, but she did not succeed. She was completely disappointed and embarrassed. Everywhere, people had become sensible and had learned to edit their own writing. Therefore, she changed jobs again.

## EXERCISE 6.4: CANADIAN VERSUS AMERICAN SPELLING

| American Spelling | Canadian Spelling |
|---|---|
| color | colour |
| behavior | behaviour |
| canceled | cancelled |
| catalog | catalogue |
| center | centre |
| fiber | fibre |
| fulfill | fulfil |
| gray | grey |
| honor | honour |
| defense | defence |
| kilometer | kilometre |
| practice (v.) | practise |
| liter | litre |
| theater | theatre |

## EXERCISE 7.2: CONNOTATION

1. The intellectually challenged child was placed in a special class.
2. The touchy sponsorship situation troubled the government.
3. The film had an odd conclusion.
4. The stench from the barbeque satiated the neighbourhood.
5. Her ideas were well stated but simple.
6. The soldiers retreated from the battle.
7. My grandmother wears some garish outfits.
8. The neon signs on the strip sang out their messages.
9. My professor is old.
10. The department store was noted for selling cheap goods.

## EXERCISE 11.1: NOUNS

1.      common               common
   After the <u>tornado</u>, they put the <u>pieces</u> of their

   common
   <u>lives</u> back together.

2. abstract    common
   <u>Equality</u> is an <u>ideal</u> often expressed but rarely achieved.

3. proper
   <u>Calgary</u> was buried under a late spring

   common
   <u>blizzard</u>.

4.                    abstract
   "We hold these <u>truths</u> to be self-evident,"

           possessive    common   abstract
   was one <u>plantation owner's vision</u> of <u>freedom</u>.

5.    collective   common          abstract
   The <u>gaggle</u> of <u>geese</u> saved the <u>city</u> from

   common
   <u>destruction</u>.

## EXERCISE 11.2: PLURALS

| | |
|---|---|
| banjoes | hippopotami |
| dwarves | encyclopedias |
| cargoes | gymnasia |
| campuses | 7s |
| thesauruses | antifreeze |
| *or* thesauri | |

## EXERCISE 11.3: PRONOUNS

1. Samuel Richardson's *Clarissa* is not only a monument of the English canon, but was for

                   intensive
   Richardson <u>himself</u> a remarkable personal accomplishment.

2. possessive relative

   <u>Its</u> heroine, <u>who</u> is kidnapped and raped,

        possessive        personal reflexive
   vindicates <u>her</u> honour when <u>she</u> wills <u>herself</u> to die.

3.                    impersonal
   By the twentieth century, <u>it</u> had become one of the greatest unread masterpieces.

4. possessive
   While <u>its</u> epistolary style is no longer popu-

                    impersonal
   lar, many scholars acknowledge <u>it</u> to be the forerunner of the stream-of-consciousness technique.

5. possessive
   <u>Its</u> interior monologues certainly enabled Richardson to convey remarkable psychological insight.

## EXERCISE 11.4: PRONOUN PROBLEMS

1. The neighbour's cattle were in the farmer's field, so the farmer went to his neighbour and told him.

2. Charles's duplicity was revealed to James by a letter to James's wife.

3. Everybody admires his or her own grandmother.

4. The student angrily left the building and drove away in her car.

5. If anybody wants to attend, he or she needs to purchase a ticket in advance.

## EXERCISE 11.5: ADJECTIVES

| | |
|---|---|
| bombast | bombastic |
| fear | fearful |
| love | lovely |
| destruction | destructive |
| light | lighted |
| rock | rocky |
| blue | blue |
| scandal | scandalous |
| horror | horrific |
| recreation | recreational |

## EXERCISE 11.6: ADJECTIVE ERRORS

1. He was the older of the two men.

2. As a result of the inclement weather, the schools were closed.

3. Each of the assistants is giving up his lunch hour next Tuesday.

4. The apples taste nowhere near as sweet as the pears.

5. That BMW is the most expensive car on the lot.

6. The bad dancers danced badly!

7. While stopping for a smoke, she missed her plane.

8. Her son likes that kind of book.

## EXERCISE 11.7: VERB CLASSIFICATION

2. *Transitive:* The cat was given some milk by her.

3. *Transitive:* A gold medal was won for Canada by the gymnast.

4. *Intransitive.*

5. *Intransitive.*

6. *Intransitive.*

## EXERCISE 11.8: VERB ERRORS

1. The programmers and the president walk to the restaurant each afternoon.

2. Although Ed died on that Juno beach, Jon, his pal, rushed on, intending to charge bravely to victory in his friend's memory.

3. Neither Tom nor Jane is running for re-election and not one of their ministers is interested.

4. A large crowd of screaming fans was present; it tried fiercely to get in the East Gate.

5. Yesterday she ran in the marathon.

## EXERCISE 11.9: SUBJECT–PREDICATE AGREEMENT

1. The teacher and her students visit the museum.

2. Bread and jam tastes good with tea.

3. The Queen has a limousine for state events.

4. The students said they saw them at the mall.

## EXERCISE 11.10: ADVERB ERRORS

1. Please carefully lock the door and tightly nail the shutters to winterize the cottage.

2. Lilacs are now blooming abundantly there.

3. The felon often answered rudely.

4. He was surely happy that the holidays had arrived.

5. Eddie has nowhere nearly enough money to buy that CD player.

6. The Niagara River roared loudly over the Falls.

7. After the final bell of June, most of the students raced quietly from the school.

8. The firefighter escaped, nearly breaking his neck when the floor suddenly collapsed.

9. Awfully silent, we watched the tornado as it ripped through the trailer park.

10. Some claim that rock music continues to be a really bad influence on youth.

## EXERCISE 11.11: ADVERBIAL PUNS
## (SAMPLE ANSWERS)

1. "My pencil is dull," Tom said <u>pointlessly</u>.

2. "Please pass the sugar," Tom said <u>sweetly</u>.

3. Tom sat in the Emergency Room, <u>patiently</u>.

4. "I work repairing photocopiers," Tom said <u>repeatedly</u>.

5. "This impressive piano costs $1000," Tom said <u>grandly</u>.

6. "I couldn't find the bananas or peaches," Tom said <u>fruitlessly</u>.

7. "This arrangement is missing a flower," Tom said <u>lackadaisically</u>.

8. "I want to take a picture now," Tom said <u>candidly</u>.

9. "Now, I'll NEVER dance," Tom said <u>flatly</u> (or <u>lamely</u>).

10. "Let's get married," said Tom <u>engagingly</u>.

## EXERCISE 11.12: PREPOSITION ERRORS

1. She was happy that the winter was over.

2. I just don't know where the time went.

3. Because of lateness, Michael was not selected when the interviews were held.

4. He plans on borrowing some money from Tom.

5. In which vehicle were you riding?

## EXERCISE 11.13: PREPOSITIONS

<u>After</u> a few minutes, I heard the creaking <u>of</u> my door, as if someone endeavoured to open it softly. I trembled <u>from</u> head <u>to</u> foot; I felt a presentiment <u>of</u> who it was, and wished to rouse one <u>of</u> the peasants who dwelt <u>in</u> a cottage not far <u>from</u> mine; but I was overcome <u>with</u> the sensation <u>of</u> helplessness, so

often felt <u>in</u> frightening dreams, when you <u>in</u> vain endeavour to fly <u>from</u> an impending danger, and was rooted <u>to</u> the spot.

## EXERCISE 11.14: CONJUNCTIONS

1. <u>If</u> you cannot make it, we will reschedule the party.

2. We must hurry, <u>since</u> the last ferry is at 1:00 a.m.

3. Either Kelly <u>or</u> I will help you move the sofa.

4. Please wait <u>while</u> the intersection is cleared.

5. Ali <u>and</u> Rachel were the best of friends.

6. Do not begin the examination <u>until</u> you are given complete instructions.

7. <u>Both</u> Sir John A. Macdonald <u>and</u> George Brown were Fathers of Confederation.

8. <u>If</u> you visit Victoria, you must have tea at the Empress Hotel.

9. My brother wanted to go to the University of Saskatchewan <u>or</u> Queen's.

10. Margaret Avison <u>and</u> P. K. Page, <u>when</u> all is said and done, are two of our best poets.

## EXERCISE 11.15: COORDINATION

1. He has a bat and a glove.

2. Spring is the most dangerous time for avalanches, yet they can happen almost any time of the year.

3. The London turnpike was busy and it was snowing but he still needed to get to Hyde Park quickly.

4. *Who Has Seen the Wind* and *Jake and the Kid*, by W. O. Mitchell, are both coming-of-age stories set on the prairies.

5. The heron, standing still and perched high on the pole, readied itself to dive into the water.

## EXERCISE 11.16: CLAUSES AND PHRASES

Key: <u>Independent clauses</u>; *Dependent clauses*; [Phrases]

1. <u>Many cures</u> [for insomnia] <u>exist</u>.

2. <u>Drinking warm milk is a common home remedy</u> [for sleeplessness].

3. <u>Milk contains calcium</u>, *which is a natural tranquilizer*.

4. *When you heat the milk*, <u>you make the calcium easier</u> [for your body] [to absorb].

5. <u>The warm milk cure does not work</u> [for everyone].

6. <u>Some people believe</u> [in counting sheep].

7. <u>This boring activity quickly makes them drowsy</u>.

8. <u>Others claim that long nineteenth-century novels will produce sleep efficiently</u>.

9. *Alarmed at such barbarism*, <u>nineteenth-century fiction scholars are frantically trying to find alternative sedatives</u>.

10. <u>Their most recent work</u>, *which is now in experimental stages*, <u>involves Wordsworth's *Prelude*</u>.

## EXERCISE 12.1: COMMAS (SAMPLE ANSWERS)

1. My father, who leads a sheltered life, took a dim view of my being arrested.

2. My mother, however, saw the injustice involved.

3. All students who cannot swim must wear life jackets on the canoeing trip.

4. Natasha's cousin, who cannot swim, has decided to stay at home.

5. Date rape, after all, occurs in a culture that still expects men to be assertive and women to be resistant.

6. Before you complete your plans for vacationing at Lake Louise you should make plane reservations.

7. Reservations, which may be submitted either by mail or by phone, will be promptly acknowledged.

8. Reservations that are not secured by credit card or cheque will be returned.

9. If you go out, please get me some cheese, crackers, pickles, and a case of cola.

10. Anyone who wants the most from a university or college education must study hard.

11. Maureen, who was born November 15, 1950, in Whistler, British Columbia, moved to Flin Flon, Manitoba, before she was old enough to ski.

12. Before getting all excited, let's find out if the money is real.

13. Irving cannot seem to pass math although he studies for hours and hours.

14. My cousin Clarice is the tall, willowy, red-haired girl with the short, bow-legged, long-haired dog.

15. Robert Frost tells of a minister who turned his daughter, his poetry-writing daughter, out on the street to earn a living, saying there should be no more books written.

## EXERCISE 12.2: REVISING

1. Many people are left-handed. Some of them belong to an organization called Lefthanders International.

2. Lefthanders International fights discrimination against the left-handed. It informs the public about the special problems of left-handed people.

3. More men than women are left-handed. Hand preference does not become established until about the age of six.

4. The right side of the brain controls the sense of space; in addition, it governs the left side of the body.

5. Left-handed people can drive or sew or paint as well as any right-hander; still, it is not easy for them to use many ordinary tools and mechanical gadgets.

6. Stores now sell objects designed especially for left-handed people. These include watches, scissors, cameras, and pencil sharpeners.

7. Creativity is not the same thing as intellect; in fact, there is no relation between intelligence and originality.

8. Intelligence tests measure knowledge and skill; however, they do not accommodate inventiveness.

9. Creative people ask questions; intelligent people want to know the answers.

10. Creative scientists have a lot in common with creative artists; they both prefer things to be complex instead of simple.

## EXERCISE 12.3: REVISING

### WATER SUPPLY

Years ago, river water and rain water provided all the water people needed. The farmer working in the fields used river water; the people in the towns used rain water. There was no shortage in the water supply; however, population growth and town development have changed the situation. Nowadays geologists are looking for new underground reserves and engineers are trying to find cheap ways to get drinking water from the salty sea. Newspaper advertisements ask people to save water and towns have passed ordinances against watering lawns in the summer. Farmers who have no irrigation system fear a dry winter. Townsfolk once disliked the winter rains; now they wait for the clouds that will bring the needed water.

## EXERCISE 12.4: REVISING

1. Next year I am going to cooking school. I got the idea from a friend of my brother's, a business manager for a cruise line. He said that cruise ships build their reputations on the meals they serve, which must be superbly prepared and elegantly presented. Consequently, cruise lines are always looking for chefs, trying to find people who are well trained as expert cooks.

2. There are many ways to exercise and have fun at the same time, such as swimming, hiking, or playing tennis. But some people are exercise puritans, insisting that exercise must be serious and painful. My next door neighbour, for example, makes fun of me because I prefer walking to jogging, but I walk several kilometres every day while he jogs only once or twice a week. I figure that exercise isn't going to help if a person doesn't do it regularly, so why not find something enjoyable to do?

3. To do their work, steeplejacks have to sit on seats that hang down from ropes attached to the very tops of church steeples. If you watch them at work, you can see them swinging gently in midair while they repair a roof or replace the old numbers on a church clock with newly painted ones. Would you have the nerve to do that kind of work? Probably not—most people wouldn't.

## EXERCISE 12.5: APOSTROPHES

1. Many adults' distrust of computers stems from a lack of understanding the way that the machines function.

2. Children's love of computers may indicate that they are not concerned with the machines' internal workings.

3. Grade school teachers are often surprised by their students' achievement on computers.

4. One student's accomplishments were the main topic of talk in the teachers' lounge.

5. Students' attendance improves when they are allowed to do assignments in class on computers.

6. When he was given a computer, James's attitude changed completely, greatly to his mother's surprise.

7. "For goodness' sake," his mother exclaimed. "I used to question James's intelligence."

8. Many of society's problems have been eased by computer use.

9. But the computer's usefulness is offset by problems caused by programmers' mistakes.

10. A computer's mistake can ruin a person's credit, for instance.

## EXERCISE 12.6: *ITS* OR *IT'S*

1. The army forces its recruits to do aerobic exercise.

2. Undoubtedly it's a good idea to keep soldiers fit.

3. The military needs its forces in fighting shape.

4. To gain its full benefits, exercise must be performed strenuously.

5. In order to exercise regularly, it's helpful to have a "drill sergeant" force you.

## EXERCISE 12.7: QUOTATION MARKS

"Motherhood is not for every woman," moaned Michelle, as she wiped up the milk. "Why doesn't anyone ever tell you that having children can be hazardous to your health?"

"Do you mean your mental health?" inquired her friend Laverne, who was holding the dripping Billy at arm's length.

"That too!" snapped Michelle, stripping off the milk-soaked T-shirt. "This makes the third time today I've changed Billy's clothes. And it's not even afternoon yet!"

"But he's so cute," observed Maureen, glancing at the grinning Billy who was already planning more mischief. "Isn't he your pride and joy?"

"Maybe, if I live through his childhood," sighed Billy's mother, "I may be able to see some profit in this venture. But right now I agree with Roseanne, 'When my husband comes home at night, if those kids are still alive—I've done my job.'"

## EXERCISE 12.8: PUNCTUATION (SAMPLE ANSWERS)

1. Matthew was not looking at her and would not have seen what she was really like if he had been, but an ordinary observer would have seen this: a child of about eleven, garbed in a very short, very tight, very ugly dress of yellowish gray wincey. She wore a faded brown sailor hat and beneath the hat, extending down her back, were two braids of very thick, decidedly red hair. Her face was small, white and thin, also much freckled; her mouth was large and so were her eyes, that looked green in some lights and moods and gray in others.

   —L. M. Montgomery, *Anne of Green Gables*

2. Robert Jordan was climbing down into the framework of the bridge. The girders were cold and wet with dew under his hands and he climbed carefully, feeling the sun on his back, bracing himself in a bridge truss, hearing the noise of the tumbling water below him, hearing firing, too much firing, up the road at the upper post.

   —Ernest Hemingway, *For Whom the Bell Tolls*

3. Above all things a hun must be loyal. Disagreement is not necessarily disloyalty. A hun, who in the best interest of the tribe disagrees, should be listened to; on the other hand, a hun who actively participates in or encourages actions that are counter to the good of the tribe is disloyal. These huns, whether warrior or chieftain, must be expeditiously removed. Their ability to influence and discourage loyal huns is a contagious disease. In cases where disloyal actions and attitudes cannot be changed, harsh action must be taken to rid ourselves of those among us who see no value in and subvert our cause.

> —Attila the Hun, *Leadership Secrets of Attila the Hun* (Wess Roberts)

4. I told some of you last Thursday of the principle of the time machine and showed you the actual thing, itself, incomplete in the workshop. There it is now, a little travel worn, truly, and one of the ivory bars is cracked and a brass rail bent, but the rest of it's sound enough. I expected to finish it on Friday but, on Friday, when the putting together was nearly done, I found that one of the nickel bars was exactly one inch too short and this I had to get remade so that the thing was not complete until this morning. It was at ten o'clock to-day that the first of all time machines began its career. I gave it a last tap, tried all the screws again, put one more drop of oil on the quartz rod, and sat myself in the saddle. I suppose a suicide who holds a pistol to his skull feels much the same wonder at what will come next as I felt. Then I took the starting lever in one hand, and the stopping one in the other, pressed the first and, almost immediately, the second. I seemed to reel. I felt a nightmare sensation of falling and, looking round, I saw the laboratory exactly as before. Had anything happened? For a moment I suspected that my intellect had tricked me. Then I noted the clock. A moment before, as it seemed, it had stood at a minute or so past ten—now it was nearly half-past three!

> —H. G. Wells, *The Time Machine*

5. "Where are you?" John asked his sister. "It is very dark in here." *or* "Where are you, John?" asked his sister. "It is very dark in here."

6. "I interviewed him before the fatal accident," the reporter said, "and he joked, 'I'm very careful. Driving on city streets is more dangerous than racing.' I can't believe he's gone."

## EXERCISE 13.1: AGREEMENT

1. A child's personality and behaviour are influenced to a great extent by environment.

2. In this new stage of our relationship come new adjustments.

3. There have never been any concerted attempts to solve the mystery.

4. Financial support, like volunteer workers and effective speakers, is hard to get.

5. Movies packed with violence are still a favourite with the public.

6. There by the bank of that stream is a mass of lovely flowers.

7. Melba Starstruck, along with her agent, her latest husband, and her Bengal tiger, is staying at the Plaza.

8. In the centre of the superstore lie various departments ranging from electronics to kitchenware.

9. Where have my toothbrush and the toothpaste gone?

10. The prime audience for advertising, mainly young people, is an easy target.

## EXERCISE 13.2: AGREEMENT

1. There are Yolanda and Chris, talking furiously.

2. Bananas and peanut butter makes a tasty snack.

3. Peanut butter and bananas make a tasty snack.

4. The major impact of these statistics has not yet been analyzed.

5. Ingesting tar, as well as nicotine, causes cigarette smoking to be hazardous to your health.

## EXERCISE 13.3: IRREGULAR VERBS

Today, I . . . Yesterday, I . . . In the past, I have . . .

| | | |
|---|---|---|
| slay | slew | slain |
| creep | crept | crept |
| flee | fled | fled |
| ring | rang | rung |
| swing | swung | swung |
| wring | wrung | wrung |
| say | said | said |
| beat | beat | beaten |
| freeze | froze | frozen |
| dive | dove (or dived) | dived |
| awake | awoke (or awaked) | awaked (or awoken) |
| eat | ate | eaten |
| think | thought | thought |

## EXERCISE 13.4: IRREGULAR VERBS

2. Yesterday I laid my watch on the sink.

3. She was so tired that she lay down.

4. I set my watch ten minutes fast.

5. We had just lain down when the telephone rang.

6. The goalie laid down his face mask and throat protector.

7. His son almost drowned in the pool.

8. It has cost me a lot to move.

9. She has gone to Montreal.

10. I have just begun to fight.

11. The director saw to it that I knew my part.

12. What have you brought to the picnic?

13. They had been soundly defeated.

14. You have done it again.

15. We swam to the other side of the lake.

## EXERCISE 13.6: REVISING

Bowser, the huge sheepdog who lives next door, has a shaggy coat and a loud resounding bark. He is friendly and loves to be petted, but his size frightens children. He gets so excited when kids come around that he knocks them down like bowling pins. So, he spends his time barking at squirrels, or else he gallops along the fence and terrorizes our tiny fox terrier. Bowser really needs to live on a farm and have animals of his own size to play with.

Bowser, the huge sheepdog who lived next door, had a shaggy coat and a loud resounding bark. He was friendly and loved to be petted, but his size frightened children. He got so excited when kids came around that he knocked them down like bowling pins. So, he spent his time barking at squirrels, or else he galloped along the fence and terrorized our tiny fox terrier. Bowser really needed to have lived on a farm and to have had animals of his own size to play with.

## EXERCISE 13.7:  REVIEW

1. It is you, not your friends, who has to take responsibility for the accident.

2. Some of the teams are coming to the celebration.

3. Cell phones and email, to a great extent, have changed the way people communicate.

4. In the dean's office were a student and his parents.

5. There are many students who have not had the pleasure of life in a residence.

6. He should not have drunk with his friends the night before the exam.

7. "The Whiteoaks of Jalna," based on the novels of Mazo de la Roche and largely scripted by Timothy Findley, was a very successful television series on CBC.

8. The manager and the assistants, working together, refuse to use those tactics.

9. Neither the winners nor the losers were happy.

10. The interior of the newest lecture theatres was not very attractive.

## EXERCISE 14.1: PRONOUNS

1. Those living outside town should leave their job early to avoid getting their car stuck in a snow drift.

2. A good student does her or his own homework. *or*

   Good students do their own homework.

3. Someone has left his or her car lights on.

4. Players wishing to improve their tennis game should work on their backhand.

5. Each must cast her or his own vote.

## EXERCISE 14.2: REVISING

1. Al asked if Jose had allowed a speck of egg yolk or a particle of grease to get into the egg whites, each of which might have kept the whites from fluffing up the way they should.

2. Meg ate Chinese food and then went out jogging, a combination that caused her to feel unwell.

3. To relax after a hard day, I prefer to eat a simple meal in an outdoor setting.

4. This activity makes all my symptoms of stress disappear.

5. I got into trouble because I was late and skipped dinner.

## EXERCISE 14.3: PRONOUNS

1. You can't win if you run against Malcolm and her.

2. At the prom next Saturday Ashley and I are going to wear blue jeans.

3. For too long we taxpayers have been at the mercy of Parliament.

4. Who is going to deliver the keynote address?

5. Stanley went to visit his mother whom he called "Muma."

6. Renato and I are planning to become vegetarians as soon as we finish our Big Macs.

7. Did both she and Cecil promise to come early to help?

8. The member of Parliament is the person on whom I base all hope for the future.

9. We should be spared commercials that are an insult to our intelligence.

10. We arranged to study for the big exam with Selina and her.

## EXERCISE 14.4: REVISING

1. After we decide which section will be sewn first, we must then cut the material.

2. After having a safe driving record for forty years, I fell asleep at the wheel the other day and had my first accident.

3. Otis was robbed at gunpoint in the elevator of the building where he lives.

4. I hope to get a scholarship so that I can attend university and start to study singing.

5. A crutch is a device that you stick under your arm and lean on to take weight off an injured leg.

6. When I am in Montreal where my Aunt Frieda lives, I do not see her much.

7. With a total lack of responsibility, she purchased more and more items.

8. Consider this letter that was written to an editor of an urban newspaper a few years ago.

9. The poem exemplifies the patriarchal socialization of women.

10. After reading the essays, students wrote papers discussing their ideas about them.

## EXERCISE 14.5: REWRITING

1. The company packages natural meals for children; these packages can be shipped anywhere.

2. North Dakota citizens' groups are sending volunteers to assist those flood relief workers already in Manitoba.

3. Next week the House of Commons plans to resume consideration of legislation to restrict campaign contributions.

4. Yesterday, Bob Gainey signed a contract to manage the Montreal Canadiens.

5. At a city hall press conference, a municipal task force announced its plan to increase the number of parking lots.

6. The plan will increase the number of lots in areas where the traffic is congested by street parking.

7. The superintendent called for a meeting with members of the school board to talk about the problem of increasing drug use among teenagers.

8. The passengers desperately wanted their ordeal to end.

9. Before their daughter was ten years old, the Grishams decided that she would be a lawyer.

10. The restaurant had many autographs on the walls of celebrities that had eaten there.

# Index

# Credits

Davey, Frank. *From Here To There*. Erin: Press Porcepic, 1974.

Davies, Robertson. "Keeping Faith." *Saturday Night* January (1987).

Dickens, Charles. *A Tale of Two Cities*. 1859. Harmondsworth: Penguin, 1976.

Erasmus, Georges. *Dene Nation: The Colony Within*. Toronto: U. of Toronto, 1977.

Frum, Linda. *Guide to Canadian Universities*. Toronto: Key Porter, 1990.

Frye, Northrop. "Northrop Frye Talks About the Role of the Humanities." *Columns* Fall (1985).

Fukuda, Mikiko. "Silence vs. Sound in Joy Kogawa's *Obasan*." Unpublished student essay. Reprinted with permission.

George, Chief Dan. *My Heart Soars*. Toronto: Clarke/Irwin, 1974.

Gutteridge, Don. *Teaching English*. Toronto: Lorimer, 2000.

Helwig, David. "Haunted by Lives Unlived." *Thinking Through the Essay*. Ed. J. Barker-Sandbrook and N. Graham. Toronto: McGraw-Hill Ryerson, 1993.

Hemingway, Ernest. *For Whom the Bell Tolls*. 1940. New York: Scribner's, 1968.

Laurence, Margaret. "Where the World Began." *Heart of a Stranger*. Toronto: McClelland and Stewart, 1976.

Leggo, Carl. "In Defence of Television: (Re)Viewing the Curriculum of Literacy." *Advocating Change*. Ed. B. Barrell and R. Hammett. Toronto: Irwin, 2000.

Library and Archives Canada. Homepage reproduced with permission. Retrieved from www.collectionscanada.ca 17 September, 2004.

Munro, Alice. "Boys and Girls." *Dance of the Happy Shades*. Toronto: McGraw-Hill Ryerson, 1968.

Phillips, Amanda. "Silence and Slow Time: Women in the Media," Unpublished student essay. Reprinted with permission.

Richardson, John. *Wacousta*. 1832. Toronto: McClelland and Stewart, 1967.

Roberts, Wess. *Leadership Secrets of Attila the Hun*. New York: Warner, 1990.

Trudeau, Pierre Elliott. qtd. in *Time* Oct. 26 (1970).

Wells, H. G. *The Time Machine*. 1898. New York: Magnum, 1970.

Wilson-Smith, Anthony. "Overemphasizing Crime." *Maclean's Magazine* Aug. 7 (2000).

---

Figure 8.1: courtesy of The New York Times Company.

Figure 8.2: courtesy of Library and Archives Canada, www.collectionscanada.ca. Retrieved Nov. 5, 2004.

Figure 8.3: courtesy of The New York Times Company.

Figure 9.1: data adapted from *CBC TV News*, *Radio 98*, and *London Free Press*.

Figure 9.2: data adapted from BBM.

Figure 9.3: data adapted from *Entertainment Weekly* and Nielsen Media Research.

Figure 9.4: data from *The Daily* and *OWO Western News*.

Figure 9.5: data extrapolated from Statistics Canada.

Figure 9.6: data adapted from BBM and Neilsen Media Research.

July 31/07